Globalized Palestine

Globalized Palestine

The National Sell-Out of a Homeland

Khalil Nakhleh

THE RED SEA PRESS
Trenton | London | New Delhi | Cape Town | Nairobi | Addis Ababa | Asmara | Ibadan

THE RED SEA PRESS
541 West Ingham Avenue | Suite B
Trenton, New Jersey 08638

First Printing 2012

Book and cover design: Saverance Publishing Services

Library of Congress Cataloging-in-Publication Data

Contents

ACKNOWLEDGMENTS

Although I authored this book personally, I feel, however, it is a product of a serious collective effort, which benefited from the various discussions I had with thousands of people, friends and organizations during the last 25 years, as well as the experiences I accumulated as a result. More specifically, this book would not have been developed and matured had it not been for the encouragement and direction I received from a number of close, committed and critical friends, who accepted, enthusiastically, to act as the rudder for this writing project. Where I erred, I was gently corrected; and where I revealed confusion and lack of clarity, I was re-directed towards more clarification and articulation, because everybody was keen on getting the message through, with sharp clarity and un-ambiguity.

At the early stages of my thinking, I want to thank specifically my friends Adel Samara and Zuhair Sabbagh for wading with me through the various scattered ideas I was pursuing as I was embarking on this enterprise, since, for me, it was indeed an enterprise.

As I started drafting, my friends Sam Bahour and Peter Schaefer, whom I burdened with this task, read and reviewed every word I put down on paper; commented and edited, as they went along; and in some cases, proposed re-directions and re-formulations, for the purpose of clarity and consistency. For them, I am so ever thankful. I am sure they can recognize their inputs as they read the printed version. As for my newly discovered colleague, Patrick Bond, whom I met in person when he came from South Africa to discuss with us in Palestine our mutual worries, and became more familiar through his writings, I want to express to him my appreciation for his encouragement to pursue the idea of this book.

As for my wife, Lois, who has been my loving partner and source of inspiration over the last forty-three years of our marriage, I want to express my deepest thanks to her on three counts: (1) for reading, reviewing and commenting on every word I drafted, with concerned and loving precision and commitment to the critical positions I am advocating in this book; (2) for acting as my responsible, consistent and reliable research assistant and collaborator, by forwarding to me and alerting me to numerous articles and sources of relevance, many of which I found very useful for my analysis, references from which are embodied in this book; and (3) for her genuine, unfathomable, and nurturing love and caring that kept me going. I hope that I was able to reciprocate at least a portion of that love and caring with her. Certainly, I could not have accomplished this mission had she not been with me.

Also, I want to thank our friend Allegra Pachecho for encouraging me to persevere in this writing project, and for reading and commenting on certain parts of the manuscript in its draft form. My friend Sari Hanafi expressed keen desire to see the manuscript published in Arabic, and did not spare pursuing any contacts towards facilitating reaching that end.

Numerous friends were un-reluctant and eager to provide background information, whenever I approached them. They are many to mention them by name here. I want to express my deep and sincere appreciation for their help and encouragement.

Finally, I want to express my deep appreciation for the anonymous (to me at least!) reviewer for his/her incisive comments on the typescript draft, and for the very useful recommendations about restructuring the flow of the text. I adopted the bulk of the comments made.

Translating this work into Arabic, for local publication, would not have been possible, at this time at least, if it were not for the un-reluctant and generous support of the Ramallah office of the Rosa Luxemburg Foundation, through its Director, who shared my commitment to circulate the book in Arabic locally. For that I am most grateful. However, putting that commitment into action was impossible had it not been for the meticulous, responsible, precise and faithful translation carried out by Ubab Murad. For Peter and Ubab I extend my genuine appreciation.

However, none of the above should be held responsible for any of my shortcomings, or the positions I hold and defend in this book.

A Necessary Preface

This preface is a form of personal confession.

For a solid twenty years, both in Geneva, Switzerland, and in Ramallah, Palestine, I was in a position where I benefited from the same processes I am criticizing in this book. I was in a position of responsibility to manage, coordinate, plan, and implement "development" projects in Palestine, while coordinating and directing funds from transnational agencies towards that end. Although I became critical early on of the objectives of the "development" process, and the controlling role of the funding sources that were paying my salary, I stayed in those positions as long as I could, because I needed the money. I adapted myself to co-exist with the contradictions that situation generated. I took decisions then, which I am criticizing in this book, to maintain my job. Now, that I am retired, some may claim that I have the luxury to advise young people to take critical positions of the whole "aid" industry, from which some of whom are making their living, and others are wishing to get there, at no sacrifice to myself. This is true to some degree.

On the other hand, I permitted myself to reflect on these cumulative experiences, to draw the necessary conclusions from them, in however critical and blunt manner necessary, and to disseminate, what I consider, an accrued benefit. For this, I may be exposing myself to paying unforeseen costs. But living with internal contradictions is a state that I don't wish for any one.

Finally, I worked on researching and writing this book, more than full-time, for an entire year, dependent on my own personal resources. The idea of writing and publishing this book is not the initiative of any funding agency. It is mine, and mine alone. However, the cost of translating the manuscript into Arabic, upon my request, was graciously, generously, and un-reluctantly supported by the Rosa Luxemburg Foundation in Ramallah.

Introduction

In the beginning of the year 2002, unknown to us then that a few months later Israeli occupation army would reinvade and physically overrun Ramallah and other Palestinian towns and villages, and destroy all physical and institutional infrastructure accomplished by "donor" funds, I embarked, with an unparalleled stamina and determination, to write a book on my direct personal engagement in trying to develop Palestinian society in, what I considered, positive and sustained directions, in response to our people's needs. I felt I was compelled by an inner driving force to reflect on these experiences, right then and there. Even though I started drafting in English (since my notes were in English, and it was easier for me to write in English then), I was determined to have the book appear first in Arabic, in order to generate local discussion.

At the onset of my writing mission, I committed myself to dedicate the next 6 months for the task. Towards the end of January 2002, I received a telephone call from the then Palestinian Minister of Higher Education urging me to join the Ministry, in order to set-up a new Accreditation and Quality Assurance Commission for Higher Education. I remember arguing with him then that I was on a mission to write a book on Palestinian development, and that I would never forgive myself if I self-renege on this mission. The Minister convinced me that the notion of the Commission was "my baby", and that it is now the most opportune time to put it into action. We bargained to cut the 6-month time—my own self-commitment, by half. Consequently, I joined the Ministry in March 2002, and I was able to establish successfully the said Commission, as an autonomous body. The Commission is still operating today under the umbrella of the Ministry, although, I believe, with a lesser degree of the foreseen autonomy. About two and a half years later, I resigned as the head of the Commission because I felt its autonomy was politically compromised, in favor of the ruling political faction—Fateh, which I could not alter from inside.

When I first embarked, in 2002, on the task of writing my first book on why "development" is not working, I was very confident that, as a result of my deep involvement at a decision-making level in the work of Welfare Association (for 9 years) and, later, the European Commission (for 8 years), I could draw important, useful and pertinent lessons to the future of the development of my Palestinian society. Based on a detailed micro-analysis of my comprehensive and well-documented field notes, and discussions with indigenous organizations and individuals, over a span of nearly twenty years, on the one hand, and my direct involvement with external sources of funds in the planning and implementing projects and programs towards that end, on the other, I concentrated on drawing useful, constructive and valuable "lessons learned" from this experience. I did not commence my book-writing "project" with the conclusion I reached at the end of the "project". However, the deeper I delved into it, and the closer I observed, the more I was led to the conclusion that what we have been doing, since the beginning of the so-called "peace process", under the rubric of "development", was an internalized comprehensive myth—an illusory self-deception that the large amounts of funds that "donors" were allocating to the West Bank and Gaza Strip would help lead my people under occupation towards a free and just society, and who, consequently, would insist on nothing other than a "People-Centered Liberationist Development" (PCLD) approach. And that, if we don't subject our basic premises to deep self-assessment, guided by more honest, objective and serious analysis and reflection, the internalized "myth of development", I observed[1] will, eventually, become entrenched deeper and deeper, as I expect to show in this work.

1 (Nakhleh, 2004)

Moreover, I realize now in retrospect that my analysis, in the first book, focused more on "the managerial culture"[2] or technical aspects of development. I did not divert much from the principles I gained in my formal American academic training, which became reinforced in actual implementation throughout my work at Welfare Association (WA). The WA was clearly priding itself, through its Berkeley Economics-trained director general, hand-picked by its capitalist founders, by following American managerial culture. My acquired experience of nine years at Welfare Association dovetailed with the much-flaunted European managerial culture, and rewarded me with a long-term technical consultancy appointment for a span of eight years, with the European Commission Technical Assistance Office in Jerusalem (ECTAO), during which I oversaw the implementation of all EU funded activities in the Palestinian education sector.

I was very critical, in my analysis and conclusions, of Welfare Association's wealthy Palestinian founding members' factionalized approach to how they wanted their funds to be allocated to "development projects", and how they pushed the Association to become closer and closer to the dominant position of Fateh, as Arafat and the PLO (from which he was inseparable) got closer and closer to clinching a "historical" deal with Israel, which would assure Arafat, his Fateh faction, and his non-Fateh loyalists who were financially tied to him, return to rule the West Bank and Gaza under the continued Israeli occupation, and the overall consent of the USA.

For me, it was painful criticism because of the depth of my disappointment in how Palestinian capitalists' funds could be misdirected and factionalized. My disappointment was deep because I joined Welfare Association with the naïve, yet sincere, conviction that with the availability of "independent" Palestinian capital we had a historical and rare opportunity to transform our society under occupation into a resilient, resourceful, integrated and steadfast society. I was aspiring towards an environment,

2 (Challand, 2009:121-122)

where, with the availability of "clean" and "unconditional" Palestinian funds, we would be able to re-direct our inherent and indigenous resources to increase the productivity of our agricultural lands and labor; to develop an independent and strong local economy; and to integrate societal energies in creating a tightly solid social fabric capable of resisting the imposed settler-colonial occupation. I was aspiring to an environment where we, the Palestinian people, would be in the position to decide about our destiny and the type of society we desire to live in.

In the first place, I was naïve to think that capital can be "independent", regardless of whether it is Palestinian, Arab, or otherwise. Furthermore, I was more naïve to believe that Palestinian capitalists, who made their wealth primarily in the Arab Gulf region, by aligning themselves with the dominant and pro-Western ruling regimes, and acquiesce themselves to their policies, would be ready to allocate a portion of that capital towards a People-Centered Liberationist Development (PCLD) of Palestine. I chose then to give them (and myself) the benefit of the doubt. In spite of my "gut-feeling" at the time, I chose not to dwell on the notion that perhaps they were seeking to assuage their guilty consciences by an emotional and impulsive little commitment of funds as a reaction to images of Palestinian youth resisting occupation forces with stones; or to images of free flowing sewers in the dismal alleys of Gaza refugee camps! Perhaps, in a candid retrospect, I chose that path consciously, at the time, to keep my job?

Similarly, I was very critical of the European Commission's approach to the "development of Palestine", being anchored on the precondition that Palestinians have to accept the imposed Western and Israeli political agenda for a solution of the conflict. At the time, as it is today, many studies were written about the negative impact of international "aid" on Palestinian society under occupation. On this point, my book was not advancing anything new, but, my micro-analysis, as a Palestinian participant-observer, was. I was showing not only how politicized the entire "aid giving" process was, but how hypocritical, deceitful and disingenuous it was.

Unsurprisingly, all parties addressed in my analysis were irked: Palestinian capitalists founding members of Welfare Association, major international "donors", particularly the EU, and the Fateh-controlled, obsequious political regime in the West Bank and Gaza Strip, and its legitimizing intellectual elite.

In a way, the current book is a sequel to my 2004 book, published under the title "*The Myth of Palestinian Development: Political Aid and Sustainable Deceit*"[3]. This book is about how truncated, distorted, and mythologized the official claim of Palestinian "development" is, and has become. Basically, this book is about the role of an informal tri-partite coalition of (1) Palestinian capitalists-political elite, (2) Palestinian "developmental" NGOs, and (3) transnational "aid" agencies in impeding, obstructing and negating, what I call, "People-Centered Liberationist Development" (PCLD).

Before proceeding any further, however, it is necessary to explain what I mean by PCLD development. In general, the concept of "development", when used without qualification, may encompass all the following terms: economic development, social development, cultural development, human development, sustainable development, and societal development, separately or together. Whenever "development" appears in this book, it refers to a "People-Centered Liberationist Development" (PCLD). It is a process of purposeful intervention whose target is the widening to the utmost of individual and collective choices of the human being, the individual, the average citizen, which is sustainable from one generation to the next.

PCLD targets the entire society in order to strengthen and enhance the indigenous resources of the society, by giving a primary focus and eminence to indigenous production rather than consumption, which leads to self-dependency, protection and maximization of indigenous material and human resources. PCLD development, in this sense, aims to liberate people from external oppression, domination, and hegemony, and from internal repression, abuse, exploitation, corruption, and privi-

3 (Nakhleh, 2004)

leged and skewed access to sources of power. It is a process that seeks to provide free and humane labor opportunities, where workers actually participate in deciding their future, by sharing ownership of their work place. Furthermore, PCLD development aims at providing the necessary tools at achieving real and genuine equality among citizens, by empowering them through quality and free education, quality and free health provisions, and humanitarian emergency support, as needed. PCLD development, thus, targets the poor, not as an object, but the reasons that make people poor, and seeks to eliminate those reasons. In the final analysis, therefore, PCLD development, as argued throughout this work, is inherently a process of social and political self-determination and liberation; and, as such, for it to be possible, it aims primarily at resisting and ending foreign occupation, colonialism and hegemony, as well as internally perpetuated apartheid, be it political, economic or social.[4]

Thus, anchored in the above, the main objectives of PCLD intervention must be embodied in the following points:

1. Empowering Palestinian individuals, local communities and the society at large, through the provision of necessary qualitative resources, skills, awareness of their legitimacy, resilience, trust and confidence;
2. Improving people's living conditions, qualitatively and sustainably;
3. Protecting people's basic human, social, cultural, economic and historical rights;
4. Providing the required conditions and expertise to help the people realize these basic rights, primarily the right to be free from occupation and exploitation, to self-determine their future, to have access to non-exploitative productive work, to develop the society so as to respond to people's basic humanitarian needs, and to sustain it for future generations;

4 Some of these thoughts were elaborated earlier in an unpublished report. See (Nakhleh, 2009).

5. Exposing publicly that all international "aid" flowing into the WBG since 1994 is "political" and non -developmental aid, in the sense that its overall objective has always been, from the onset, to ensure the success and maintenance of the political Oslo Process. In other words, to ensure that the "Oslo-invented" PA adopts a negotiated peace settlement, acquiesces to Israeli and Western (US) imposed political and economic agenda, develops visible (but artificial) PA institutions and agencies (as symbols of a sham "sovereign entity").
6. Identifying and analyzing the most pernicious and destructive sources of aid that lead to the pauperization of the society, the shackling of present and future generations in debt to corporate financial institutions, and weakening of the cultural social fabric, and work towards their active boycott.
7. Setting-up relevant mechanisms to actively apply the gained information, skills, and the revived awareness.

To sum up, the approach and ultimate objective of the PCLD development, therefore, is to create a resilient and solid "social fabric" permeating Palestinian society under occupation.

In a pioneering work on "assessing the strength of the social fabric in Canada", Raymond Breton and his colleagues[5] launched a social science analysis of what constitutes social fabric of a society, and how, when that is impacted negatively, it could have serious implications on the social and normative quality of life. Such an analysis has a direct bearing on the impact of aid and conflict on Palestinian society under occupation. They asked, for example, "*What if people feel that they are not treated fairly; that they cannot trust one another and their business and political leaders? What if they find that their contribution to society is not recognized; that they do not feel at home in their community or society? ... What would this say about the quality of their lives?*"[6]

5 (Breton, 2004)

6 Ibid: 4

Social fabric refers to the "social and normative infrastructure" that determines "the quality of life of individuals, the functioning of institutions, and the governance of the society." Analysis of social fabric addresses issues of "belonging", "inclusion/exclusion", "participation", "recognition" and "legitimacy"[7]. Thus, whenever it is stated that the impact of aid, the ongoing state of occupation, colonialism and apartheid is weakening, or fragmenting the social fabric of Palestinian communities, the reference is to the normative and value social infrastructure. Thus, the decline in the strength of the social fabric of the Palestinian society under occupation, since the establishment of the "Oslo invented" Palestinian Authority, evidenced by high level of fragmentation, lack of trust and confidence in the imposed political and capitalist elite, increasing gaps between rich and poor, absence of meaningful and sustained employment, rush to normalize relations with the occupation structures, etc, is an indication that PCLD development is not taking place, and that what's happening is a camouflage for something else. It is obvious, in general, that under a persistent occupation of the people, the land, the water and other natural resources, etc, and the absence of real sovereignty and national decision-making powers of the PA, no PCLD development is possible.

This is an analysis of the various truncated attempts to develop Palestinian society, over the span of the last thirty years. My analysis in this study will portray how disingenuous the claims to develop Palestinian society have been, and how distorted and mythical the developmental outcome is. This is a study of Palestinian development: the development of people, society, economy and polity. It is not a comparative study of third world development examples. It is a study that interweaves the personal, the experiential, the political economic, and the comprehensive view of the aspired future developmental path of Palestinian people and society, if genuine interventions are undertaken. I write here as a "critically engaged actor",

7 Ibid: 7

to borrow Graeme Chesters and Ian Welsh's term from their book.[8]

I am basically trying to focus on the role of what I describe as a tri-partite coalition, namely, (1) **Palestinian capitalists and Oslo political-economic elite**, (2) **the newly emerging Palestinian "developmental" NGOs,** and (3) **the transnational aid agencies** in the re- entrenchment of the "myth" I addressed in my earlier book. I am not claiming that this is necessarily a conscious coalition, i.e., pre-planned by the three parties involved. However, the longer the current status-quo, which is built on the internalized and marketed premise that there is no contradiction between being under colonial occupation and "economic development", is accepted and internalized, the more this tri-partite coalition becomes purposeful and intentional. I am claiming in the current analysis that this is what we are observing today. The closer this tri-partite coalition becomes, the more mythological and deceptive the officially claimed "development" becomes. And, in other words, the more removed people become as its central concern.

The argument I am making is simple; it rests on three anchors.

The **first anchor** focuses on the relationship between PCLD development and capitalists. There is an inherent incongruence between Palestinian capitalist class and PCLD development, as discussed above, unless of course the expected outcome of their financial intervention is foreseen to enhance the opportunity for increasing their accumulations and personal business involvement.

The **second anchor** focuses on the relationship between PCLD development and sovereignty under a prolonged military and economic colonial occupation and apartheid, surpassing 43 years in its direct form, and 62 years in its quintessence. There is an inherent incongruence between seeking to effect a PCLD development of the Palestinian society and people under a situation devoid of real, not putative, political and economic

8 (Chesters and Welsh, 2006)

sovereignty, notwithstanding the deceitful and devious trappings, or marketing labels of "self-rule", "government", "ministries", "parliament", and continued occupation. In other words, acquiescing to a continued system of occupation, whether enforced directly by the occupying colonial power itself, or through an indigenous Palestinian sub-contracting system of control, is contradictory to developing Palestinian people and society. Elimination of the colonial occupation and apartheid, and its direct or sub-contracted systems of control, is a necessary pre-condition.

The **third anchor** focuses on the relationship between PCLD development and the exclusive societal dependence on external financial resources. There is an inherent incongruence between Palestinian absolute dependence on Western international aid, and official expectation that financial aid, whose primary source emanates from Western governments or agencies, is the avenue to developing and emancipating Palestinian people and society from the poverty and pauperization created by the imposed colonial system of occupation that is supported and sustained by these same sources. This is political aid *par excellence* advanced to the Palestinians, specifically to acquiesce and submit to an imposed political agenda and program. It shackles, mortgages, and holds hostage the entire current society and future generations in political and economic debt. It is not intended to stimulate and maximize indigenous creative and productive abilities that, if properly directed and utilized, will work against societal fragmentation, and will eventually lead to a state and culture of genuine independence. It is aid that focuses on consumption and mortgaging people. It is aid that is anti-production and anti-liberation.

My main concern in this analysis is not "state formation in Palestine" under occupation. My concern is how to participate in the genuine development of Palestinian society to strengthen its resilience to resist occupation, and emancipate itself from the shackles of the imposed status quo. This is a nationalist and human struggle of a higher magnitude in which all Palestinians, especially those classes with vast resources, should be involved.

In this study, I am trying to analyze why there is dissonance between speech, discourse, words, etc., that appear "nationalistic" and "patriotic", at face value, and action on the ground that is strengthening the hold of colonial occupation, and seeking to normalize relationships with it.

I am not interested in the type of the "illusionary state" Palestinian capitalists and the Oslo political elite, and their intellectual legitimators, are seeking, in tandem, to create under colonial occupation. Nor I am interested in their dubious claim that its creation is feasible in the next couple of years. I am interested to show in this analysis that the Palestinian capitalist class in both of its wings, expatriates (*shatat*) and indigenous, are inherently and principally unwilling, unconcerned, and incapable of "developing" the type of resilient society needed to resist occupation and get rid of it. Their primary concern is how to initiate, sustain and expand capitalist consumptive projects in collaboration with occupation structures (physical, human and economic), thus aiding, in reality, the entrenchment of occupation, albeit under different names. I am interested in showing that the reiterated and overt claims that Palestinian capitalists are the "levers" of development, and that their financial and technological investments are its "engine", is nothing but a mythical mirage. What is being created is nothing more than a Development Business, a Development Industry, a Development Share-Holding Company (Limited)! It's a rush for mercantilism in which the paramount activity is the interplay between capital, political elites, NGOs, and international funding. It's an advancing "Globalized Development Business" program that uses, at this time, the occupied Palestinian areas in the West Bank and Gaza Strip as its hub and as a testing case. In such a "Globalized Development Business", Palestinian capitalists, the Oslo political bureaucracy (and its intellectual legitimators) , and the newly-emerging "developmental" NGO structures, are nothing more than the localized agents, brokers, for Western capital centers and for transnational funding agencies (euphemistically referred to as "donors"!).

I am cognizant of the fact that our case is not unique, and we need to be aware of similar examples from the rest of the world. In reality, the external experiment of funding, controlling and impeding the "development" of Palestinian society, is not different of the experience of much of Africa, where the externally imposed so-called "development" was "only an ideological framework for ensuring the perpetuation of capital's domination of the peripheries – the so-called 'developing countries'".[9] Likewise, this experiment does not deviate much from similar experiments in Latin America, where multitude of examples attest to the rise of neo-liberal "developmental" NGOs as a replacement for mass movements, supported by international capital through transnational funding agencies.[10] Nevertheless, we keep behaving as if we have escaped this historical orbit; and as if we are not subject to the same forces that decimated and gutted other non-Western cultures, societies and economies the world over!

Although this book is about Palestine; it's not really and completely. Because it is also about the important lessons that we can learn from South Africa since 1994, when apartheid was transformed into a social category of control , oppression, and a system of exploitation by the people's own indigenous self-proclaimed leadership. It is also about Latin America, and about many other struggling peoples, in whom current Palestinian struggle is embedded, and cannot be but embedded, thanks to the global process of colonization and emerging re-colonization.

Through this work, the evidence will show that the experience of Palestine under occupation since 1994 is not unique. It is, as one of the small peripheries of the colonial, capitalist Western Center, subjected to the process of "re-colonization of the 'third world'" by hegemonic Western financial systems, which Andrew Gavin Marshall so aptly analyzed and sum-

9 (Manji, 2010)

10 See Petras and Veltmeyer, 2001, and Petras, 2009.

marized.[11] In this context, the analysis in this book benefited greatly from the research and analysis on "global economic crisis" carried out by Michel Chossudovsky, Andrew Gavin Marshall and their colleagues at the Global Research Center in Canada.[12]

Furthermore, the current work will present evidence to approximate the critical analysis of the actual state of failing "war on poverty" programs, and the emergence of ruling elites of the formerly colonized South Africa, as agents of international financial capital, working against empowering their own people. This will be anchored in the critical work of Patrick Bond and his colleagues. It benefits directly from their work on the failing 'War on Poverty'.[13] Since Palestine is still effectively under the hold of Zionist settler colonialism, this work benefits from re-reading, and carefully reviewing the work of Frantz Fanon[14] about colonized countries in Africa, and countries where colonization formally was terminated, but where developments there strike an eerie resemblance to 21st century Palestine. From this vantage point, the current analysis cannot be only an analysis of Palestine today; it is an analysis of a wider scope: how the "political economy of the oppressed", or the "political economy of the occupied" may look like in globalized 21st century.

STRUCTURE OF THE BOOK

Thus, this analysis will be carried out through four main chapters, in addition to this introduction. Chapter one leads by locating our current situation in its global context, and how we in Palestine, like the rest of the "third world", are subjected to, and affected by, the same global forces, especially corporate finance capital and global governance. I present necessary ideas for action, which, in my view, are required for laying the ground

11 (Marshall, 2010)

12 For further detail, see http://www.globalresearch.ca.

13 See Maharaj, Desai, and Bond 2010; and Bond 2007.

14 (Fanon, 1963)

for a People-Centered Liberationist Development (PCLD) environment in Palestine.

Chapter two analyzes the role of Palestinian capitalists in investing in the Palestinian areas, and in actively opening this part of Palestine to international corporate investments, through a collaborative effort with the Oslo political elites and the occupation machinery, thus declaring it "open for Business". By doing so, I focus on the role they play in impeding a "People-Centered Liberationist Development"(PCLD) approach.

Chapter three focuses on the role of "developmental" NGOs as depoliticized sub-agents of transnational aid agencies, being created by them as a replacement for mass-based movements. Additionally, it focuses on analyzing the process of aid-brokering of Western transnational aid by presenting a detailed analysis of the role that the Palestinian Welfare Association (WA) plays in this. This part of the book will give a special attention to the shifting role and approach of WA since it moved to the Palestinian areas under the jurisdiction of the Palestinian Authority. The case study of the WA acquires special importance in this analysis, because it is a case of an international and indigenous NGO, simultaneously, in which the role of its Palestinian capitalists' founders, its "developmental" claims, and its newly-devised role as a channel of international aid, are deeply intermingled.

Chapter four takes theoretical excursions in the various critical sources, writings and concepts that aided me in the current analysis.

A NOTE ON METHODOLOGY

Being a participant-observer native anthropologist, I will follow a micro-analytical, qualitative approach, through well-grounded case studies. My methodological and analytical strength stems from the fact that I have been an engaged and continuous "participant-observer" in and of the Palestinian "development scene" for over 25 years, at the senior decision-making level in the funding organizations that granted "development" aid, and in local Palestinian NGOs and GOs, that became recipients of some of that aid. Furthermore, my participant- observer status and approach spanned over actual participation in numerous local and international conferences and workshops, which deliberated some of the issues/problems I am addressing in this work.

In addition to my own observations, field notes, reflections and earlier writings, I rely, in these analyses, on information gathered from a wide array of published sources, unpublished reports and studies, personal interviews and focus groups.

Being an anthropologist, I am biased in focusing my analysis at a "low culture" (versus "high culture") level, which reveals under a sharper prism the unevenness in localized power relations, the vulnerability of "national leaderships" to abuse, corruption and exploitation of weaker segments of the society, and the consequent weaknesses of the societal social fabric. Here, as in other situations of prolonged oppression, occupation, apartheid, on one hand, and struggle for independence and freedom, on the other, national elites (economic, political and intellectual, governmental and non-governmental alike) get transformed to become agents and sub-agents for their current and former oppressors, under the mantle of "nationalism", and under the claim of not enticing the wrath of transnational funding agencies and, thus, risking interruption in the flow of international capital. From this level of localized analysis, economic, political and cultural forces of fragmentation of the people, along class, ethnic or sectarian lines, emerge. However, under the weight of globalized economic and political forceful trends coming from the Western centers of capital, the perceived "uniqueness" of present-day Palestine gets diluted and generalized. In other words, it gets comparable to other experiences in the so-called Third World, which in themselves are being transformed, specifically South Africa and Latin America.

This book is not an impact assessment of international aid; it goes beyond it and precedes it at the same time. It is not my intention to assess the value and impact of specific individual "development projects". As specific "interventions" at a certain definite time may have been inherently and structurally worthwhile, with an honest intention to improve, or alter, the specific state of things. I am not assessing intentions. I am focusing on cumulative results. My primary and major focus in this analysis is on the collective impact of the sum-total interventions, over the last quarter of a century, on alleviating poverty, strengthening people's resilience to withstand and struggle against the continued colonial occupation, and creating a coherent and tightly-knitted social fabric that undermines societal, political and cultural fragmentations, and liberates people, ultimately.

Chapter One

IDEAS FOR ACTION: REQUIREMENTS FOR LAYING THE GROUND FOR PEOPLE-CENTERED LIBERATIONIST DEVELOPMENT (PCLD) ENVIRONMENT IN PALESTINE

> *Vietnam was allowed to join the World Trade Organization and qualify for World Bank loans provided it embraced the "free market," destroyed its free public services and paid off the bad debts of the defunct Saigon regime: money which had helped bankroll the American war.*
>
> *The Vietnamese were finally being granted membership of the "international community" as long as they created a society based on inequity and exploited labor, and abandoned the health service that was the envy of the developing world ... along with a free education system that produced one of the world's highest literacy rates. Today, ordinary people pay for health care and schools, and the elite send their children to expensive schools in Hanoi's "international city" and poach scholarships at American universities.*[1]

1 (Pilger, 2010)

INTRODUCTORY CLARIFICATIONS

In certain ways, this chapter will be different from the rest of the chapters. Here, I write in a language of frustration, pain, anger and determination that current prevailing trends must change. I write also as a Palestinian living and experiencing what's happening to us, as a people, but with determined humility to propose futuristic ideas that, I believe, should halt this cascade of societal deterioration. I claimed in the 'introduction' to this book, as I started writing, that what we're experiencing is a rush for mercantilism in which the paramount activity is the interplay between capital, political elites, the newly-created NGO class, and transnational funding agencies, in advancing what I called a 'globalized development business' enterprise. I claimed, further, that this enterprise uses, at this moment at least, the occupied Palestinian areas in the West Bank and Gaza as its hub and testing grounds.

It is not unusual for the writer to grow with his text, as he writes. My ideas became more sharpened as I proceeded and reflected on the global trends shaping the world, and us, of course, as a part of it. Now I cannot look at what is happening to us as an accidental development, influenced only by a ruthless structure of military occupation and racist apartheid ideologies, detached from these global trends. This forced me to reflect on 'my—our Palestine', twenty or fifty years hence; and which 'Palestine' it is? Also, this reflection forced me to veer away from, and devalue the formal claims and incessant public Palestinian preoccupation with the establishment of a totally unviable, dependent, non-sovereign 'national state', just to be listed as such in the UN registry, and without necessarily providing its people—my people—with the freedom and justice the world owes them, and for which they for so long struggled and suffered. I am totally convinced that, through our struggle, we should redefine and redirect our collective perception of the 'highest Palestinian national interest' to focus, instead, on creating a viable, but unbounded, homeland, whose essence ought to be a self-liberated, resilient and energetic Palestinian society.

The excessive concern with the establishment of a "national state" is, in my view, misguided and anachronistic. The global trend is to create a corporate-controlled world, circumventing and undermining the nineteenth century notion of a "national state", and supplanting it with regional (if not global) economic-political corporate structures.

In order to do that, we need to understand the global trends that are affecting us or that are shaping our struggle most directly; what are they, and what should we do to contain and reverse them? I argued throughout this study, primarily, that our objective should be to undermine and expose the prevailing state of mythological "development" in the occupied Palestinian areas, and to replace it with a People-Centered Liberationist Development (PCLD). In this part of the book, I am exploring and delineating the substantive requirements necessary for laying a solid ground for a PCLD environment in Palestine.

As a prelude to this, I feel it is imperative to discuss certain dimensions of how the emerging global governance system is affecting us. I shall focus on:

- The indebtedness trend to corporate transnational financial systems,
- The increasing gap between rich and poor,
- Our failure, or unwillingness, to learn from some examples where, supposedly, "liberated" national states betrayed their people's interests,
- How we became, through transnational corporate aid, mortgaged, re-politicized, re-colonized and privatized, and, finally,
- What type of action steps we need to embark on in order to ensure laying a solid ground for a PCLD environment Palestinian society.

GLOBAL GOVERNANCE AND US

Although at face value we may be a unique case, incomparable to other entities in the world; in terms of emerging global trends, however, we are very similar to other entities in the peripheries of the Western capitalist centers. We are, indeed, a hub of experimentation. Our small size; the invention by Western centers of capital of our imagined self-rule authority, as a sub-agent to a settler colonial occupation and to transnational corporate aid agencies render us a target for experimentation, par excellence. Actually, it looks increasingly so that the PA was invented to be a control model for experimentation and re-engineering. The essence of experimentation seems to revolve around the question: how a fabricated, non-sovereign "national state" can be re-casted and remodeled into a manageable size modern corporation, run by "political" CEOs, managed by a re-politicized and re-engineered NGO class, and regulated and kept in order by a well-trained security apparatus.

In a recent article in which he explained the status of what he termed "global governance", Andrew Gavin Marshall wrote:

> *We now stand at the edge of the global financial abyss of a 'Great Global Debt Depression,' where nations, mired in extreme debt, are beginning to implement 'fiscal austerity' measures to reduce their deficits, which will ultimately result in systematic global social genocide, as the middle classes vanish and the social foundations upon which our nations rest are swept away.*[2]

The Bank for International Settlements (BIS), which was created in 1930, had two functions: the management of German reparations payments, and the coordination of central banks around the world. BIS became, essentially, "the central bank for the world's central banks", as described by historian Carroll Quigley:

2 (Marshall, 2010)

> *The powers of financial capitalism had another far-reaching aim,* ***nothing less than to create a world system of financial control in private hands able to dominate the political system of each country and the economy of the world as a whole.*** *This system was to be controlled in a feudalist fashion by the central banks of the world acting in concert, by secret agreements arrived at in frequent private meetings and conferences. The apex of the system was to be the Bank for International Settlements in Basel, Switzerland, a private bank owned and controlled by the world's central banks which were themselves private corporations.* [3]

This is essential to our current discussion regarding the indebtedness of "national states" in the world, particularly in the third world, and the ensuing control and management of these nations by global corporate finance, the more they fell into debt, as global interest rates were jacked up. For example, following the "oil shock" in late 70s and early 80s of the last century, interest rates were raised by nearly ten folds.

> *The effect this had was that the countries of the developing world suddenly had to pay enormous interest on their loans, and in 1982, Mexico announced it could no longer afford to pay its interest, and it defaulted on its debt, which set off the 1980s debt crisis – collapsing nations in debt across Latin America, Africa and parts of Asia ... .*
>
> *It was the IMF and the World Bank came to the 'assistance' of the Third World with their 'structural adjustment programs', which forced countries seeking assistance to privatize all state owned industries and resources, devalue their currencies, liberalize their economies, dismantle health, education and social services;* ***ultimately resulting in the re-colonization of the 'Third World' as Western***

3 As quoted in (Ibid); emphasis added.

> ***corporations and banks bought all their assets and resources, and ultimately created the conditions of social genocide, with the spread of mass poverty, and the emergence of corrupt national elites who were subservient to the interests of Western elites.***[4]

Like the rest of the world, albeit at a smaller scale, we are faced with a "global debt crisis", affecting not only "nation states", but individual citizens to a large degree. It is estimated that today the average Canadian citizen, for example, is $39,000 in debt, not to mention university students who graduate without the possibility of jobs, but with loans that they cannot pay. ... "Thus, we see the emergence of a process towards the formation of a global central bank and a global currency, **totally unaccountable to any nation or people, and totally controlled by global banking interests.**"[5] Perhaps we may be very fortunate that we do not have our own "national" currency!

With the beginnings of, what Marshall labeled as "the Great Global Debt Depression", global nations will "cut social spending, create mass unemployment by dismantling health, education, and social services. Further, state infrastructure – such as roads, bridges, airports, ports, railways, prisons, hospitals, electric transmission lines and water – will be privatized, so that global corporations and banks will own the entirety of national assets." [6]

If this is the global trend, whose impact is felt not only in third world countries, but also in the centers of Western capital, e.g. some states in the USA and some EU member states, e.g. Greece, Ireland, etc, why are we acting as if we are immune to its effects; and as if it does not concern us?

Why aren't we discussing, with worry, current and future indebtedness of Palestinian society in the West Bank and Gaza?

4 (Ibid); emphasis added.

5 (Ibid); emphasis added.

6 (Ibid); emphasis added.

I am not aware of any discussion groups, forums, community deliberations, professional seminars, etc, focusing on this subject. Some concerned economists or development practitioners have addressed the issue, albeit opaquely, but not as a platform for serious action. In her presentation to a "United Nations Seminar on Assistance to the Palestinian People" in Vienna, Ghania Malhis wrote:

> *Despite donors' generous assistance and contribution, we witnessed an incessant increase in the need for the Palestinian Authority to borrow from local banks to meet its obligations whereas the accumulated public debts of the Palestinian Authority to the local banking system has exceeded 733 million dollars in mid 2009 with accumulated arrears payments to the private sector of 188 million dollars."*[7]

This is not the complete picture. The figures listed above are increasing gradually, but steadily. Today (2010) the PA's debt to the local banking system is estimated at over $800 million, and the external debt in corporate loans that the PA committed itself, and with it our future generations, is put at about $2 billion.[8] Furthermore, the above quotation does not address the average individual indebtedness to local financial institutions for housing, businesses, consumer items, higher education, etc., which is proliferating in the context of what was described by a former PA minister of national economy, as a "consumer explosion" economy.

Moreover, it is essential that the indebtedness of both the PA and individual citizens is discussed in the context of the increasing gap between rich and poor, and how and why the Palestinian rich is becoming richer and the Palestinian poor is becoming more pauperized. So my question is: when will the "global political awakening", to use Zbigniew Brzezinski's term, that began stirring globally, become a part of our own activa-

7 (Malhis, 2010: 5)

8 (Al-Wazir, 2010)

tion and awareness of the inequalities, exploitation, privilege and dependence on transnational aid agencies, etc, that underpin our indebtedness?

The "crisis of capital accumulation" that characterizes the current phase of global development, as discussed by Samir Amin, is generating new and "modern" phenomena of social dislocations and poverty. He labeled these phenomena as a form of "modernized poverty", where peripheral societies

> *suffer from a huge volume of 'reserve army' of manpower, which is impossible to absorb under the dominant logic of capital accumulations, especially in the context of the opening of local accumulations and markets towards neoliberal globalism, without any form of regulation. Competition in these open markets presupposes the concentration of investments in big projects that have the capacity to absorb huge capital, considering the requirements for modern technological needs. Consequently, concerns in raising levels of productivity in sectors that employ the majority of labor force have regressed.*
>
> *Consequently, dislocations in social equilibria in favor of the unilateral control of capital represent the main reason behind social inequalities and poverty, albeit in modernized forms.* [9]

Based on the political economic analysis of the real causes of poverty and social inequities, the World Bank-type projects of "poverty alleviation" remain in the realm of ineffective slogans, unless the principle of "open market sovereignty" is completely discarded and replaced by the principle of market regulations. For this to happen, it requires:

- At the local and regional levels: the institution of radical democratic governance systems with real social content;

9 (Amin, 2008:4)

- At the global level: the establishment of an alternative, multi-polar globalization that allow popular classes a significant margin of mobility, as a replacement for the dominant neoliberal globalization.[10]

Amin concludes that, in the final analysis, we cannot escape the stark fact that "to bridge the gap between rich and poor, globally and regionally, entails a process of dual liberation from liberal globalization and American hegemony, since both are two sides of the same coin, and separating between them is impossible.[11]

To foresee where we could be going, as a society, and as a political entity, embedded in the prevailing process of neoliberal globalization, it is instructive for us to reflect on some of the observations by critical analysts characterizing the emerging, corporate, anti-people situations in the USA, and South Africa. These situations are referred to here for the sake of illustration; they may provide us with a glimpse of what kind of future we could be heading into, and, hopefully, an advance notice of how to circumvent it. These situations emerged supposedly as a result of people-mass-based struggles against foreign occupation, oppression and racial apartheid.

In his recent article, "A Recipe for Fascism", Chris Hedges alerted and cautioned about the evolving prevailing situation in the US, in the following words:

> *The Sarah Palins and the Glenn Becks use hatred as a mobilizing passion to get the masses, fearful and angry, to call for their own enslavement as well as to deny uncomfortable truths. ... Our dispossessed working class and beleaguered middle class are vulnerable to this manipulation because they can no longer bear the chaos and uncertainty that come with impoverishment, hopelessness and loss of control. They have retreated into a world of illu-*

10 (Ibid:5)

11 (Ibid:6)

> *sion, one peddled by right-wing demagogues, which offers a reassuring emotional consistency. This consistency appears to protect them from the turmoil in which they have been forced to live.*
>
> *The liberal class, which remains rooted in a world of fact, rationalizes placating corporate power as the only practical response. It understands the systems of corporate power. It knows the limitations and parameters. And it works within them. The result, however, is the same. The entire spectrum of the political landscape collaborates in the strangulation of our disenfranchised working class, the eroding of state power, the criminal activity of the financial class and the paralysis of our political process.* [12]

With a simple replacement of the names of the two ultra-right politician-capitalists at the lead of this paragraph, the reader would be hard put not to think that this is not a description of our current Palestinian situation, and where it could lead to.

The "elite interpreters of globalism", Hedges concludes further,

> *are the vanguard, the elect, the prophets, who alone grasp a great absolute truth and have the right to impose this truth on a captive people no matter what the cost. Human suffering is dismissed as the price to be paid for the coming paradise. ... They lack the vision to offer any alternative. They can function only as systems managers. They will hollow out the state to sustain a casino capitalism that is doomed to fail.*
>
> *We are ruled by huge corporate monopolies that replicate the political and economic power, on a vastly expanded scale, of the old trading companies of the 17th and 18th centuries. ... The political*

12 (Hedges, 2010)

> *theater funded by the corporate state is composed of hypocritical and impotent liberals, the traditional moneyed elite, and a disenfranchised and angry underclass that is being encouraged to lash out at the bankrupt liberal institutions and the government that once protected them. ... All these political courtiers, however, serve the interests of the corporate state and the utopian ideology of globalism. Our social and political ethic can be summed up in the mantra let the market decide. Greed is good.*
>
> *We believe, like the Spaniards in the 16th century who pillaged Latin America for gold and silver, that money, usually the product of making and trading goods, is real. ... Today's use in the United States of some $12 trillion in government funds to refinance our class of speculators is a similar form of self-deception. Money markets are still treated, despite the collapse of the global economy, as a legitimate source of trade and wealth creation. The destructive power of financial bubbles, as well as the danger of an unchecked elite, was discovered in ancient Athens ... But we seem determined to find out this self-destructive force for ourselves. And when the second collapse comes, as come it must, we will revisit wrenching economic and political tragedies forgotten in the mists of history".*[13]

Trading in the Palestinian Securities Exchange, one of the subsidiaries of PADICO, which is mesmerizing the average person through the deceptive claim to generate fake wealth, represents one of those "financial bubbles", discussed above.

The struggle against apartheid in South Africa is rightly considered one of the greatest liberation struggles in contemporary history. However, increasing evidence shows that it is failing its citizens. We need to learn from it, and avoid falling

13 (Ibid)

into its "destructive political economic logic", as Patrick Bond describes it.[14]

Bond, who is a professor in the School of Development Studies at the University of Kwazulu-Natal, identified in a recent article some major aspects of how this political economic logic can be destructive. It is destructive, he maintained, by

- building or renovating infrastructure geared to society's richest residents and visitors (luxurious airports and fast trains);
- ensuring that tenders go to a new breed of crony capitalists (many associated with Zuma's [South Africa's current president] family and friends);
- hiring tens of thousands more police trained to withhold civil liberties on behalf, mainly, of those who stroll through high-profile tourist sites and inhabit upper-income residential zones; and [by]
- doing all this with massive increases in foreign debt, reaching nearly $85 billion at present, up from less than $25 billion inherited by Nelson Mandela in 1994." [15]

Concomitantly, there has been an actual increase in urban poverty, from 1993 – 2008, or since the liberation from racial apartheid, and decline in rural poverty, due to the movement of the rural poor to the cities, and the extension of the "welfare grant system". Additionally, "the state is also losing its so-called 'War on Poverty', and instead ... what is more apparent is Pretoria's war on the poor: repression and disconnections of water/electricity to people who cannot afford their fast-rising utility bills ... ."[16]

Exacerbated by these phenomena, Bond poses two pertinent questions about current South Africa, also appropriate to

14 (Bond, 2010, October 6).

15 (Ibid)

16 (Ibid)

our Palestinian situation, and would demand serious and deep reflection on our part:

> *Why? Our economy is structured so as to generate poverty-expanding 'growth' of GDP. As accumulation of capital occurs in much of South Africa, the rich grow richer and the poor grow poorer.*
>
> *"Why? The large corporations mainly responsible for these problems have a tight-knit 'crony capitalist' relationship with the ruling party, bordering on outright corruption".*[17]

HOW AND WHY DID WE BECOME DEPENDENT ON TRANSNATIONAL CORPORATE "AID", AND RE-POLITICIZED AND RE-COLONIZED BY IT?

In formal economic terms, "aid dependency" is the ratio between aid and the gross national income. According to this, aid dependency in the PA areas "has been gradually increasing since 1999", where in 2006 the PA areas ranked "as more aid dependent than most other countries worldwide." [18] Locally, however, in real perceptional and behavioral terms, there appears to be a total paralyzing dependence on external aid that undermines any initiative for local action, big or small. External aid has been allowed to acquire almost a tyrannical controlling power, and, consequently, subjugation to the sources of this aid. Statements such as: "the abrupt cessation of aid could have catastrophic repercussions for the Palestinians, including mass famine and thousands of deaths ...", [19] feed into this manufactured phobia and expected submission. Thus, considering that the EU countries, the US and Japan constitute the major source of external aid, it is easy to see, then, how subserviently indebted PA policies are towards this capitalist bloc of countries.

17 (Ibid)

18 (Hever, 2008:29-30)

19 (Ibid:48)

According to a recent "Congressional Research Service" report,[20] the US has committed over $3.5 billion in aid to the Palestinians in the West Bank and Gaza, since the signing of the Oslo Accords. Since the death of Arafat in 2004, US aid has been averaging about $400 million per year.[21] However,

> *Since [the Hamas take over in Gaza], the United States has dramatically boosted aid levels to bolster the PA in the West Bank and President Mahmoud Abbas vis-à-vis Hamas. The United States has appropriated or reprogrammed nearly $2 billion since 2007 in support of PA Prime Minister Salam Fayyad's security, governance, development, and reform programs, including $650 million for direct budgetary assistance to the PA and nearly $400 million (toward training, non-lethal equipment, facilities, strategic planning, and administration) for strengthening and reforming PA security forces and criminal justice systems in the West Bank. The remainder is for programs administered by the U.S. Agency for International Development and implemented by nongovernmental organizations in humanitarian assistance, economic development, democratic reform, improving water access and other infrastructure, health care, education, and vocational training.*[22]

Globally, on the other hand,

> *The average annual contribution from 1994-2000 represented 500 million dollars and jumped to an average of 1 billion dollars a year from 2001-2005. Although 2006 witnessed a slight decrease registering 716 million dollars, the numbers rapidly esca-*

20 (Zanotti, 2010)

21 (Ibid)

22 (Ibid)

> *lated to 1.5 billion dollars in 2007, 1.7 billion in 2008, 1.8 billion in 2009 and is expected to reach almost 2 billion dollars in 2010."* [23]

Likewise, there was an increase in aid from Arab official sources that came to represent 25 percent of the total. Thus, since 1994 total external aid amounted to no less than $18 billion.[24]

Despite the above volume of external aid that was poured in, and the fact that the PA areas of the West Bank and Gaza ranked in 2006 as 11th highest recipient of per capita aid worldwide,[25] Ghania Malhis stated in her report that

> *it has been almost impossible to trace any positive impact of these mobilized resources on the ground, even when taking into consideration the substantial investment carried by the Palestinian private sector in the occupied Palestinian territories, including those made by the Palestinian Diaspora ....* [26]

She elaborated, furthermore, about the "structural distortion in public expenditures", where the share of security represents 33 percent, "while health and education combined correspond to no more than 29%."[27] Having been closely connected to the PA, as she occupied official and semi-official posts, she concluded her report to the UN Seminar by the following:

> *It goes without saying that mistakes were made and resources were wasted. It is also obvious to us, that a paradigm shift is needed when assistance is concerned, and mindsets need to be shifted from*

---

23 (Malhis, 2010:3)

24 (Ibid: 4)

25 (Hever, 2008:28)

26 (Malhis, 2010:4)

27 (Ibid:6)

> *donations to focus on socio-economic investments in order to provide sustainable solutions."*[28]

For any honest observer of the "aid/development" scene, this conclusion is public knowledge, and any person on the ground would be able to reiterate it without hesitancy, perhaps with lesser articulation in English! Advocating a "paradigm shift", however, is always an acceptable and less challenging position to take. What is required, as I shall discuss below, is not only a shift in the paradigm, or model, or pattern, etc. of the aid, but a serious re-thinking of the existing paradigm; dismantling it; and replacing it with a "people-centered" paradigm of "liberationist development".

On another plain, Yezid Sayigh expressed his worry about the role of the "international community" in "inducing a failed state in Palestine". He stated that

> *What may be harder for the international community to accept is that its policies have contributed materially to systemic, probably irreversible collapse – 'state failure' – in the Palestinian Authority. It has more than doubled financial assistance to the Palestinians since 2000, yet is locked into policies that are bringing about the very humanitarian crisis it seeks to alleviate, while generating long-term dependence on external funding.*[29]

To illuminate what needs to be dismantled and replaced, through innovative indigenous strategic thinking, I delineate below the major destructive trends that are overtaking our Palestinian society, economy and polity in the PA areas as a result of the "Oslo process", and have invaded our current collective mindset.

- The Oslo Accords, sanctioned by Western centers of capital, became a substitute for liberation from occupation;

28 (Ibid:10)

29 (Sayigh, 2007)

- Our historical revolutionary creative opposition to oppression and occupation has been substituted by a well-financed and domesticated "court opposition" from the left;
- Presence and involvement of transnational corporate and governmental aid agencies through funding have assumed a tyrannical control, and became a substitute for local governance;
- Professionalized, managerial, de- and re-politicized NGOs, invented and sustained by transnational corporate and governmental aid agencies, became a substitute for mass-based grassroots politicized social and economic movements;
- Mechanical and measurable economic growth became a substitute for production-based development;
- Dependence on salaries from an artificially-created public sector became a substitute for a sustained employment generation by the productive sector;
- Capital investments in consumption, in monopolies and holding service companies, acceptable to the occupation and dependent on collaboration with it, became a substitute for small and lasting indigenous productive enterprises;
- Substituting what we can do, with our indigenous skills, resources and expertise, with what funds we need, and muster from external aid agencies; thus, leading to a prevalent normative system which respects externally funded projects, than those initiated through local volunteering energies and resources.

IDEAS FOR ACTION: REQUIREMENTS FOR LAYING THE GROUND FOR PEOPLE-CENTERED LIBERATIONIST DEVELOPMENT (PCLD) ENVIRONMENT IN PALESTINE

What I am proposing below is basically an approach of counter re-engineering at the societal level. It is long-term and multi-faceted. I shall try to dissect it in different interrelated segments. I am not claiming that this is the panacea for all our ills, but I am maintaining throughout this work that until and unless we start embarking on this approach, we shall not be able to liberate ourselves, and genuinely develop our society. I maintain, further, that Palestine is not a unique case, and the PCLD approach which I am advocating is engaging and liberating, whether in Palestine or in other similar situations.

THE PREVAILING POLITICAL ENVIRONMENT

To ensure a conducive environment for a People-Centered Liberationist Development, the current prevailing political environment has to be transformed. The Oslo generated process, which was imposed on the people, has to be abrogated and decisions about it should be returned to the people. This means that the promise of achieving an independent Palestinian state in the context of the Oslo Accords, and in collaboration with the Israeli occupying power and the apartheid system it imposes, has been shown over the last 17 years to be a mirage, a mythical illusion. The lie that has been marketed, namely, that with the funds from the corporate agencies that are responsible for this lie, we can build the institutions of an independent Palestinian state, as the current plan of the current illegitimate government maintains, has to be exposed, and the average citizen has to become aware of it.

Briefly, the current truncated self-rule, which was created by, and is responsible for the alliance of Western-Zionist capitalist centers, is antithetical to Palestinian people's concerns and interests. It is more responsive to Israeli concerns, and, consequently, the invented so-called Palestinian "leadership" has to act as a sub-agent of these concerns, and it cannot be responsive to Palestinian people's needs, notwithstanding the public rhetoric.

Altering this political environment is necessary in order to lay the ground for a proper PCLD environment. Although it is a necessary pre-condition for it, it does not mean that we should sit idly by and do nothing until the Oslo process and its derivatives are abrogated.

The Prevailing Investment Environment

Formally at least the prevailing economic policy was codified in the Fayyad government's "Palestinian Reform and Development Plan" of 2008. The Plan uses the World Bank language of neoliberal development. The Plan is premised on "free market" economy; its neoliberal agenda opens widely Palestinian areas to foreign investments, from Western corporate sources and Arab and Palestinian capitalists; and it barely mentions the presence of Israeli occupation. Its main concern was to present attractive appeals to corporate and governmental transnational funding agencies. The appeal was considered by the Fayyad government as highly successful in that transnational funding agencies pledged funds in excess of 37 percent of the budget requested.

The main concern is that this plan did not reflect people's needs and concerns; the people were not consulted. It was the Oslo political and economic "leadership" plan. It was the Plan of transnational corporate finance and Palestinian capitalists. It was justified as an investment framework which is the most conducive to creating jobs and employment, and to eliminate poverty. A successful investment environment, it was argued, needs "security and the rule of law", which allows for the build-up of a police force loyal to the government, as a tool for violence and suppression of dissent.

Since then, steps to declare that PA areas are open for business, irrespective of the buyers, have rapidly escalated. The claim that aid from transnational corporate agencies and wealthy capitalists that is invested largely in profitable services and consumption projects, generates sustainable employment, is deceptive at best, in the absence of serious focus on equity in wealth and income distribution. To quote Michael Hudson, "The argument is made that 'The rich create jobs.' After all, somebody has to build the yachts. What is missing is the more general principle: Wealth and income inequality destroy job creation."[30]

It is clear by now that investing in opportunities to create sustainable employment to politicized Palestinians under occupation is the antithesis of the objective of corporate and governmental transnational agencies. What about Palestinian capitalists? If they are really concerned about alleviating poverty and investing in creating sustainable jobs, with dignity, to the average unemployed Palestinian, the true test would be to contribute to a transformation in the prevailing investment environment, through:

- Discussing the issue of sustained employment with actual and potential workers, employed and unemployed, not as individual investment projects, but as national projects;
- Focusing on initiating and investing in small productive enterprises, in developing the agricultural lands and food production, that are workers-planned, owned and run;
- Focusing on medium to long-term investments, geared towards liberation from occupation, in innovative training programs for necessary skills to sustain those productive projects, all the way from project planning to production engineering. This could utilize the existing network of community and technical colleges and universities.
- But since capitalists compelling motive is maximization of their profits, perhaps pressure should come from newly-devised, workers-based unions and coalitions, reformed and re-generated political parties on the left, etc.
- People's "monitoring committees" should be formed to assume the responsibility of monitoring how profits from current investments of financial institutions,

30 (Hudson, 2010)

> service monopolies, etc, are being used, for what purpose, and where. Regular reports and community-based discussions should be held regularly to hold investors accountable for their alleged commitment to societal responsibility.

I present below two illustrative cases (out of many) to show the distorted capitalist investments, under the guise of "developing" the place. The first case took place during the pre-Oslo period (i.e., pre-1994), while the second case took place during the post-Oslo period (i.e., post-1994).

ILLUSTRATIVE CASE 1: THE RASHAD SHAWWA PYRAMID IN GAZA, OR THE "SHAWWA CULTURAL CENTER"

Rashad Shawwa was the former mayor of Gaza City. He was an indigenous capitalist and feudal land owner, well-connected with the British Mandate authorities, pre-1948, and the Israeli occupation authorities, later on. Having been, or at least self-perceived to have been, of the same economic class standing as Hasib Sabbagh's, one of the leading "shatat" capitalists and one of the founders of WA, the two traditional capitalist personalities developed a certain affinity. Both had mansions in London, and in those dimensions they were considered neighbors, but both utilized their privileged economic positions and resources to gain access to people in power.

During the time when I was the Director of Programs at the Palestinian Welfare Association (WA) in Geneva, I had the opportunity to meet Rashad Shawwa twice, once in May 1984 and the second time in January 1987, nearly a year before the beginning of the first intifada.

> *Whilst planning my first field mission following the first annual meetings of the decision-making bodies of the WA, in May 1984, I was instructed [at the prompting of Hasib Sabbagh] to visit the 'Cultural*

> *Center' of the former mayor of Gaza and to identify its needs. Unknown to me then, his contact in the Executive Committee [Sabbagh] had already promised him support for the Center's library, from his own funds. I arranged to meet with the former mayor and toured the facility for about an hour. I observed a huge 'fortress-like' structure, with 'Danish-Interiors' imported shelves for the library and very fancy marble. At the time, the building, which was basically completed, had been sitting idle for the last two years. During the course of our discussion, the mayor admitted that there was about US$400,000 in the Center's account. My assessment, based on this field visit, was that "he needs no help from us [i.e. WA]." Sensing the critical tone in my questions and comments, the message the mayor then conveyed to the Executive Committee [of the WA] (as I was told later) was, 'Who is this Communist that you are sending me?'* [31].

The "critical tone in my questions and comments", to which I referred in the above quotation, had to do with my expressed incredulity and astonishment at his proud reiteration and haughty declaration, during my tour of the edifice, that everything for the "center" was imported from the West: marble tiles from Italy, wooden shelves from Denmark, etc. When I probed to understand why, since we had many unemployed carpenters and metal workers in Gaza, and a potentially strong, albeit fledgling, stone and marble Palestinian-owned industry, both in the West Bank and in Galilee (Israel), we had to import these materials from foreign countries, the answer was adamant and defensive. "We deserve the best and we should show the world how civilized we are!"[32] There was total and utter disregard for local production, manufacturing, and expertise; and absent concern—almost contempt—for local employment needs and local labor.

---

31 (Nakhleh, 2004:78)

32 Author's field notes

Upon my second visit, nearly two and a half years later, "the 'Cultural Center' was still standing an empty edifice, although it had received considerable amounts of financial contributions in the meantime, but without any real evidence, then, of embarking on any actual cultural activity. Thus, in reality, the stone and marble edifice was standing idly for nearly 5 years, symbolizing and reinforcing the Shawwa imminence in Gaza, while overlooking the squalid al-Shate' refugee camp. The justification given then for the absence of cultural activities' program was that the building was not completed yet. Such a claim was absolutely fictitious, and it was used as a pretext to elicit additional "donor' funds for "development" projects in Gaza!

To give himself prominence as a local institutional development figure, who is responding to people's immediate needs, Al-Haj Rashad Shawwa created in Gaza what was known as the 'Benevolent Society.' The 'Benevolent Society' became the official conduit for supporting and marketing the Jordanian Plan in Gaza [supported by the Americans and the Israelis]. The offices of the Society were open for people to come in and submit proposals for possible help from funds channeled through Jordan, from a variety of sources. The Society became the official address in Gaza to coordinate permits to Jordan and to Israel. This was then the most visible address and symbol of normalizing acquiescent and simultaneous relations with the Israeli occupation structure, on the one hand, and with the Jordanian regime, on the other. The Society was an example par excellence of enforcing the control and authority of the ruling capitalist elite.

ILLUSTRATIVE CASE 2: THE MUNIB AL-MASRI "HOUSE OF PALESTINE", AN ANACHRONISTIC PALACE IN NABLUS[33]

Munib al-Masri is one of the well known "shatat" capitalist tycoons, who was permitted to return with the entourage of Arafat in 1994, as part of the Oslo package. He is from Nablus,

33 I relied for information about this case on a number of sources. Some were published, for example, BBC, 2007, Peraino, 2007, and Macintyre, 2008.

but studied in the US, and accumulated his vast wealth in the "shatat". I got to know him well for the duration of my work as the Director of Programs at Welfare Association in Geneva, where he was one of the leading founders and executive committee members. He surfaces and re-appears in different sections of this work, due to his multiple capacities, and initiatives, that pertain directly to the major issues addressed in this book, particularly in the analysis of the role of capital in impeding PCLD development (Chapter II), and his role in sustaining the work of Welfare Association (Chapter III). Furthermore, Munib al-Masri is relying visibly on his strong capitalist standing and his close relationship with the Oslo political elite, to forge for himself a public political standing, by initiating and assuming visible role in reconciliation between Fateh and Hamas, and between the political leadership in Ramallah and its counterpart in Gaza. He is maneuvering all of this without impacting negatively his privileged relationship with the Israeli occupation, or his connections with the Oslo political elite and his intellectual/academic legitimizers. He is not a traditional party politician, but he emerged over the last few years to stand behind a middle of the road "forum" or "current" that could easily grow into a political party, when the conditions are conducive, and unconnected, at the face of it, to either Hamas or Fateh. He, however, is known to be close to Fateh, as a result of his close historical relationship with Arafat. He continues seizing political opportunities, as of this writing, to insist on his political visibility, and to portray himself as a very cautious critic of certain PA policies. An example of this was his participation in the public gathering at the central square in Ramallah (called *al-Manarah*), on 1 September 2010, which was organized by center-left political parties and trends, against Palestinian participation in direct negotiations in Washington. He read a brief prepared speech filled mostly with inane words and aspirations. I read his participation, however, as an opportune gesture to those left of center forces that he is on their side, and that he is clearly looking for a certain political forum to buoy him.

Yet since his return, and in an effort to assert his visible prominence and economic prowess in the West Bank, particularly, in his hometown of Nablus, he erected, what Donald Macintyre of the *Independent* described as "a jaw-droppingly ostentatious home on the edge of his beloved Nablus". Al-Masri's palace is built on an estate of over 70 acres, on the summit of Mount Gerisim, a stone-throw from Balatta refugee camp. The ostentatious palace is a Palladian-style mansion, "a replica of La Rotanda, Antonio Palladio's 16th century high renaissance architectural masterpiece."

"Almost all of the building materials, including the gravel and sand, were imported from France". The palace includes a staircase "imported from Sicily", and a "Gothic fire place from Versailles". "In the courtyard is a swimming pool whose walls are inlaid with ancient stones imported from France, and alongside the pool is an enormous jacuzzi and sauna". To deflect from this obscene extravagance, al-Masri reiterates, with a "nationalist" pride, that the height of construction was done during the second *intifada* in 2000, where 500 people from Nablus and the surrounding villages were given employment, and participated in the construction of this palace. In one of the interviews al-Masri gave, he made a point in strongly connecting the process of building this palace to Palestinian national struggle for independence, economic development, peace and tolerance. Building this palace, he stated, "gave me a lot of enthusiasm to show to the Israelis and to the world that Palestinians have the urge, the perseverance and the stamina to do something like this"! And that "for the last 45 years I have worked for peace with Israel …". To insist, further, that whatever he is doing is doing it from the perspective of serving his people, as they proceed to achieving their independence, he created fake and artificial apolitical and human discourse, as an embellishment to this anachronistic edifice. "The central structure is called the Dome of Tolerance and includes tributes to the three Semitic religions: Judaism, Christianity and Islam."

While al-Masri dubbed his palace, disgustingly, as the "House of Palestine", or the "People's House", he, himself, was dubbed by foreign reporters (to his liking, I am sure) as the "King of the West Bank" and the "Messiah on a Hill"! This type of anachronistic and dissonant structure is the farthest from the people, and bears no relation whatsoever to economic and political liberation or independence, nor does it have any relation to the architectural culture of Palestinian building.

The Prevailing "Aid" Environment

It has been discussed earlier, here and in numerous other studies, the extent of external aid that is being made accessible to the PA as an enticement to accept the imposed political agenda on us that falls much shorter than our minimum demands for justice, equality and freedom from occupation in a liberated society. This has been made very clear, and repeatedly. The prevalent environment of aid is that of, what I would describe, as the "tyranny of aid" and aid agencies. Major transnational corporate and governmental aid agencies are permitted to be "tyrannical" because they pay the salaries of some 170,000 employees, on which no less than 1-1.5 million Palestinians depend, whether through direct employment in the PA or in various NGOs. The challenging question is how to regain control over our decisions and public policies, and to undermine that "tyranny".

The aid that we are receiving is not a humanitarian charity; it is political aid that Western centers of capital extend to ensure the success of their political agenda. It may be also a symbolic compensation for the massive historical evil they inflicted on us. However, this is the extent of it. Being our entitlement, is not a sufficient justification to allow external aid to permeate the core of our society and value system, and to supplant and take over our governance structure. How to challenge that, reverse our engulfing dependence on it, and replace it with our own indigenously accountable resource system is the crux of our struggle.

Dalia Association's approach towards advocating the development of "community philanthropy" as the "antidote to dependence on external aid" could be the correct approach. However, it is too early to tell because Dalia itself is struggling to survive in the prevalent aid industry atmosphere.[34] Such a system of philanthropy is based on identifying and valuing our indigenous resources, rather than determining what funds we need to get from outside, and what compromises we should be willing to do to get them. How do we confront this hegemonic external "aid" challenge?

First, we need to embark on a process of self-liberation and true consciousness that our life is NOT dependent on funds we get from external agencies. Conversely, we need to stress that our life is truly dependent on local solidarity and mutual communal popular support and protection, through collectively generating local resources for what we really need to survive and plan for our future sustenance and resilience. The important point here is not the amount of resources (funds, etc), but the pride and national identity in generating these resources locally, as a result of our determination and conviction. While this is a gradual and long-term process, the end result should be a decrease in our dependence on external funding sources, and regaining our strength in our auto-strength and confidence in our indigenous ability to support what we really need.

Second, we need to apply, what I call the BDS rule, albeit more stringently. In this transformational process, we need to form "community-based development committees", whose primary task would be to research external funding agencies, not in terms of what they fund, but in terms of who funds them. Transnational funding agencies whose sources of funds are Western corporate and governmental capital, who are against Palestinian self-determination and true liberation, should be boycotted, and that information should be disseminated and deliberated publically.

Third, we should emphasize that it is the people's prerogative—I mean the average person's prerogative—to participate in the decisions of what "development" they need, and how to do it.

34 (Murad, 2010); Thanks to my friend Sam Bahour for his insightful comment.

ILLUSTRATIVE CASE 3: CONSTRUCTING AL-JIFTLIK SCHOOL—A CASE OF INDIGENOUS INITIATIVE MARRED BY POLITICAL FUNDING[35]

Al-Jiftlik is a very poor area in the Jordan Valley Rift (*al-Ghor)*, in which currently some 4000-5000 Palestinians live. The area has been completely neglected since the early fifties of the last century, by the Jordanian Government and since the Israeli occupation in 1967. According to the Oslo Accords, al-Jiftlik is classified as area "C", i.e., it falls under exclusive Israeli jurisdiction.

Pre 1948 the people who owned the land and lived on it were Al-Masa'id Bedouin tribe, their social allies and affines from other neighboring tribes, and the people who tilled the land and managed their livestock for them. "Al-Masa'id tribe had no school to teach their kids, even though 35 men among them were literate. No better indication of Al-Masa'id's passion for learning and education than the fact that they sent their sons to Al-Najah school in Nablus to get their education. Ten of their sons were studying at Al-Najah school in 1944." [36] This prompted the Damen family of al-Masa'id tribe to establish their own school on their land, in 1944, to ensure that their sons get educated. They hired at their own expense a teacher from *Ma'had Akka al-Shar'i* (Akka Religious Institute), who came to al-Jiftlik, lived with them, and taught their sons. And gradually, as they completed the available grade at this school, they were shipped to Nablus to continue in the next grade at Al-Najah school. There, they were placed in the appropriate grade after they were tested.

Following the *Nakba* of 1948, the social composition changed. Refugees from different locations in Palestine streamed

35 I relied for information for this case on interviews conducted with the Director General for Buildings at the MoEHE, the Director of the Jericho Educational District, the Principal of the school, and a member of the family that owns the land on which the school was built. Interviews were conducted in August-September 2010, by phone and in person).

36 (Al-Dabbagh, 1970: 570).

into al-Jiftlik area. In 1951, the Jordanian Government agreed with UNRWA to open an elementary school in the area, on the condition that the school would provide the service to both refugees and non-refugees alike. UNRWA established a school in tents. According to the historian Al-Dabbagh,[37] UNRWA had established two elementary-preparatory schools (the first 9 grades), one for boys and one for girls. In 1966/1967, the boys' school had 674 pupils, while the girls' school had 248 pupils.

Since the establishment of the PA and the Ministry of Education in 1994/1995, The Damen (Al-Masa'id) family kept looking for ways to have a secondary school in the area to provide education until the end of the 12th grade to all boys and girls in the area. They donated the necessary land for the project, and they urged the Ministry of Education to secure the required funding for construction and equipping. Finally, a commitment of nearly $1 million was made by USAID for the new school, to be implemented through ANERA (American Near East Refugee Aid), an American PVO (Private Voluntary Organization) active in the area. After a long bureaucratic process, the bid for construction was launched, and a winner was selected.

After Hamas won the legislative elections in January 2006, and a "national unity" government was formed, led by Hamas but including Fateh and other political factions, the US decided to boycott the new government. USAID's financial commitment to build the school in al-Jiftlik was frozen, and the entire project was in limbo. In the meantime, the Government of Malysia allocated some funds for the new government. These funds were allocated for projects in various governorates. The share for the Jericho governorate was about $300-$350 thousand, which, initially, was to be used to remodel and upgrade the "muqata'ah", the President's headquarters, in Jericho. However, the then governor of Jericho argued that the priority is for building al-Jiftlik school, and the Malaysian funds should be used to replace the frozen US funds. With an additional contribution of $90,000

37 (Ibid.: 571)

from the Moroccan-Palestinian solidarity Committee, al-Jiftlik secondary school was built.

However, following the botched coup against the Hamas-led government by US-trained Fateh forces in Gaza, Abbas, in collusion with the US and Israel, formed a "care taker" government, with Salam Fayyad as its Prime-Minister. This was openly hailed and welcomed by the US, Israel and other Western powers. To show its support to the President and his "care taker" government, and to reward it, the US released some of the funds that had frozen earlier, directly to the new Ramallah government, and flaunted them visibly. Some of these funds were allocated to add a few rooms to the existing school structure, including computer rooms, administration, etc. Because of this, the entire school structure became identified as having been constructed thanks to USAID funds!

This is one of multitude of cases where Western aid is a political aid par excellence. It is granted as a reward to those who acquiesce to the imposed political agenda. This case amplifies the fact that actual people's priorities are identified and highlighted by the people themselves on the ground, and that political aid impedes the realization of indigenously-identified priorities.

The Prevailing Civil Society and Socio-Cultural Environment

Although the concept of "civil society" is reiterated frequently, in conferences, reports, publications, etc, the particular reference is to non-governmental organizations. Under the tyranny of Western corporate funding, critical viable components of civil society have been degraded, and rendered almost obsolete. Based on our analysis in the previous parts of this book, which focused on how external funding sources are targeting the proliferation of "developmental" NGOs at the expense of politicized mass-based movements, it is evident where the challenge lies. To facilitate the formation of a PCLD environment, our target should be the reformulation, re-activation and re-engineering of a viable, critical, membership-based political-economic-social mass movement. The main components of which ought to be political parties on the left, workers unions, independent local community press, student movement, youth movement, and coalitions of various voluntary work groups.

Since the *intifada* of 1987 was terminated through containment by the deceptive promise of an end to the conflict by political means, and since the promise for a just solution was overtly false and misleading, the socio-cultural environment sled into gradual dilapidation. The daily *modus operandi* was directed by an ad-hoc conglomeration of eclectic cultural values, which permeated the existing traditional system of values. In the context of the prominence of capitalist cronyism, corrupt political clientilism, abuse of power and privilege, collaboration and normalization of relations with the occupation structure, absence of personal security, increasing poverty and unemployment, it became clear that the essence of action was based on quick and maximized profit motives, willingness to do all that is necessary to obtain funds from NGOs and transnational agencies, no social collective solidarity and voluntary initiatives, and individual concerns and interests were pegged against communal and collective concerns. Such a situation provided the ground for self-salvation, prominence and success through access and extreme loyalty to influential individuals in the ruling political and economic elites.

This process gave birth to new and hybridized classes, unrelated to the means or the process of production, e.g., the NGO class, the "policing" class, the "bureaucratic" class, etc. This is an offshoot of the Oslo process, and whose function is the entrenchment of this process.

The challenge confronting us is: how to re-engineer this artificially-imposed environment in order to render it people-centered and liberation-prone?

First, I maintain that liberationist development starts with self-liberation;

Second, self-liberation requires, as Fanon[38] maintained more than half a century ago, real (not false) consciousness, indigenously-generated and nurtured, and embedded in people's history, strength, and value system;

Third, to create and nurture an indigenous consciousness[39] that evolves an integrating identity and collective strength, we need to revise our basic educational curricula in order to counter the re-engineering approaches, imposed from outside, by redefining the content of what it means to be a Palestinian in our context, and how to re-integrate the new notion of Palestinian hood with that of the rest of the Palestinian people. This is an integrative process that should involve and empower parents committees.

Fourth, the people, through their various formations, i.e. parents, youth, workers, etc, should be involved in determining the type of quality education offered, and by whom. Quality education is not a market function; it is a critical nationalist enterprise aiming at how to train generations to be willing and ready to safeguard a resilient social fabric that resists fragmentation and all forms of oppression. This is a nationalist strategic endeavor, the support for which must come from indigenous resources. We, as a people, should resist any attempt by external funding sources to circumvent it.

Fifth, creating a conducive environment for People-Centered Liberationist Development is a long-term collective struggle, yet it is essential if we are to be really free.

How do we proceed from here? I offer the following suggestions and justifications.

1. The reader of these chapters may come out with the conclusion that this is a lost cause, and we cannot do anything about it. I do not share this position. We can do a lot about it, if we realize that ...

38 (Fanon, 1963)

39 Refer also to (Freire, 1971)

2. Our people are our greatest and most important asset. This asset cannot be effective unless it comes together, with the determination and conviction that our Palestinian communities need our support. Among us, we own and control a huge reservoir of indigenous resources that we can regenerate and put to use, exactly as we did admirably during the first intifada. These resources were put to use effectively then not because they were funded by external agencies and "donors", but because the people identified with the needs of their communities; believed in their inherent collective strength; and they internalized the commitment to struggle against an occupying and oppressive power, and the determination to end it. The same occupying and oppressive power is still controlling us albeit more perniciously, through the direct use of some of our people, our so-called leadership, our police, our capitalists, etc, as sub-agents for this control.
3. Generating productive, sustained and dignified work: It is imperative that our young people find opportunities for productive work, which allows them to make a dignified living; which provides them with job security; and which imbues them with personal and national pride that they are doing something meaningful for their families and society. The emphasis here is on "productive" work during which they develop new skills, or hone their existing skills, and strengthen their Palestinian Arab affiliation and identity. Most of the jobs in the public sector—PA ministries, security agencies, other agencies—are non-productive hidden unemployment, based on factional loyalties and wasta. This is a colossal human and national waste. Many of us keep repeating the question of why are not the right-skilled people put in the right place? Why are many highly-skilled individuals roaming around looking for jobs, and not finding them, in a supposedly "state building" situation? We need to reverse that. We should demand

to know, publically, why is the ruling party affiliation is the major criterion for placing young people in these PA positions? Places of potential employment, whether private or public sectors, need, too, to reverse that, and we must hold them accountable.

4. Monopolies that were established under the pretext of investment in the development of our society, e.g., Paltel, Jawwal, etc, cannot just provide temporary employment for qualified young people, for batches of 2-3 years at a time, in order to avoid having them accumulate social benefits, and to increase the monopoly's profits. It is well known that if young people feel secure in their jobs, they produce more, and develop job loyalty. I am not against the simple principle of profits for investments. I am, certainly, against the principle of greed; the accumulation and maximization of profits at the expense of workers' decent living and job security. Greed, as many others have recognized, leads to control, abuse and corruption. Many of our Palestinian capitalists, who navigated and maneuvered the political elites to establish these monopoly companies, were already billionaires in their own right. If they are investing in these companies, as they claim, to "develop" Palestine, why do they insist on accumulating more profits, and to where these profits are redirected? This is a legitimate question all of us must insist on receiving truthful and convincing answers for. It is our right—the average citizen's right—to know, since these profits are generated by investments that are made in our name.
5. The right skills, what should they be, and who decides: It has been said repeatedly that ours is a "university degree" culture, where having a formal degree is more important than the skills or training it embodies, or the way it was obtained. Our universities persist in producing thousands of graduates every year with new degrees, but with lesser and lesser quality, and with hardly any job potential. The financial reward,

through salary increments of public sector employees, for formal academic degrees, the higher the degree the more money, is an additional driving force behind this trend. We need to re-think this entire trend of employment criteria. I suggest that we should largely ignore academic degrees, and focus more on actual –not putative, experience, skills, and aptitude and drive to learn and acquire new skills. On the other hand, the market, in the liberal capitalist sense, should not be the determining factor in what are the needed skills; our needs to develop a resilient and sustained society should. The community-based development committees, suggested earlier, should have the determining say in this.

6. For example, all necessary skills needed for food production, organic agriculture, organic food -processing, etc, by and large, are not taught, developed, and learned. Agribusiness and corporate agriculture is not the correct approach for us; small community-based food production is. We should insist on the values of food production that produces healthy and nutritious foods for our people. We have to believe in these values, for the real well-being of our future generations, and in order to give us the drive to initiate and sustain profit-sharing adventures.
7. We need to be aware that at certain times in our history, we were the food basket for the region. Currently, we have no food security in most of the basic things we need for our communal health and well-being. We should go back to farming our lands the way we knew best; develop this farming in ways that are not dependent on external inputs; and, to do that, we should invest all our financial and human resources in feeding our people, not depending on others, especially our enemies, to feed us. We cannot continue allowing Israel and its occupation structure to persist in controlling our most fertile farmlands.

8. Under the drive of the funding we receive from transnational aid agencies, and embroiled in pseudo-academic culture, most of us became involved, enthusiastically, in a non-productive industry of conferences, workshops, seminars, forums, etc, during which we spend hours regurgitating the obvious, and avoiding real action. This gets us nowhere, and it must be stopped. No one seems to be raising questions about the cost-effectiveness (donors' pet term!) of these activities. On the contrary, these proliferate towards the end of the year because allocated budgets have to be spent. They proliferate, not necessarily because there are important and critical issues to deliberate, but because reporting to funding sources must be prepared on time. Of course, I am not against deliberative (not rhetorical) and action-oriented seminars; but I am, certainly, against resource-wasting, non-productive, and not-cumulative activities of this sort, which are geared primarily for public consumption and dissemination.
9. This brings me to my final point. If we are to reverse this entire global trend, and if we are committed to self-liberation, we must stop lying to ourselves, and stop the useless and non-productive search for a "quick fix" by declaring that "Palestine is open for business", and by perpetuating the deceit that neoliberal capitalist investments is the road to our liberation.

I am very aware that I am only scratching the surface. Many of you have other and more developed ideas. I cannot offer magical recipes or solutions; such things do not exist in my lexicon. I can, however, suggest ideas for real action, and urge you, as you read and reflect on this book, to offer your own suggestions for what needs to be done. Only together we will create the necessary environment for a People-Centered Liberationist Development.

CHAPTER TWO

PALESTINIAN CAPITALIST CLASS: ITS ROLE IN IMPEDING THE PCLD PROCESS

INTRODUCTION

The focus in this chapter is on the role of Palestinian capitalists (both "shatat"—Diaspora—and indigenous capitalists), as they become the primary instrument in thwarting PCLD development.[1] The analysis will focus on the interplay between politics (the PLO/PA) and capitalists, as both become the main constituents of the Palestinian ruling bourgeoisie, since the PLO was transformed from being a "revolutionary" movement in the mid-seventies to a ruling political-bourgeois class, in the mid-nineties of the last century, with the establishment of the PA. It will show that the over-riding interest of the emerging class configuration puts it in total alliance with the interests of regional politico-financial interests, (including Israel and the Arab countries) as they form the true periphery of the dominant Western Center of capital.

1 For the purpose of this analysis, I use the term 'Palestinian capitalists' to refer to all those individuals who seek actively to maximize their capital accumulation, regardless of the size of that accumulation. Intentionally, I am trying to avoid the use of the unclear label 'rich', 'wealthy', etc.

This analysis is framed in the evolving context of money and bureaucratization of the PLO since the mid-seventies, and their enticement under the threat of annihilation and rendering them irrelevant, to accept and buy into the notion of dependent self-rule in minute parts of historical Palestine under Israeli-Western hegemony, as a substitute for a liberated and independent Palestine. Money and "aid" played, and continue to play, a key role in making sure that this process stays on track and does not deviate from its prescribed objectives. We will address the role of Palestinian capitalists in fueling this process of concession and acquiescence to an ongoing and sustained colonial occupation, under the "nationalist" guise of seeking an "independent state", to be realized through adopting a free market economy, open economic borders, service monopolies, providing opportunities for cheap labor, etc. All to be achieved through rent-economy, profit-seeking investments, an accelerated and above-board economic collaboration with Israeli capitalists, and ensuring that financial aid from Western states and transnational agencies is secure and maintained. "Development" became the code for this process. Thus, "development" became the code for exploitation, monopolies, misuse and corruption of available funds, securing dealerships for non-productive consumer goods and services from regional and international companies, conducting business deals with Israeli capitalists to expand the profit base for both sides, with the support of the entire gamut of the dominant colonial structures, the control and possession of economic assets that PA bureaucrats managed and regulated earlier, through coalitions, often fabricated, by their capitalist allies, etc.[2]

It is clear that any insightful analysis of the "impact of aid" should be done on the macro level. It should be directed to show to what degree "aid" (whether from Western or Arab sources) is pushing Palestinians under occupation to acquiesce and submit to the imposed plan of dependent self-rule, and the consequent

2 See (Klein, 2007:190ff) for similar processes in China, Poland, etc, under the guise of "reform".

creation of a dependent and subservient population, economy and society.

THE NATURE AND FORMATION OF PALESTINIAN "SHATAT" (OR DIASPORA) CAPITALISTS

Palestinian capitalist class is dualistic with two distinct branches shaped by the occupation and destruction of Palestine. The capitalists, or potential capitalists, who were forced out of Palestine in 1948, are dubbed as "expatriate". They are dispersed throughout the world. The capitalists, or potential capitalists, who remained in Palestine after its destruction, or who became refugees in 1948 and resettled in the West Bank and Gaza, are dubbed here as "indigenous". Whereas the Palestinian "shatat" capitalists "were more developed than capitalists in many other developing countries with equivalent per capita incomes"[3], the "indigenous" capitalist class was "under developed because of decades of Israeli occupation." Such a duality, according to Hilal and Khan[4] "resulted in an implicit PNA strategy of trying to accelerate economic development by prioritizing the needs of the expatriate bourgeoisie while ignoring for the time being the demands of smaller and less advanced indigenous capitalists.". By itself, however, this bias does not explain the discrepancies in capital investments from one sector to the next. Notwithstanding the volume of required investments, which would favor "shatat" capitalists, the priority sectors of the economy are determined by the occupation and the "Oslo Agreements" to which the PA is subject.

"*Shatat*" is a Palestinian term for "dispersal" following the occupation, and the ensuing ethnic cleansing and destruction of Palestinian society in 1948. The reference here to the "shatat" capitalists denotes those Palestinians who had already accumulated capital and were forced out of Palestine in 1948, and were dispersed throughout the world; and to all those who became capitalists in their countries of refuge, and their descendants.

3 (Hilal and Khan, 2004:101)

4 (Ibid)

Thus, the reference here is to Palestinian capitalists outside Palestine, or what some refer to as the "Diaspora", or the "expatriates". These are spread through most countries in the world, from Jordan to South America, most particularly Jordan, the UAE, Egypt, the USA, Canada, Chile, and Western Europe.

In a detailed sociological field study about "Palestinian Businessmen in the Diaspora and the Emerging Palestinian Political System", sponsored by the Egyptian Center for Economic, Legal and Social Studies and Documentation, and funded by the Ford Foundation and the European Union, Sari Hanafi, a Palestinian sociologist and chief researcher, provided us with detailed and comprehensive analysis of the sociological characteristics of this strata. The data are culled from interviews with more than 600 capitalists throughout the world. This section relies heavily on both of Hanafi's books, which he published so far, based on this field study.[5]

In its attempt to arrive at a reliable and comprehensive inventory of Palestinian businessmen in their places of dispersal around the world, in order to gauge their economic capacity and political willingness to support the newly established PA, the study focused on Palestinian Diaspora communities in North America, Chile, the UAE, Egypt, and Syria. After identifying some of their general characteristics, I shall give more particular attention to the emerging Palestinian capitalist class in Egypt, due to its unique and historical relationship with Gaza, and their involvement in the triangle of circulating capital accumulations between Egypt, Gaza and Israel.

"The state of dispersal," Hanafi concludes, "contributed to the creation of new social and bourgeois strata ... and it circumvented the recycling of existing class structure."[6] It seems, however, that this applies most appropriately to the Palestinian communities in North America only.

Most of the Palestinian capitalists studied expressed their support for the "Oslo Process" (keep in mind the context of this

5 (Hanafi, 1997, 2001)

6 (Hanafi, 1997:70)

comment, which was made during the euphoric short period after the signature of the DOP in 1993, and which, in this case, did not deviate from the view of the rest of Palestinian social strata). As to their readiness to invest in the PA areas, the general tone was "wait and see", and "leave all options open". Palestinian capitalists' willingness to invest in the occupied PA areas "depends on pragmatic economic considerations, not political", i.e., regardless of their views of the Oslo Process. The case of Palestinian capitalists in Syria is illustrative. Hanafi reported that, in principle, they are not opposed to peace with Israel, "but they are dubious about the meager results that the Oslo process produced so far." [7] The door for profit is always left ajar! On the other hand, some of the Oslo supporters invest because, as one capitalist in the US commented, "strengthening the economy is the only antidote to violence".[8]

As an archetype of influential and powerful "shatat" capitalists, we shall focus on two examples: Abdul-Majeed Shoman (the Arab Bank) and Hasib Sabbagh (CCC).

ABDUL-MAJEED SHOMAN (THE ARAB BANK)

Being eulogized on his death in 2005, Shoman was characterized as the "builder of one of the Arab world's biggest financial institutions"[9]. Upon the death of his father, Abdul-Hameed Shoman, in 1974, the son, Abdul-Majeed, became the chairman of the Arab Bank, which his father founded in Jerusalem in 1930.[10] "During his career at the helm, he opened 378 branches in 27 countries across the Americas, Europe, Asia and Africa, and made Arab Bank one of the most widespread Arab-owned financial institutions in the world."

Following the first occupation of Palestine in 1948, the Arab Bank moved its headquarters to the Jordanian capital, Amman,

7 (Ibid:63)

8 (Ibid:74)

9 (http://www.timesonline.co.uk)

10 On the detailed process of establishing the Arab Bank, see (Shoman, 1982)

although a few branches remained open in the major cities of the West Bank until the second occupation in 1967. However, benefiting from the "Oslo-generated environment", the Arab Bank became very active again as an important financial institution in the WBG, where 22 branches mushroomed in various locations.

"It is a testament to the quality of the Shoman family's management and foresight — and particularly that of Abdul Majeed — that Arab Bank not only survived the political and military turmoil of the Middle East, but also thrived. His actions during the 1989 economic collapse, and his support of the Jordanian dinar after the death of King Hussein, are now thought to have saved the country from crisis." [11] Intervening to rescue some Arab leaders and regimes from possible collapse, thus ensuring the stability of its own operating environment, has been noted by other observers. For example, Lawrence Joffe commented in the "Guardian" that "often Shoman rescued Jordan from fiscal disaster. In 2000 he released funds to support the Jordanian dinar, which had collapsed after King Hussein died. And Shoman's bridging loans were rumoured to have saved Arafat's Palestinian Authority from bankruptcy."[12]

Shoman served as the first chairman of the Palestine National Fund, the PLO's financial institution. During the 1980s and 1990s, the Arab Bank managed tens of millions of dollars for the PLO.

Shoman was one of the founders, with other "shatat" capitalists, of the Welfare Association in Geneva, and became its chairman until his death.[13] He served as a Member in the Jordanian Upper House of Parliament for two terms (1987-1990 and 1993-1997). He also served as the chairman of the Shoman Foundation in Jordan.

11 (http://www.timesonline.co.uk)

12 (Joffe, 2005)

13 See Chapter III in this book

HASIB SABBAGH (CONSOLIDATED CONTRACTORS COMPANY INTERNATIONAL)

On his death at the age of 90, in January 2010, Hasib Sabbagh's net worth was put at USD 4.3 billion. Nearly eleven years after he graduated with a degree in civil engineering from the AUB, he co-founded with his brother-in-law, and life-long partner, Said Khoury, and other partners the Consolidated Contractors Company (CCC), in Haifa in 1945. The company was reconstituted in Lebanon after the fall and destruction of Palestine in 1948. CCC "evolved from a modest local enterprise into the giant global multinational corporation that it is today".[14] CCC had its headquarters in Beirut until the break of the Lebanese civil war in 1975, where the company was relocated to Athens.

Benefiting from the economic construction boom of Dubai, CCC provided offshore services to the oil and gas industries in the countries of the Persian Gulf. Its project portfolio includes: the construction of Iraq's Abu Ghraib prison, a terminal extension at Washington's Ronald Reagan National Airport, the Azerbaijan section of a 1,770-kilometer pipeline to the coast of Turkey for a group led by BP Plc, Europe's largest oil company, and a Dubai shopping mall. CCC today has over 140,000 employees and annual sales of about $5 billion. CCC is ranked within the top 20 of international contractors globally, according to the company's Web site.[15]

In an interview with *Bloomberg Business Week* at the occasion of Sabbagh's death, a former Jordanian prime-minister characterized Sabbagh as having "maintained relationships with very senior and key decision makers around the world … Hasib went from being a Palestinian refugee to being a citizen of the world."

Sabbagh was a member of the Palestine National Council and helped former Palestinian Authority President Yasser

14 (Khalidi, 2010:52)

15 (Derhally, 2010)

Arafat to get into a dialogue with the U.S. Former U.S. President Jimmy Carter, whose Center received financial support from Sabbagh, characterized him as "one of my earliest and strongest allies in pursuing peace in the Middle East. ... Hasib's integrity and judgment ... made him a successful businessman ... (and) a trusted adviser."[16]

With Shoman and other "shatat" capitalists, Sabbagh founded the Welfare Association in Geneva. He remained on its Board until that position was passed on to his son.

PALESTINIAN CAPITALISTS IN EGYPT

Below, we shall look in detail at the group of Palestinian capitalists in Egypt, focusing, in particular, on their relationship with Gaza since the establishment of the PA.[17]

The presence of the Palestinian community in Egypt dates back to as early as the 1930's and 1940's. During that period the British Mandate authorities were encouraging Palestinian emigration as a means of support for the Zionist project in colonizing Palestine. The Palestinian minority in Egypt, most of whom are from Gaza, due to physical proximity, became solidified in the aftermath of the ethnic cleansing of Palestine in 1948.

During the Nasser regime, opportunities were open for Palestinian students to study in Egyptian institutions of higher learning. Many did. Thus, Hanafi's research shows that 74% of his sample of Palestinian capitalists in Egypt had university degrees, one-third of whom in economics and commerce and 13% in engineering.[18] So, it is not surprising that the major economic activities, in which they are involved, are commerce, trade, services, construction, tourism, agriculture, etc.

Following the 1967 occupation of the West Bank and Gaza, a number of Palestinian capitalists from Gaza embarked on investments in Egypt. This expanded particularly in the after-

16 (Ibid)

17 (Hanafi, 1997)

18 (Ibid:45)

math of the peace treaty between Egypt and Israel, and the "opening of the economy" during the Sadat regime. A number of investments followed a triangular path between Egypt, Palestine and Israel. The case of Walid Shawwa, the owner of the "Unified Plastics Company for Modern Irrigation" is a good illustration. After he studied agriculture in a vocational institute in Gaza, he received a number of training courses in Israel, and became the Gaza representative for Israeli companies specializing in irrigation networks and equipment. After gaining the necessary experience, he started his own private service of selling, installing and maintaining drip irrigation equipment. With the peace treaty between Egypt and Israel, he decided to settle in Egypt in 1977 where his company became involved in production. In 1994, the company employed 80 employees, and it was the only company in the Arab World that specialized in the comprehensive production of equipment or drip irrigation.[19]

There are other similar cases of Palestinian capitalists who transferred to Egypt the knowledge and the experience they acquired from Israel in advanced methods and research in agriculture, and settled in Egypt during the Sadat period. In one such case, a Palestinian capitalist established in Egypt a successful company specializing in genetically modified plant production, through the transfer of Israeli knowledge in this area. However, he was reluctant to admit that he was engaging in business deals with Israeli Jewish capitalists until the signature of the "Declaration of Principles" between the PLO and Israel.[20]

While these, below-the-surface, normalized economic relations between Palestinian capitalists living in Egypt and Israeli capitalists are ongoing, the surface discourse is anti-normalization and, on the whole, nationalist and patriotic! Overtly, Palestinian capitalists in Egypt insist on remaining on good terms with the PLO. In September 1995, the "Association of Palestinian Businessmen in Egypt" published a full-page ad

19 (Ibid:47)

20 (Ibid:50)

in the leading Egyptian official daily (Al-Ahram) in support of Arafat, as soon as he arrived in Gaza.[21]

Historically, on the other hand, the PLO interfered and railroaded earlier attempts by Palestinian capitalists in Egypt to organize themselves in federations or associations. Earlier attempts in 1985 and 1989 by Palestinian capitalists to establish a federation for themselves were circumvented by the PLO until after the establishment of the PA in 1994. Then, the PLO/PA encouraged Palestinian capitalists in Egypt to organize in the hope of enticing them to invest in Gaza.[22]

It should be noted that all other organizing attempts by "Shatat" capitalists, initiated during the period when the PLO leadership was at its weakest, following its expulsion from Lebanon in 1982, were undermined by the PLO leadership. The obvious explanation is that a weak and humiliated PLO leadership feared that such initiatives may generate new centers of economic-political power, which could have the potential of challenging its geographically disbursed political-symbolic legitimacy, for example, the "shatat" capitalists' "London Conference" in 24 June 1982, while Beirut was besieged by the Israeli army, is a case in point. This is not to say, however, that an organic interplay between the two elites—capital and political—did not take place for the duration of the period, since the rise of the PLO. On the contrary, a fairly integrated interplay between the two, based on an understanding of some sort of "division of labor", whereby capital would support the claimed PLO leadership position, as it is being guaranteed ample opportunities for profitable investments in Palestine, disguised as "national development", abound.

THE INTERPLAY BETWEEN ECONOMICS AND POLITICS: CEMENTING THE "DEVELOPMENT BUSINESS"

Of course, the interplay between economics and politics is not new in human history. Each side's goal in this process is to use the other side to help him in maximizing his capital accu-

21 (Ibid:46).

22 (Ibid)

mulations, whether it is financial, political or social capital. This section, however, will concentrate on the process of interaction between Palestinian capitalists, especially those in the "shatat", and the PLO/PA political elite, through which each tried to maximize its profit-base—political, economic, or symbolic. Regardless of how this process was dubbed, the overall result which we have been witnessing over the last some twenty years is, what I am referring to here, the "development business".

My focus is on the last 20-30 years of Palestinian history. The analysis will go in depth in this process of interplay between Palestinian capitalists and the ruling political elite (the PLO, Fateh, etc.) to show that what is taking place is a "development business", or "development industry", in which capitalists increase their opportunities for profit, as they legitimize and consolidate the acquiescent position of the ruling political class to a continued and normalized Israeli colonial occupation of this part of Palestine (the West Bank and Gaza). In this process a **dependent** self-rule is justified and internalized; the right of return of Palestinian refugee communities is abrogated and re-defined; the society itself is transformed into a pool of controlled and pauperized workers; the use of land as an agricultural productive source is undermined and ignored; indigenous energy and voluntary initiatives are determined by the amounts of available "donor' funds; and the genuine "development" of Palestinian society is transformed into a deeply entrenched myth.

This generates a number of critical questions that need to be explained. How do we sort out fact from fiction? Talk from action? Form from content? Etc. How can we explain the apparent contradiction between the publically reiterated and repeated *ad-infinitum* official slogans of seeking Palestinian independence (an independent state); ending the occupation, etc., on the one hand, and joint political economic ventures with the agents and structures of the occupation, on the other? How can we explain the flagrant push of the politico-economic ruling elite to normalize relations with Zionist capitalists (Jewish-Israelis and Jewish-Americans), while the people remain under actual, ongoing and legitimized colonization, camouflaged with the rubric of "economic peace"?

This analysis is anchored in the premise that there was a gradual shift of the PLO, from being a "revolutionary movement"(barely, the first ten years of its life) seeking to liberate Palestine from colonial occupation, to a "bourgeois movement" seeking to invest in any part of occupied Palestine given to it as long as it acquiesces with the international plan of continued colonization. This strategic shift required an unambiguous shift of the PLO to the right, portrayed clearly by the continued hegemony of Fateh in the PLO and the PA, later on. This shift started becoming clear by the mid-seventies when the survival of the PLO became totally dependent on funds from regional Arab countries, especially Saudi Arabia, the price of which was its acceptance of Western imperial plans for the region. This process became more crystal clear with the effective replacement of the PLO by the PA, as a result of the "Oslo Process", and the consequent absolute dependency of the PA on foreign aid for its survival.[23]

In this section, we will trace and analyze the interplay between Palestinian capitalists in the Diaspora (*shatat)* and the PLO leadership since the Israeli invasion of Lebanon in 1982, whose explicit objective was to end the PLO as the then recognized leadership of the Palestinian people, and to force them out of Lebanon. This analysis will show that the "shatat" capitalists could not have succeeded at "moderating" PLO position towards accepting the US-Israeli dictat of a political submission agenda, without the PLO leadership itself having taken that position much earlier. Palestinian "shatat" capitalists accepted willingly to be used as a "political-economic" tool to reach an objective beneficial to both. In reality, they aspired to play that role in seeking influence; and when the opportunities presented themselves, they welcomed them.

This is not an analysis of Palestinian politics or the evolution of political institutions during this period. This is outside

23 For an in-depth analysis of this process, see (Samara, 1993 and 2007)

the purview of this book. This is, however, an analysis of the major actors who are moving Palestinian political economy into a threatening direction. They are transforming the needed "development" of the PA areas into big business, an open market place. Palestinian capitalists are leading this process in total coordination—not contradiction—with the ruling political elite, and major Western and transnational "donor" agencies.

PRELUDE TO THE ENTRENCHMENT OF THE "DEVELOPMENT BUSINESS"

The 1974 Ten-Point Program which was adopted by the Palestine National Council (PNC) paved the way for the PNC's "declaration of independence" in 1988, and the subsequent PLO aspiration and acceptance to participate in the 1991 Madrid conference, the follow-up initiation of the "Oslo Process" in 1993, and the evolution of the status-quo of a Palestinian Authority truncated and dependent self-rule in the West Bank and Gaza.

The Israeli invasion of Lebanon in 1982, and the subsequent expulsion of the PLO and the termination of its political, military and economic presence in Lebanon, accelerated the PLO's moves towards accepting some kind of an American-Israeli legitimized physical, political, economic, and symbolic presence in parts of Palestine, namely the West Bank and Gaza.[24]

The PLO, in effect, had accepted in 1974 the idea embodied in UN resolution 242 that the West Bank and Gaza were occupied Palestinian areas, and that it is willing to set-up authority in those areas, or in any part thereof, alongside Israel. However, the US Administration at the time insisted that the PLO adopts a public and unambiguous position in which it accepts resolution 242 and "renounces violence", as a price for American recognition of its leadership.

Thus, the years between 1982 and 1988 were replete with political machinations that appeared to "pressure" Arafat, the PLO Chairman at the time, to modulate his position (which

24 Numerous studies and political analyses have shown the advantages accrued to the PLO by accepting this position.

he had taken earlier) in order to satisfy American conditions. In this process, Arafat used well-known Palestinian-American academics and top Palestinian "shatat" capitalists to "mediate" with the Americans.

In his detailed account, as a participant-observer of these political machinations within the PLO, since they were forced out of Lebanon in 1982 until the "declaration of independence" in 1988, and the subsequent deliberations about the Madrid Conference in 1991, Mamdouh Nofal [25] documented how Abu Ammar (Arafat) choreographed these machinations. It was documented before how he utilized, earlier, two well-known Palestinian-American professors, Edward Said and Ibrahim Abu-Lughod, to convey messages on his behalf to the US Secretary of State at the time. Both professors, thanks to Arafat's appointment, were members of the PNC until the PLO's signature of Oslo.

Arafat always made sure to nurture and maintain strong relations with Palestinian capitalists. He always favored to refer to them as the "Palestinian Comprador". Some went as far as claiming that "the PLO emerged from the bosom of the capitalists"[26]. The relationship goes back to the fifties when Arafat headed the Palestinian Students Union in Cairo. The Union, and later Fateh, included in its management committee some members who later became leading capitalists, e.g., Zuhair al-Alami, the CEO of one of the largest engineering consulting firms in the Arab World; Jaweed al-Ghussein who, through his construction companies, was instrumental in building the UAE, and who later became a member of the PNC and the head of the PLO National Fund, a member of the PLO Executive Committee, and a member of the Board of Trustees of Welfare Association.

Since its establishment, Fateh included a number of Palestinian capitalists, through Arafat's nurtured contacts when he was the owner of three contracting companies in Kuwait.

25 (Nofal, 2000)

26 (Hanafi, 1997:86)

Of course not all his business contacts joined Fateh, but, nevertheless, they maintained active contacts with Arafat, not as a contractor (in the economic sense), but as the chairman of the PLO (a contractor in the political sense!). They were the main financiers of the new political movement. Most important among them was Abdul-Majeed Shoman, the then president of the Arab Bank.

During the bloody conflict between the PLO and the Jordanian regime in 1970, the capitalist tycoon, Munib al-Masri, the founder and owner of the Engineering and Development Group (EDGO), and the then Minister of Public Works in the Jordanian government, and the tycoon of finance capital, Abdul-Majeed Shoman, the owner and president of the Arab Bank, used their influence to mediate between both sides of the conflict. The result, which they achieved was to extract the PLO from Jordan, intact.

It has been public knowledge that Arafat relied on a small circle of influential and well-connected capitalists to "mediate" and "ameliorate" the PLOs' positions in critical crises, to render them amenable to the demands of the US-Israel for humiliating surrender. It is moot whether the initiatives came from the capitalists or from Arafat. It is not really important. What is important is the fact that both sides were working gradually towards reaching a platform that was not inconsistent with the US-Israel plan of subjugating the Palestinian political "leadership". Such a platform would lead them eventually into a truncated and totally dependent self-rule on some areas of the occupied Palestinian lands, which they would be able to claim then that this is an "independent Palestinian State", and that this is a visible result for what they have been struggling for all along!

The litmus test for pushing this process forward is the visible and public acceptance by the PLO/Arafat (since the two were synonymous!) of the so-called "peaceful settlement" to the conflict, as was expressed then in the acceptance of UNSC Resolution 242. Just prior to the Israeli invasion of Lebanon—whose clear target was the dismemberment of the PLO—and which was, most probably, coordinated with the US, the Reagan

Administration pushed clearly for this position. To have a backup for his position, Arafat urged certain Palestinian and Arab quarters who were in favor of this approach in the first place, to generate position papers about the proposed "peaceful settlement". Three such papers were presented: one from indigenous capitalists and their supporting intellectuals (primarily from the West Bank); one from "shatat" capitalists and their supporting intellectuals (primarily, Abdul-Majeed Shoman and others); and one from a former Egyptian prime-minister[27].

Taking a clear and unequivocal acceptance position of Resolution 242 was the precondition for starting a PLO-US "dialogue". Machinations towards achieving this goal were intensive, overtly and covertly, until they culminated publically in the 1988 press conference in Geneva. A small circle of "shatat" capitalists played an instrumental role in brokering this process. Most notable among them is the late Hasib Sabbagh, the wealthy tycoon of one of the most successful contracting construction corporations in the Arab World (CCC), and Basil Aqel, his "political advisor". Both were among the founders of Welfare Association. [28]

Concurrently, CCC was involved in construction projects and other business deals in the Gulf region with the multinational Bechtel Corporation. George Shultz, who became the Secretary of State in the Regan Administration, was Bechtel's CEO. Arafat exploited this channel in the hope that the Sabbagh-Shultz "connection" would streamline and facilitate reaching his desired goal of PLO-US "dialogue", without considerable public humiliation. As a result, the atmosphere was prepared for Arafat's/PLO's public concession, but which Arafat insisted that it should take place in the UN body. However, after the US refused to grant Arafat a visa to enter New York to address the UN general assembly, the venue was moved to Geneva, where Arafat gave his long-awaited speech, on 13 December 1988. In that speech, he publically rejected "all forms of violence", and

27 (Wallach, 1992), as quoted in (Hanafi, 1997:87)

28 See Chapter III of this book

accepted Resolution 242, which guarantees the right of all states in the region to survive.

Present during Arafat's speech at the UN General Assembly in Geneva, according to a participant member of the PLO "were many of the cadres and representatives of Fateh, and the independent Palestinian nationalist personalities, among them Hasib Sabbagh and Basil Aqel who played an essential role in the formulation of the American position in the dialogue with the PLO."[29] In an explanatory endnote, Nofal elaborated further:

> *Hasib Sabbagh and Basil Aqel, members of the PNC since its establishment, are independent nationalists. The first is one of the large Palestinian capitalists and the founders of the PLO; and the second is a veteran politician. ... Abu Ammar [Arafat] always consulted them and always used them to transmit his views to various international parties, benefiting from their wide network of relations, especially among the American politicians and capitalists. Abu Ammar was keen on having both next to him when he delivered his speech in Geneva, and benefiting from their relationship with Shultz before he became the US Secretary of State.*[30]

The humiliation did not stop with refusing Arafat a visa to enter New York, but the American position following the speech was that "it did not go far enough". They claimed that he was ambiguous; and he did not utter the magic words of "renunciation of violence" and "recognizing Israel's right to exist". A flurry of activities by three "shatat" capitalists, namely, Shoman, Sabbagh and al-Masri, focused on pushing Arafat to abide by the US-Israel condition, to the letter, and to express it, unequivocally, in a press conference; a process which Arafat himself referred to as "strip-tease". A new text was then drafted, and Sabbagh "transmitted it word by word" to the Americans, before they finally

29 (Nofal, 2000:258)

30 (Ibid.: Endnote 13)

consented.[31] When the entire scenario was fully cooked, Arafat expressed that position later in a press conference in Geneva.[32]

A Palestinian sociologist friend on the left, who was with the PLO in Beirut at the time, commented to me how the Left, at the time, was antagonistic to the Palestinian bourgeoisie and attacked the two Palestinian-American professors for their role in mediating between the American Administration and the PLO. Fateh, he commented further, had good relations with finance capital and no doubt the bourgeoisie felt more affinity with Fateh than with the Left. "My feeling at the time ... is that Palestinian capitalists were very much in favor of a state on part of Palestine (West Bank and Gaza)." His feeling is that their position was influenced by "political" reasons where they wanted a state to represent them, where they would have political influence.

Following 1982, "shatat" capitalists embarked on initiatives to fill what they perceived as a political vacuum created by the expulsion of the PLO from Beirut, and their dispersal in a number of Arab countries distant from the immediate borders of Palestine. Except for their capital and their possible influential connections with American and regional capital, they lacked political legitimacy and real constituencies on the ground in Palestine. They tried and failed. The "London Conference" of 24 June 1982, which was, as Samara claims, "in preparation for inheriting the PLO" should be viewed from this vantage point. Arafat, however, succeeded in undermining and thwarting this initiative. He may had acquired a more correct reading of Israel's position, where it would be more beneficial for it to negotiate with a Palestinian group who claimed political leader-

31 (Hanafi, 1997:88)

32 At the time, I was in Welfare Association offices in Geneva. I can't help but recall the excitement and enthusiasm that Munib al-Masri displayed that day, following the US approval of the text. Munib came into my office and hurled with glee his "visitor pass" for the press conference for that afternoon on my desk, as an undisputable evidence that it is finally happening. This was considered a prized achievement by these "shatat" capitalists for their skillful mediating effort and interplay between capital and politics.

ship, and who enjoyed legitimacy on the ground, i.e., the PLO. If, as it is very clear, that capitalists' approach to the conflict has always been through negotiations and compromise, then it was obvious that any adversary would conduct negotiations with those who have the power to deliver, or "to sell". That was, and is, the PLO/PA. For them, "as people of capital, the Homeland is a Business. That is why when the PLO started negotiations with Israel, Palestinian capitalist elite supported and became closer to Arafat and his bureaucratic capitalist structure. Thus, inside the occupied Palestinian areas, a large section of the capitalists became sub-contractors and formed, essentially, a Palestinian comprador".[33]

Consequently, and within these parameters, Palestinian "shatat" capitalists must have come to realize that the most effective and profitable approach they could play is to broker effective **economic** interplay between the political leadership (the PLO/PA), on the one hand, and the structure of Israeli occupation and Western capital centers, led by the US, and supported by European centers, global corporations, and transnational funding agencies, on the other. This approach would not alienate them from the dominant political leadership of the day; thus they can maintain the façade that they are investing "Palestinian nationalist capital" in the "development" of Palestine. This would ensure their largely "profitable" influence without rocking the political boat, as it were.

The "shatat" capitalist initiative of founding the Welfare Association (WA) in 1983 in Geneva, as a "development association", with benign and philanthropic implications embedded in the name, through which they decided to invest some of their wealth, should be viewed from this perspective. Likewise, the bulk of subsequent financial investments, which the "shatat" capitalists decided to commit in the areas under the PA jurisdiction, follows the same path, and allows them to buy (and sell) parcels of WBG, through politically facilitated and

33 (Samara, 2007)

sanctioned multi-year monopolies in a "captive economy". To do that, they have to maintain and nurture close and coherent relationships with the political bureaucracy, while maintaining and nurturing close and coherent relationships with the structure of real power, i.e., Israeli colonial occupation and the US. This is inherently and ideologically an antithetical approach to the "people-centered, liberationist development" (PCLD), as discussed earlier, and that is being advocated here.

THE NATURE AND FORMATION OF PALESTINIAN INDIGENOUS CAPITALISTS

In the present context, "indigenous" capitalists refer to the group of Palestinian capitalists in the West Bank and Gaza, who had to develop their businesses under occupation since 1967. Economically, this group is much less developed than the "shatat" capitalists because of restrictions imposed by the occupation structure. The colonial occupation undermined "the power base of the traditional landed and commercial capitalist classes and ... it erected insurmountable obstacles for further indigenous economic development and the emergence of an industrial capitalist class."[34]

Thus, the industrial base was small and undeveloped. By the time the PA was established, "the Palestinian economy remained dominated by small, family-owned firms".[35] According to the Palestinian Central Bureau of Statistics (PCBS), in 1998 "more than 90 percent of firms in the WBGS employed less than 10 workers, only 20 establishments hired more than 100 people ...". [36] Prior to the advent of the PA, many Palestinian firms, especially in textiles and footwear, depended on subcontracting activities for Israeli businesses. Basically, the indigenous capitalist class was "integrated within and dependent upon Israeli capital".[37]

34 (Kimmerling and Migdal, 1994), as quoted in (Hilal and Khan, 2004:71)

35 (Nasr 2004:173)

36 (PCBS 1998:42-6), as quoted in (Ibid:173)

37 (Samara, 2007)

In their discussion of "PNA political institutions and the future of state formation", Amundsen and Ezbidi concluded that indigenous capital provided no "internal strategic partners for the state in its capitalist development strategy. ... Privileged access to rent granted to expatriate capital inevitably left indigenous small and medium capitalists further marginalized. ... Investments of some size were dependent on state protection and privileges, and were made by people with close ties to the political leadership. ... Maintaining good relations with the political leadership was a necessary expense for protecting investments".[38]

Palestinian indigenous capitalists were infuriated by the visible pre-eminence of the "shatat" capitalists, and their overt influence on the PA's economic plans, and their almost unfettered access to the new "Oslo political bureaucracy", and the consequent privileged monopolies. After having been suppressed and beaten by the occupation, they witnessed their "shatat" counterparts, who were permitted to accumulate huge capital outside Palestine, coming back to reap profits with ease. The first public indication of this dissatisfaction surfaced in May 2000, during the Palestinian Trade Center's (Paltrade) "First National Trade Dialogue Conference". Many viewed this Conference "as an early attempt by local capital to exercise its influence". As an influential business association representing mainly large businesses, Paltrade attempted to engage the new political bureaucracy in facing and listening to the concerns of indigenous capitalists.

The Conference "demanded that a law regarding monopolies and privileges be established ... (and that) the private sector should participate in the formulation of this and other economic laws, express its opinion on the final status negotiations ...". [39] As we see below, all major monopolies are controlled by "shatat" capitalists, and the role of indigenous capitalists remains subsidiary.

38 (Amundsen and Ezbidi, 2004:158)

39 (Paltrade, 2000:23-4), as quoted in (Nasr, 2004:174)

INVESTMENT IN A FREE-WHEELING MARKET ECONOMY

Immediately following the signing of the Oslo Accords, the PA reiterated clearly and unambiguously that the "new Palestine" will abide by "free market" economy; and, consequently, it is wide open and very hospitable to all types of economic investments—the bigger, the better. In 1996, the PA prepared, with the assistance of the World Bank and the IMF, a "Palestinian Development Strategy", and submitted it to the "Conference on the Assistance to the Palestinian People" in Paris.[40] "Four areas were identified as urgent needs areas, namely physical infrastructure, business development, financial systems and the legal and regulatory framework." The document stated also that the PA "would support an open, export-oriented, private-sector led market economy".[41]

Appeals to invest in Palestine for the purpose of effecting the necessary "economic development" were launched recurrently, by Arafat and his "Oslo regime", and were then enshrined in the Basic Law. The first rent-seeking move was the Telecommunication Law (Law # 3, 1996).[42] After the "Law on Encouragement of Investment in Palestine, 1998" (passed in 1995 and modified in 1998) was promulgated, an autonomous public agency was established. The "Palestinian Investment Promotion Agency" (PIPA) was established in 1998. Its stated mission is "to build a better future for all Palestinians by providing constantly improved customer service to foreign and domestic investors, by utilizing an effective One-Stop-Shop, special investment incentives and state of the art technology to attract investment. We facilitate cooperation between the private sector and the government, thereby creating and maintaining a more competitive investment environment".[43]

40 (PNA, 1996)

41 (Nasr, 2004:174)

42 See (Bahour, 1998 and 2000), for more details

43 (http://www.pipa.gov.ps)

The website identifies a number of "investment incentives", as follows:

- "The fixed assets of an enterprise receive various exemptions on customs duties for a defined period …";
- "Exemptions on income taxes are granted to investments of greater than $ 100,000 …";
- "Additional exemptions may be granted to enterprises engaged in export activities";
- "Special incentives and exemptions apply to investments in hospitals and hotels." [44]

It was argued that the new Law and the investment instruments that were set-up were "biased toward large firms and thus promoted monopolies for politically influential groups in the Palestinian economy".[45] Furthermore, it is very clear from the above that there is no emphasis on, or encouragement of investments in production and agriculture. The emphasis is on services and export-oriented economy, whose success is totally dependent on collaboration with the Israeli economy and Zionist capitalists. But, after all, this is not a deviation from the essence of the "Oslo Accords"!

This drive continued afterwards through, what was referred to as, the "Annapolis Process" that was instigated by the George W. Bush regime in 2007. The Annapolis Process "effectively depoliticizes the conflict by converting it into a Palestinian project to earn international recognition as a state, not dissimilar to the old League of Nations mandate and UN trusteeship and decolonization systems. … The thrust of the Annapolis process indeed focused more on how reform and development could help reconsolidate power for the discredited Ramallah-

44 (Ibid)

45 (Nasr, 2004:176)

PA led by Mahmoud Abbas than on how capacity building could lead to meaningful sovereignty".[46]

The political tier of the "Process" started in Annapolis, under the controlling eyes of the Bush Administration, in which formal declarations of support to the Ramallah-PA were induced and reiterated publically by the dominant political powers. However, the economic tier of the "Process", with a Paris venue (on 17 December 2007), focused on pledging funds to the Ramallah-PA in response to a masterfully prepared, technocratic plan for Palestinian reform—The Palestinian Reform and Development Plan (PRDP), under the control of Salam Fayyad's government. Although the Fayyad Government requested the "donors" to cover the total bill of $5.6 billion for the PRDP, the "donors" pledged, instead, $7.7 billion, which exceeded the original request by about 37 percent! It's an unusual step in the annals of allocating foreign Western aid for a specific Project, unless, of course, it's a reward, or compensation, for something else.

The PRDP had three general aims. The clear focus was on the economic development through various institution-building projects, in preparation for statehood.[47] None of the aims, however, focused on independence or sovereignty, or on how to achieve it. Furthermore, and in the absence of sovereignty, the Plan did not address the macro-implementation impediments, which will certainly arise due to the complete control of the process by Israel. On the contrary, it is obvious that the Plan was premising its successful implementation on the integration of Palestinian economy with the Israeli economy, and the essential collaboration of Israeli and Zionist capital in pushing the process forward.

Following the Paris Donor Conference on 17 December 2007, a flurry of heated efforts to attract Palestinian and foreign investors into the PA areas came to the surface. These efforts materialized in The First Palestine Investment Conference

46 (Tilley, 2010:54-5)

47 (PNA, 2007)

which was held over two days in Bethlehem on 21-23 May 2008. The Investment Conference "will showcase business opportunities in the West Bank and Gaza and forge links between the Palestinian private sector and international investors. The conference is a top priority for the Palestinian Authority (PA), which considers it a follow-up to December's donor conference in Paris. The message of the conference is clear: Palestine is open for business".[48] More than 1,800 invitations were sent out. "The majority of potential investors, many of them members of the Palestinian Diaspora, will be coming from the UAE and Jordan. Israel has promised to ensure their access to the event is as smooth as possible. In addition, official delegations from China, Japan, Russia, Sweden, the UK, France and the US will attend, in most cases led by government ministers.[49]

"Palestine is open for business" indeed. All the more than one thousand potential investors, including Palestinian "shatat" capitalists, Palestinian indigenous capitalists, foreign investors, and diplomatic corps, were welcomed officially by a clearly visible and well-marked poster, crowned by the clear insignia of the State of Israel, the Israeli police, and the occupation army. The poster stated "Welcome to Investors Conference-Bethlehem". The sole reminder that the PA existed, or that it could have had anything to do with this, was a small sign at the right bottom of the poster "Palestine investment conference", as you see it on the cover of this book.

Fifty projects in agriculture, finance, ICT, infrastructure and real estate, manufacturing and tourism, with a total budget of $1.073 billion were presented to the Conference, in addition to 59 "project concepts". About one-half of the budget was for infrastructural and real-estate projects. Most of the infrastructural and real-estate projects were presented by "shatat" capitalists under the monopolies that they had established.

The momentum of the first Palestine Investment Conference (PIC) held in Bethlehem in 2008, was formally main-

48 (MAS, Palestinian Economic Bulletin, 2008, Issue 19)

49 (MAS, Palestinian Economic Bulletin, 2008, Issue 20)

tained through other international and local fora. Internationally, a "Palestine Business and Investment Forum" was held in Washington, D.C in October 2008, which was followed by the "London Business Forum on Trade and Investment", held in London in December of the same year.[50] The local forum, dubbed as the "North Forum", was held in Nablus in November 2008.

The "North Forum" was organized and driven by Munib al-Masri, the capitalist tycoon from Nablus, and the Chairman of PADICO, to give a special focus to the North of the West Bank. "The Conference," he said, "was dedicated to businessmen from Nablus, Jenin, Salfit, Qalqilia and Tulkarem in the northern West Bank with the overall aim of boosting business competence in the northern region of the West Bank". The Palestinian Economic Bulletin reported that "70 projects with thousands of job opportunities across the north of the West Bank were presented in four sessions at the conference. Over 1,200 participants attended, including foreign dignitaries, the international community, 300 Palestinian and Arab businessmen (200 from the Palestinian Diaspora), 50 Palestinians living in Israel and members of the PLO executive committee. 100 business leaders from Gaza were denied permits and unlike the conference in Bethlehem last May, no Israeli businessmen attended".

The coordinator of the Conference, Samir Hulileh, PADICO's CEO, "stated that the organizers had targeted Palestinians from the Diaspora to attend the conference. The Diaspora is an important and largely untapped resource of potential investment. ... We believe that Palestine is a good place for new investments. **We guaranteed their smooth entry [?]** for the conference and their attendance was crucial to its success".[51] It must be noted that neither PADICO nor its CEO can "guarantee" anything unless there was an Israeli consent to hold the conference!

50 (PIPA, 2010:4)

51 (MAS, 2008, Palestinian Economic Bulletin, Issue 27; emphasis added).

The slogan of "Palestine open for business" of the first PIC in Bethlehem was maintained and showcased in the public preparations and documents of the second PIC in Bethlehem in June 2010, under the label of "inspiring business"! Such an event, as it was reported, will "highlight successful Palestinian companies that are competing in international markets and promote Palestinian products". Some of the major monopolies and their subsidiaries were directly involved in sponsoring the event. Major funding for the Conference, however, came from the USA (through USAID) and the UK (through DFID), and the Islamic Development Bank. "The conference hopes to encourage business relations between regional and international investors and the Palestinian private sector".[52]

The Palestinian Investment Promotion Agency (PIPA) claimed in its more than 400-page document of the Conference, voiced by President Abbas, "will reflect a different face of Palestine. A Palestine that is ..., a place where you can witness the veracity of the Palestinian people, their steadfastness, and persistence to stay and build a better future ... [where all are invited] to witness firsthand the outstanding achievements of the Palestinian private sector at the industrial and investment levels and the Government's progress in economic and administrative reforms".[53] The Conference was a public marketing campaign for the "Fayyadism", which maintained that "all efforts will be geared towards building the institutional, social and economic infrastructure that will underpin a viable Palestinian State and enhance the ability of Palestine's citizens to prosper in parity with other nation states".[54]

In the second investment conference, 123 projects, available for equity investment, were presented, with budgets totaling in excess of half a billion dollars. About two-thirds of the proposed budgets were concentrated in projects in construction, real estate, and building materials. The lion's share of these projects was pre-

52 (MAS 2010, Palestinian Economic Bulletin, Issue 44)

53 (PIPA, 2010:4)

54 (Ibid)

sented by companies established by "shatat" capitalists, and big indigenous capitalists, or a coalition of both.

Behind the fancy glossy paper and the professional "state of the art" presentations, with detailed SWOT analyses and financial projections, one is really hard put to find what is actually taking place on the ground. What is the status of these more than 200 proposed projects with total budgets of about $1.6 billion? How many of these projects were realized, and how much foreign direct investment they generated? The only obvious indication on the ground is a wave of construction of apartment units, many are completed but empty; some are partially completed and standing idly; and yet some are at the stage of ground breaking. This is all in addition to an active movement of "ready mix concrete" trucks, where we mix the raw cement, which we diligently import from Israel, Egypt, Turkey? No one seems to care!

Our analysis in this section will focus in particular on how the investments of a small, but influential, band of "shatat" capitalists flourished in the PA-controlled areas as part of the "Oslo package", under the wing of, and in cahoots with, the already compromised and subservient PLO leadership. Some of them returned physically to the Palestinian areas; others remained outside. But since this is a transnational process, fueled by transnational capital, it did not matter whether the capitalists themselves physically returned to the WBG or not. They have been successful in this process with the support of other capitalists who remained in the "shatat", indigenous capitalists, Western "donor" countries, and the transnational finance agencies. They coalesced in selling and re-buying Palestine in retail; turning it into their own private farms; mortgaging future generations to cheap slave labor opportunities, totally dependent on the continued occupation, Israeli economy and international financial donations. They, with their supporters, beneficiaries and benefactors in the PA corrupt bureaucracy, came to be dubbed, and often hailed, as levers, or drivers, of future economic "development" of Palestine.

In such an inviting "investment" environment, there was a rush by capitalists to get as close as possible to the "Oslo" political elite, in order to secure the most profitable economic investments for both sides. Public and private monopolies were established. Capitalists, with the support of the World Bank, the IMF, major "funders" of the PA, major UN agencies, aspiring-capitalists within the corrupt political bureaucracy created by the "Oslo Process", pushed and exacted a number of regulatory measures to ensure profitable investments. Big "shatat" capitalists realized, from the outset, that they would have greater profits if they could have a say in determining these regulatory structures, and general economic policy. Thus, it is understandable within this context that "immediately following the Oslo Agreements, a number of large expatriate capitalists offered Arafat a partnership in which they would come up with significant investments in return for involvement in policy-making from the outset. Arafat refused. It was only after the PNA had achieved a degree of entrenchment following the general elections in 1996, and Arafat had secured substantial funding from the international donor community, that he contemplated developing the partnership with expatriate capital."[55]

From what follows, one cannot escape the feeling that we are watching the emergence of an "economic Sykes-Picot" process, albeit at a much lower scale!

NATIONALIST APPROACHES TO MONOPOLIES

As mentioned above, the competition over access to monopolies and privilege resulted, not surprisingly, in the "shatat" capitalists having the upper hand. Two main reasons are responsible for this situation: their control of huge capital accumulation, and their direct interplay with the PLO and loyal support of its political agenda. Indigenous Palestinian capitalists "lacked serious capital and political legitimacy since it had played a marginal role in the national liberation movement. ... The expatriate Palestinian capitalists, located in the oil-rich Gulf states, North America and Europe had significant blocks of capital. They were also eager to invest in Palestine for a com-

55 (Hilal and Khan, 2004:102)

bination of nationalistic and profit-seeking motives. ... The PNA opted for a strategy relying on big expatriate capitalists ... capital intensive investments in services and manufacturing, e.g., hotels, telecommunication, etc, ... It was easier to share rents with a few large capitalists than many small ones." [56]

The following quotation from Nasr's analysis about "monopolies and the PNA" explains clearly the approach used by the PA.

"The PNA followed a number of parallel strategies. First, the PNA granted monopolistic concessions to private investors in large infrastructure projects such as telecommunications and electricity ... . Second, in some cases it went into partnership with private firms in business activities such as hotels, casinos, cigarettes and flour milling. Finally, ... the PNA monopolized the imports and distribution of certain strategic products such as cement and petroleum. Each of these strategies involved discriminatory support for large firms".[57]

The ownership of the PA of the major monopolies ranged from a complete ownership of equity (100%), e.g., the cement, petroleum, and various real estate monopolies, to 80% ownership in the "Palestinian Cigarettes Company", to about 50% in the "Palestinian flour mills", to about 34% in the, so called "Peace Technology Fund", which was a subsidiary of the "Peres Peace Center" and the World Bank! What is more pertinent for our current analysis is the economic decisions that the PA undertook, within the context of the "Oslo Agreements", to cement its dependency on Israeli capital and economy. Many of the PA's holdings "were in commercial enterprises distributing Israeli imports". These products, however, could be imported from other countries at lower cost.[58]

By monopolizing the import of cement, the PA controlled and limited the import of cement, primarily, to the Israeli Nesher Company, which claims in turn that it "supplies most

56 (Ibid:101)

57 (Nasr, 2004:176)

58 (Ibid: 184-5)

of the cement needs of Israel and the Palestinian Authority".[59] Since it sells more than 85% of all cement in Israel, Nesher is directly involved in the construction of the Separation Wall, the checkpoints and terminals, settlements, roads and the basic infrastructure for occupation.

This monopoly "was sustained with the collusion of Israeli border and security forces", and it has been criticized "because it created a powerful coalition against the development of a Palestinian cement industry".[60] The Israeli supplier, Nesher, played a critical role in hampering indigenous capitalist efforts to establish a cement industry in the PA areas, through the nurturing of a network of powerful allies from the PA political bureaucracy, supported by the colonial occupation bureaucracy.

In 1994, the PA concluded an import monopoly agreement with the Israeli Dor Energy Company. According to this franchise, the Israeli company would have the sole right for supplying petroleum products. This was done without any bidding. The Dor Energy (Israel) combined since then with the Alon Company that monopolizes the supply of gas to Gaza, to become Dor-Alon, which is classified now as "one of the 4 largest fuel companies in Israel."

Until it was "reformed" in 2003, the highly corrupt "Palestinian Petroleum Authority" was in charge of this petroleum monopoly, which was chaired by the Minister of Finance, Salam Fayyad. Rents from it were not channeled into the national budget (Ministry of Finance), but to Arafat-controlled "secret" accounts in Israeli banks. This arrangement was openly criticized by many Palestinians. See, for example, the position of the Nablus-based Palestinian "Center for Private Sector Development".[61] As to these "secret" accounts, however, they "were not secret at all and Israel and the external powers colluded in allowing the Palestinian leadership to exercise non-transparent control over part of its tax revenues. Israel even

59 (http://www.nesher.co.il)

60 (Nasr, 2004:184-5)

61 (http://www.cpsd.ps)

paid some Palestinian tax revenues into these 'secret' accounts. ... some of the money in these accounts was possibly from sources such as kickbacks that could not be audited".[62]

ENTICED AND GLOBALIZED CONSUMPTION AT THE EXPENSE OF INDIGENOUS PRODUCTION

Below, we shall focus in some detail on selected economic enterprises, which were created in the context of the "Oslo Process" as the flagships for the proposed and imposed "economic peace", with the initiative of Palestinian, Zionist, and regional capitalists. All are premised on the false assertion that since the "occupation state" is not transmutable, i.e., occupation becomes a constant, then the most effective way of achieving "economic development" in the occupied Palestinian areas is through positive and mutual coordination with the occupation structure. Within this frame of mind, the conceptualization of "nationhood", "independence", "building state institutions", "security", "development", etc. are forced to acquire their opposite "Orwellian" meanings ... their inherent negation. A new lexicon is devised and permeated, focusing, in principle, on how enterprises and capitalists can be successful in attracting investments to "develop Palestine in conjunction with, and in support of, occupation". Thus, according to this newly-formulated conceptual lexicon, coordination and collaboration with the occupation structures, from the top political echelons to the localized military commanders, through joint ventures with Zionist capitalists, become a welcome precondition for successful projects. Furthermore, all "economic instruments" that could generate profitable investments, whether private or public, are allowable and encouraged; the more dubious and corruptible, the better and the more successful.

The following is a case in point that shows the trajectory of how a corrupt, somewhat "secretive" and dubious, PA-owned "slush fund", which was set-up by Arafat and his inner circle of

62 (Hilal and Khan, 2004:79)

economic "advisors" following the signing of the Oslo Accords, acquired a public face as soon as it was subjected to "public" scrutiny. What was dubbed as the "Palestinian Commercial Services Company", which owned, completely or partially, many of the dubious private monopolies that were established, primarily, by "shatat" capitalists, to provide a lucrative base for the new Oslo elites, was allowed to exist. This was achieved thanks to the direct support and consent of the Israeli occupation and the political elite structure, in conjunction with major Western "donor" sources and transnational "funding" agencies. This is what became later on as the "Palestine Investment Fund" (PIF).

PALESTINE INVESTMENT FUND (PIF): FROM A "SLUSH FUND" TO A "PUBLIC INVESTMENT COMPANY"

The private monopolies that were permitted to be established by the new PA, and were owned, fully or partially, by it, were all lumped under the Palestine Commercial Services Company (PCSC), and were privately controlled by Arafat's economic "hit man", Khaled Salam (AKA Mohammad Rashid), away from the public eye. The first public scrutiny of PA's commercial holdings came to light with the production of the first report of the "Palestinian Public Monitoring and Audit Department" (AMAD) in 1997. The report was debated by the Palestine Legislative Council (PLC) and generated public discussions. In its defense, the PA issued a statement to the "Donors" Ad Hoc Liaison Committee meeting in Washington, D.C, denying any serious violations or mismanagement. The PLC, however, was not satisfied with the PA's statement of denial, but opened the subject widely, by publishing a lengthy report showing the various types of mismanagement and violations "including public monopolies, government interventions in the market, and government participation and shareholding in private enterprises".[63]

Finally, in 2000, the PA published a document under the title "West Bank Economic Policy Framework: Progress

63 (Nasr, 2004:180)

Report", prepared in collaboration with the IMF and the World Bank. In this report, the PA revealed a list of all PA investments. "Almost all the enterprises in which the PCSC held equity were monopolies or oligopolies and therefore enjoyed considerable market power.[64]

In the same year, the IMF and the World Bank succeeded in pressuring the PA (Arafat) to restructure the public investments. Arafat agreed to set up a Palestine Investment Fund (PIF) to which all PA holdings were to be transferred. The PIF was set up finally in 2002 under the Ministry of Finance, and managed by Arafat's economic "hit man". It was speculated correctly that "the reason why the IMF and the WB were excited about the creation of the PIF is that they saw it as the first step towards privatization, which they assume will help to create a viable capitalism."[65]

Thus, "PIF's establishment was marked by the transfer of assets previously managed by the PA. ... PIF today is a publicly limited company, fully owned by the people of Palestine. It is financially and administratively independent and is governed by an independent General Assembly and Board of Directors".[66] However, the truth is that neither the general assembly nor the board of directors are independent from the PA, since the board of directors' members, as well as PIF's CEO are appointed by the PA president. Furthermore, the PIF's CEO is the economic advisor to the President of the PA.

In 2003, Dr. Mohammad Mustafa, a Palestinian economist who worked for 15 years in the World Bank in Washington, DC, and who was responsible for setting up PALTEL immediately following the setting up of the PA, was appointed as the chairman and CEO of the PIF, doubling at the same time as an economic advisor to the PA president. He was brought back from Washington, D.C. with a mission to clean up the "slush fund" that became PIF. Was he the World Bank's choice for this

64 (Ibid:182)

65 (Hilal and khan, 2004:90)

66 (http://www.pif.ps)

mission? The PA's? Or, was it the PA conceding to World Bank and other major funders' pressure? In any case, his zigzag line of mobility from the World Bank in Washington to the economic advisor of the PA President in Ramallah is telling.

Oversight over all PIF's activities is the responsibility of a seven-member Board of Directors, appointed by the PA president for a three-year term.

A close look at the current BOD members is instructive:

1. Mohammad Mustafa, PIF's Chairman and CEO;
2. Samer Khoury, Deputy Executive Chairman of CCC, Consolidated Contracting Company, member of WA's BOT, and member of MAS' BOT;
3. Mazen Sinokrot, Chairman and CEO of Sinokrot International Group, and former Minister of the Economy, PA;
4. Nabil Sarraf, Chairman of Palestine Real Estate and Investment Compnay, a PADICO subsidiary company, and Deputy Chairman of PADICO;
5. Mohammad Abu Ramadan, Chairman of Abu Ramadan Investment Group;
6. Tarek Aggad, Chairman and CEO of Arab Palestinian Investment Company (APIC), and Executive Director of Aggad Investment Company, Riyad, Saudi Arabia;
7. Azzam Shawwa, General Manager of Al-Quds Bank, and Chairman of Al-Reef Company.[67]

Four BOD are "shatat" capitalists who were permitted to return in conjunction with the "Oslo Process". They are involved in the monopolies that were established concurrently with the establishment of the PA. They are part of the "Oslo Process" and are active in normalizing economic relations with Zionist capitalists, as a parallel track to occupation. At the same time,

67 (PIF, 2010).

PIF's CEO complained about "Israel's complete control of our movement and access," and acknowledged publically that Israel "stifles job creation and upholds a choking dependency," and that "Palestine's airports, seaports, and bridge crossings – the gateways to world trade – are not under our control. ... Yet without control of our economic gateways, the task of building an economic foundation for statehood is daunting".[68]

PIF owns direct majority and minority stakes in companies, including several fully owned subsidiaries. Since its inception in 2003, PIF transferred approximately $606 million to the PA treasury. In 2009, PIF achieved a profit of approximately $60 million.[69]

According to its 2009 Annual Report[70], PIF invests, in partnership with "Palestine's public sector", local, regional and international private sector companies, and international financial institutions, in 9 major sectors, as follows:

1. Housing: Al-Rihan neighborhood (Al-Bireh and Ramallah) and Al-Jinan neighborhood (Jenin);
2. Real estate and hospitality: Convention Center (Bethlehem), Grand Park Hotel (Ramallah), Intercontinental Hotels (Jericho and Bethlehem), commercial Irsal Center (Ramallah);
3. Telecommunication: Wataniya mobile company;
4. Power and energy: Gaza Gas, Palestine Electric Company (Gaza), WB power station (WB);
5. Trade and industry: Palestine Commercial Services Company (PCSC), National Aluminum Profiles Company (APIC's subsidiary), Nablus Crafts Complex, the Palestine Food Industries Company (APIC's subsidiary);
6. Financial services: mortgage and Loan program;

68 (Mustafa, 2010)

69 (http://www.pif.ps)

70 (PIF, 2010)

7. SME's;
8. Capital markets: local, regional and international; and
9. "Strategic development zones": Jordan Valley and Dead Sea Region.

PIF is instrumental in generating foreign direct investments (FDI). Its major partners in these investments include: Qatar Telecom Company, PADICO, CHF International, Middle East Investment Initiative, the Jordanian-Saudi Land Company (Al-Ard), and the Abraaj Capital, a Dubai-based private equity group. The Abraaj Capital and the PIF just revealed at the World Economic Forum in Davos the launch of the first equity fund dedicated to the PA areas. PIF's CEO stated on the occasion: "The Palestinian economy offers excellent opportunities to investors – despite the political difficulties. Abraaj is a big company and the fact that they have chosen to invest in Palestine is an important signal".[71]

In a recent lengthy interview with PIF's CEO,[72] he affirmed that when he took over the management of the Fund, his mandate was two-fold: "to move the Fund in the direction of investment development and to encourage domestic investment." In 2003, "more than 75 percent of the Fund's capital was invested abroad, and we brought the greater part of this back." The biggest such investment was the partnership between the Wataniya International of Kuwait, the majority of which is controlled by the Qatari telecommunications giant Qtel and PIF, in creating the Wataniya Mobile. Out of this venture, the PA "received $354 million for the license plus 7 percent of all Wataniya Mobile revenue."[73]

The Head of the Palestine Investment Fund was exuberant in cloaking this investment project in "nationalistic" terms. "One could even say we liberated a part of Palestinian space!

71 (Buck, 2010)

72 (Abdul Karim, Tamari, and Farraj, 2010:40-51)

73 (Ibid:49)

This is what it means to control our natural resources: today it is frequencies, tomorrow it will be water, and next, land"! [74] Either there is a deep leap of faith on the part of this investment economist—the economic advisor to the President—or there is basic naiveté about how prolonged settler colonial occupations may be broken, or, worse yet, there is a conscious attempt at poeticizing and mythologizing segments of certain existing oppressive realities to render them palatable to the average citizen. At any rate, I do not recall a sense of elation in the street when the deal with Wataniya was signed. But I do recall, however, that it generated a renewed and more vehement discourse about pervasive privilege and corruption among the Oslo-created political and economic elites.

There is an internal and ongoing debate regarding the accountability of the PIF between the Fayyad government and the PIF. The essence of the debate lies in who actually controls the PIF, the Ministry of Finance or the BOD's tycoons, whose companies are direct beneficiaries of the PIF. This led some observers to raise the question of "conflict of interest" potential, and the independence of the PIF. It is clear, however, that the PIF is not, nor can it be, independent from the Oslo political and economic elite.[75]

PADICO (PALESTINIAN DEVELOPMENT AND INVESTMENT CO. LTD.)

Since the beginning of the "Oslo process", Arafat used the opportunity of granting capital monopolies to capitalists loyal to and supportive of his policies. "During the PLO's initial attempt to organize the sector ... in 1994, prior to the existence of the Palestine Telecommunications Company (PALTEL), a shady American firm, International Technologies Integration (ITI), was originally contracted to set up the first Palestinian phone company. ... In addition, two US firms MCI and AT&T were promised licenses

74 (Ibid)

75 For a summary of this debate, see Adam Entous's story in Reuters (Entous, 2009)

at the same time, one from Tunis and the other from Gaza, only to later learn the PNA decided to pass the sector to its own private sector".[76] ITI, which was headed by "a person associated by marriage with Arafat, was given the sole right to operate telecommunications in the West Bank and Gaza for 25 years. Once a deal became public knowledge, a lobby was formed by a group of expatriate capitalists to persuade Arafat to rescind the deal ... Arafat eventually granted the license to a Palestinian company formed by expatriate capital, Paltel, in which the PNA became a shareholder.[77] Breaking the contract with ITI was settled in an arbitration case, in November 1998, for a $18.7 million award against the PA. The settlement amount was paid and the file was closed.[78]

PADICO is an off-shore registered company in 14 October 1993, or exactly after one month from the signing of the DOP in Washington between the PLO and Israel. PADICO was established as a holding company, which had a declared capital of USD 1 billion and a subscribed capital of USD 172 million.[79] It included the who's who of "shatat" capitalists whom, at the time, Arafat described as "the tigers of the Palestinian economy" who were expected to develop the new state.[80] The initiative came largely from the "shatat" capitalists with the enticement of the PLO leadership that already accepted the US-Israel imposed political plan embodied in the Oslo Accords.

PADICO describes itself and its mission in the following terms:

> *PADICO is a limited public shareholding company that has a paid in capital of USD 250 million, and is traded on the Palestine Securities Exchange (PSE). Since its inception in 1993, its mission has been to develop and strengthen*

76 (Bahour, 2000)

77 (Hilal and Khan, 2004:104)

78 (Bahour, 2000)

79 (Nasr, 2004:175)

80 (Ibid)

> *the Palestinian economy, through investing in vital economic sectors. This mission was initiated by several Palestinian and Arab investors who had a clear patriotic goal, but also had the belief that the Palestinian market was a unique business opportunity, and offered substantial returns.*

The number of PADICO's investors has gradually increased over the years from a mere 710 shareholders in 1998 to over 12,000 shareholders in 2008. The profile of PADICO's shareholders is diverse, constituting major investors from Palestine, the MENA region, and international markets."[81]

The first elected board of directors, who was elected for a 4-year term, included the leading big "shatat" capitalists, notable among whom is the Palestinian tycoon Munib al-Masri, who played, among others, an important role in bringing Arafat to accept the American-Israeli agenda for maintaining the WBG under continuous Israeli control, as discussed earlier in this chapter. It must be noted that at least 80% of the members of the first board were, or continue to be, members of Welfare Association, which they founded about ten years earlier, immediately following the expulsion of the PLO from Lebanon by the Israeli invasion in 1982.

Some of the main objectives of the new company, as stated in its literature , were: to attract Palestinian, Arab and international investments that will help rebuild the economic infrastructure of the Palestinian economy, particularly in industry, real estate, tourism, housing, and other service and technical projects; establishment, or participating in pioneering projects of economic, social and financial feasibility; investment in existing projects for the purpose of developing them technically and administratively and opening external markets for their products.[82] To achieve these objectives, and to diversify and ensure a wide profit base, the new company decided from the start to

81 (http://www.padico.com)

82 (Hanafi, 1997:79); (Nasr, 2004:175)

establish a number of subsidiary companies in critical sectors in order to involve indigenous capitalists in its projects, and to minimize the friction between the two capitalists groups, and the brewing criticism by indigenous capitalists that they are being swallowed from the outside. It was decided that the subsidiaries will be public holding companies in which PADICO will have 49% of the shares in each.

The subsidiaries are:

1. The first subsidiary was the Jerusalem Investment in Tourism (JIT) with headquarters in Jerusalem. PADICO's share is 35%. The rest was covered by investors from Jordan and Palestine. The main investment activities are in purchasing land, building hotels, and rehabilitating and upgrading existing hotels.
2. The second subsidiary is "ALAQARIYA", investment in real estate, where PADICO's share is 49%. The headquarters of this company are in Gaza City. The company reached "an understanding in principle where the PA identified parcels of land for development and investment in partnership with the PA".[83] These will be primarily residential housing suburbs and commercial centers. The technical and architectural designs are carried out primarily between Jordanian and Palestinian design companies.
3. The third subsidiary is an investment company in Industry (PIIC), where PADICO's share is 70%. The headquarters are in the city of Nablus.
4. The fourth subsidiary is a public shareholding company in telecommunications (Paltel). It was established in May 1995, with an initial authorized capital of USD 63 million (45 million JD). Major shareholders owned 68% of the company. In addition to PADICO, whose share was 23.29%, the Palestinian Commercial Services

83 (Hanafi, 1997:117)

Company (an investment company fully owned by the PA, which became the PIF) owned 6.78%, the Arab Bank owned 7.78%, The Arab Palestine Investment Company Ltd owned 5.93%, and the Cairo-Amman Bank (Sabih al-Masri,[84] another capitalist tycoon) owned 3.99%. "Paltel was granted a license from the PNA for a 20 year period to operate, maintain and manage the telecommunications sector in Palestine. The license covers both voice and non-voice, fixed and cellular networks. A separate subsidiary called Palcel provided mobile GSM services, and was 65% owned by Paltel and 35% by the PNA. Branded as Jawwal, this service began operations in October 1999." [85]

PALTEL partnered with the Palestine Commercial Service Company (PCSC), the precursor of PIF, to create a new private (not publicly traded) company called the Palestine Cellular Telecommunications Company, with a registered capital of JD 25 million. The move was done in violation to PALTEL's registration, and without bringing it to PALTEL's general assembly for discussion and approval. At least one of the shareholders in PALTEL raised serious questions about this step in a letter to the Board of Directors and all relevant PA ministries.[86]

In a report in *Al-Ayyam* Palestinian daily,[87] it was stated that the "Peace Technology Fund" (or Peres Fund—PTF), has purchased 3.3% of Paltel's shares.

84 Sabih Al-Masri is the chairman of the Astra Industrial Group, the Cairo-Amman Bank, and was the vice-chairman of the Palestinian Investment Fund (PIF) until he was pushed aside by the new PIF CEO. The Astra Industrial Group "is engaged in producing a wide range of pharmaceutical products, plastic coloring, fertilizers, agricultural pesticides, Fungicides, prefab steel buildings, and steel structures, in addition to producing and distributing fiber cables, mattresses, pillows, and blankets" (http://www.astra.com).

85 (Nasr, 2004:177-78)

86 (See Bahour, 2001)

87 (Al-Ayyam, 25 May 1999)

The PTF is an Israeli institution named after the then Israeli foreign minister and the current Israeli president, Shimon Peres. In 1999, Paltel made around USD 9 million in profits, which were distributed to foreign shareholders, such as the PTF! Even a Palestinian very classical, US-trained, economist had to arrive, in his analysis of "Monopolies and the PNA", to the conclusion that "it is doubtful whether the purchase of these shares by PTF added any new productive capacity in the Palestinian economy and clearly, the rents collected by PTF have not been reinvested in the WBGS. The issue, in this particular case, has an added importance because the fund … is in practice controlled by Israel, which increases the dependency of the Palestinian economy on Israel, contrary to the declared Palestinian strategy."[88]

5. The fifth subsidiary is the Palestinian Securities Exchange with headquarters in the City of Nablus, according to directions from Arafat.
6. The sixth subsidiary is the Palestinian Industrial Zones. We will come back to it later in greater detail and deeper analysis due to its importance in illustrating the major thesis of this work.

In a very recent interview with Reuters news agency, PADICO's CEO, Samir Hulileh, claimed that stability in the West Bank has helped his company increase its profits this year. However, the expansion planned by the company through investments in the real estate market, the energy sector, water resource management, agriculture and solid waste recycling, etc, was curtailed due to the "political uncertainty".[89] The "bleak prospects for the Middle East peace process … makes PADICO cautious about investing in major industrial projects". PADICO's CEO claimed also in this interview, "we are maintaining the minimum required: not just

88 (Nasr, 2004:179)

89 (Reuters, 2010)

surviving, but sustaining an operation ... we are not aggressive. We tend to be very cautious. ... [The West Bank] is becoming very secure. This is important. Security is extremely important". Hulileh indicated, however, that he intends to consolidate PADICO's real estate ventures, by selling off "loss-making investments in industry and replace them with finance and real estate ventures".[90]

PADICO owns 71 percent of the Palestine Securities Exchange, which it established, and manages 13 companies listed there. PADICO's shares have traded between $1.17 - $1.50 in the last year. PADICO's CEO expects 2010 net profit to range from "$42 million to $45 million", in spite of the fact that PADICO's investments of $66 million in Gaza are on hold. However, the Ramallah Movenpick, which is being built by a PADICO subsidiary, is due to open in 2010, and the Bethlehem Intercontinental, where PADICO owns 40 percent, "is making its first ever profit this year thanks to steps to ease its debt burden".[91]

THE ARAB PALESTINIAN INVESTMENT COMPANY (APIC)

Following the establishment of the PA, one group of investors who responded to Arafat's call to "invest in Palestine" was Al-Aggad Group of Companies, which set-up the Arab Palestinian Investment Company, Ltd., (APIC). APIC is described as the "leading Palestinian investor". It is made up of a group of subsidiary companies dealing in a "wide range of products and services." Currently, APIC's subsidiary companies comprise the following:

- NAPCO (National Aluminum and Profile Company);
- Siniora (food industries);
- UNIPAL (general trading company);
- Hyundai (Palestinian Automobile Company);
- MSS (Medical Supplies and Services Company);

90 (MAS, Palestinian Economic Bulletin, Issue 20, 2008)

91 (Ibid)

- PLAZA (The Arab Palestinian Shopping Centers Company).

The stated "vision" of APIC is "to provide superior products and services of quality and value, leaving a positive and lasting impact on Palestinian society."[92]

It is clear that APIC's investments are largely in services, consumer goods, car distribution, shopping centers, etc. Also, APIC is a founding share-holder in Paltel, the Arab Islamic International Bank, and others.

Omar Al-Aggad, the founder of the Al-Aggad Group of Companies, is another Palestinian capitalist tycoon. He is a Saudi national, and is one of the original founders of Welfare Association. His first major investment in the West Bank was the construction of the engineering faculty building in Birzeit University, in the early eighties of the last century.

MAJOR SHAREHOLDERS

- The Aggad Investment Company - Saudi Arabia
- Palestine Investment Fund (PIF) - Palestine
- Sheikh Mohamad Al-Amoudi - Saudi Arabia
- Sa'id Khoury - Greece
- Prince Al-Waleed Bin Talal Bin Abdul Aziz - Saudi Arabia
- Menavest Corporation - British Virgin Islands
- Jerusalem Development and Investment Company, Ltd. - Jordan
- Sheikh Mohamad Imran Bamieh - Saudi Arabia
- Unity Trading Establishment - Jordan
- General Hashim Said Hashim (retired) - Saudi Arabia
- Hassib Sabbagh - Greece
- Dr. Nasser Al-Rasheed - Saudi Arabia
- The Ahmad Juffali Foundation - Saudi Arabia

92 (http://www.apic-pal.com)

- Olayan Financing Company - Saudi Arabia
- Abdul Aziz and Mohammad Al-Jomaih Company - Saudi Arabia

An intricate network of dealers, sub-dealers, and free agents to entice consumerism of global products in the Palestinian market is in place.[93]

Since the beginning of the Oslo-phase, a number of foreign car dealerships, e.g., Peugeot and Hyundai, were established as a result of concerted effort by "shatat" and indigenous Palestinian capitalists. Like the so-called "national beverage company", which is a Coca-Cola franchise, the Hyundai car dealership was dubbed as "the Palestinian Automobile Company"! Like Coca-Cola franchise, nothing in it is "Palestinian", or "national", except for the workers.

In addition to popped-up dealerships of solid consumer goods of globalized brands, from cars, to TVs, to electric kitchen appliances, etc., whose import process is greatly facilitated by Israel and its occupation structure, the elaborate network of dealers, sub-dealers and free agents that flood the local market with foreign produced food stuffs is worth examining in detail. This is where avenues for quick profits and corruption are wide-open. And this is where normalization and collaboration between Palestinian capitalists, the Oslo economic and political elites, on the one hand, and Israeli authorities, both civilian capitalists, security apparatuses, and political elites, on the other, are at their peak, day in and day out.

Furthermore, a deep examining look at this aspect of our local economy reveals how this market is indeed an unregulated (and dangerous) dumping ground, and how, more seriously, the coalition of greedy and corrupt capitalists, greedy and corrupt political elites, and low-level functionaries is working to impede and circumvent local production, and tighten and

93 The information in this section was gathered through a series of personal interviews by the author with suppliers, in a Ramallah grocery store, which markets all of these products.

maximize dependency on the Israeli economy, often under the deceptive umbrella of "national economic development".

The following are cases in point.

1. UNIPAL, the "general trading company", which is a subsidiary of the APIC monopoly, is the dealer for the occupied Palestinian areas of all Proctor and Gamble products, through, of course, key Israeli agents. These products include: a variety of cleaning agents, e.g., "Ariel" washing machine soap, shampoos, mainly "Head and Shoulders" and Pantene, "Gillett" shaving blades and cream, American cigarettes, mainly, Marlboro, LM, Parliament, "Post" cereals, "Always" sanitary napkins, "Duracell" batteries, "Heinz" tomato juice and paste products, "Tang" (artificial) drinks, "Kraft" cheeses, Pastas, and many more.

   Concurrently, indigenous capitalists, who had the advantage and the precedence of cooperating with Israeli capitalists much earlier than "shatat" capitalists who came in the Oslo package, jumped in full force to reaffirm their position and to show, that in the game of profit accumulation, they can be serious and successful contenders, and, consequently, partners. A number of them rushed to strike exclusive dealerships with Israeli companies to market their products in the occupied Palestinian areas. Some competed effectively by becoming dealers of globally-manufactured products, either as direct importers, or through sub-dealerships for Israeli agents. Yet others were ready to play the role of "free lance" dealers. To maximize their leverage, and learning from the successful experiences of "shatat" capitalists, some indigenous capitalists took the initiative to restructure their existing companies into "a group of companies". Thus, they believed, they would enhance their scope of profit and market share. The following are some illustrative cases.

2. The "Anabtawi Group": This is comprised of two companies for two Anabtawi cousins in Nablus: The Near East Trading and the International Overseas Company. There is some kind of a division of labor between them. The Near East Trading is the dealer for Lipton tea (UK), "ready cake", shampoos (Dove and Lux), Delmonte canned foods, etc. It is the sub-agent for "Unilever" (whose main agent is in Jerusalem). It distributed "Safi" cooking oil, after it refills it locally from big barrels, and markets it as "product of Palestine". After some questioning, it is dubious that the origin of this oil is Palestinian. If so, there is a serious problem about false marketing, especially since Palestine produces olive oil.
3. The second branch of the Anabtawi Group is the International Overseas Company. It is the dealer for French and German cigarettes, Italian pasta, all kinds of biscuits and cookies, "bic" shaving blades, canned meats (cornbeef), cereals from the UK, "Persil" washing machine soap, etc.
4. Al-Tamimi Company in Hebron is the dealer for distributing the products of the Israeli company Osem. Also it imports food stuffs from Saudi Arabia and Morocco.
5. Al-Hilal Company in Bir Nebala is the dealer for the Israeli company Elite. Also it markets Israeli cigarettes e.g., Time.
6. The Nabulsi Company is a sub-dealer for the Israeli dealer for sweet products, such as Mars candy bars, Twixt, M&M, etc.
7. Al-Safi Company in Ramallah and Gaza is the dealer for Egyptian and Turkish products.
8. Palco Company in Ramallah is the dealer for "Huggies" diapers, "Diamond" tin foil, "Detole" cleaning agent, and "Finish" dishwasher soap.
9. Eka Company in Bethlehem is the dealer for the Palestinian areas of Hadar Israeli company. It markets "Carlsperg" beer, "Meron" water, "Prigat" juices, Turkish margarine, etc.

10. We have dealers for "Strauss" dairy products; dealers for the Israeli Tenuva dairy company; dealers for Nestle coffee, water and ice cream, etc.

Basically, it is very clear that, since the beginning of the Oslo process, we have been flooded with dealers and sub-dealers for every conceivable, consumable product, from Israel and the West, either directly, or indirectly through Arab countries. The market is flooded with products that our enemies and oppressors produce, from the soap we wash with, to the candy bar, pasta, bottled water, canned foods, etc, that we eat. Some dealers market cooking oil and soaps, at a time that we are a major producer of olive oil and olive soaps!

When asked about what they are doing in terms of development, the owner of a local dealership company for Israeli products said: " No money is invested here; all of us are employed by a few companies; all consumption is dependent on Israeli dealers; we are all sub-agents".

THE "NATIONAL BEVERAGE COMPANY"- COCA-COLA

In 1995, a group of "shatat" capitalists established the "Palestinian National Beverage Company", which manufactures and markets Coca-Cola products under official franchise in the West Bank and Gaza. Dubbing a company that is franchised to encourage and market consumptive addiction to harmful and unhealthy beverage—Coca-Cola—is anti-developmental par excellence! The Chief Executive Officer and Chairman of this company is Zahi Khouri, a "shatat" capitalist who moved back to the Palestinian areas, from the US, following the signing of the Oslo Accords, seeking to establish business ventures.

Zahi Khouri joined forces with other "shatat" capitalists in forming PADICO, the largest Palestinian investment company (discussed above), and is the chairman of one of its subsidiary companies, Palestine Tourism Investment Company. He is also an Advisory Board member at HBG Holdings Ltd. Khouri holds a number of civic positions, three of which are directly relevant to our analysis. They are: the chairmanship of the Board of NDC, the NGO Development Center in Jerusalem; the chairmanship of the Palestine International Business Forum (PIBF); and the chairmanship of the Palestine Business Committee for Peace and Reform (PBCPR) in Washington, D.C. Khouri was trained in Engineering and Business Administration in Germany and France. In 1967, Zahi Khouri moved to the US where he made his career with multinational corporations in New York City, Brazil, Puerto Rico, Lebanon and Saudi Arabia.

Khouri displayed his views in recent editorials and interviews, over the last five years.[94] He believes in the "power of business and brand names to build peace". He stated that "when the first McDonald's opened in Russia, it made more headlines than people going to the moon. ... For me, it wasn't about money. Coke could put Palestine on the map," he said. "I knew people would think that if Coke is investing in Palestine, there must be something here, and there would be followers." Khouri maintains that his commitment is to build businesses and a nation. ... The best engine driving peace, stability, and growth is a healthy business environment," he emphasized. In the meantime, he is proud that his company "sells 10 million cases of Coke a year", to Palestinian communities in PA areas.

In an op-ed piece in the *Wall Street Journal* on 30 Sept 2006, he, as a Palestinian-American, explained in dramatic and even emotional terms how he saw the connection between Coca-Cola and peace: "*Each gleaming bottle, with that red Coca-Cola swirl in both Arabic and English, would be a miniature ambassador from America. And each potential investor who saw that Coke was successful might decide to invest as well. It seemed the perfect strategy: to promote American interests while helping to build an economy that could serve as the foundation of a viable, independent Palestinian state*".[95]

94 See, for example, Wall Street Journal, 30 Sept 2006, and San Diego Union-Tribune, 10 Nov 2006.

95 Khouri, Wall Street Journal, 30 Sept 2006

In another op-ed piece, nearly a month later, he elaborated how, in the throes of euphoria generated by the Oslo Accords, he and "*many Palestinian Americans returned to Palestine to invest in businesses. I did that in 1996, when I launched the Coca-Cola franchise there. I also formed, with European and Israeli businesspeople, the Palestine International Business Forum. We hoped to bolster this new political agreement with economic cooperation that could benefit both Palestinians and Israelis. ... New economic opportunities could turn Palestinian despair into hope. We had visions of tourists streaming into the Palestinian city of Bethlehem to see where Christ was born. We hoped Gaza could one day become another Mediterranean vacation destination, welcoming Arabs, Israelis and others alike*".[96] It is clear by now that the only thing his company made was more money and profits, but neither "peace" nor "development"!

One can arrive at the following initial conclusions from the above sections. In this political-economic investment game, it is clear that the PA has been a serious economic contender, vis-à-vis Palestinian capitalists, both the "shatat" and the indigenous capitalists. In other words, the PA did not play the role of the political elites only, but it combined it heavily with a serious contention as an economic factor. It used its political and regulatory leverage to attract foreign direct investments, through the PIF, for example, to undermine the economic weight (and potential political threat) of "shatat" capitalists. Also, it played the "shatat" and indigenous capitalists against each other. Of course, major Western funding agencies, e.g., the World Bank, the US, the EU, etc. were never absent throughout. In the final analysis, however Israel was calling all the shots.

PUSHING EASY CREDIT: MORTGAGING CURRENT FAMILIES AND FUTURE GENERATIONS

Easy access to credit through loans from formal and informal financial institutions is a necessary ingredient for increased consumption of goods that are being made readily available

96 Khouri, San Diego Union-Tribune, 10 Nov 2006

in the Palestinian market. This is in addition to the various schemes for housing mortgages. Analysis in this section will show that there is a direct connection between Western aid agencies and the availability of credit that is directed towards consumption rather than industrial production. The network that is at work here in achieving this objective is composed of the banks (10 local banks, 2 Egyptian, 1 British and 8 Jordanian, with 207 branches), the Palestinian Monetary Authority (the banks' regulator), the micro-credit institutions (11 institutions in 2010, mostly NGOs), and a network of Western aid agencies, including GOs, NGOs, and private sector organizations.

As a case in point of such private sector organizations, we focus on the "Portland Trust". This company, which is a private British foundation, claims to believe that "peace and stability between Palestinians and Israelis" can be achieved through "economic development". In this context, it "promotes initiatives to develop the private sector, particularly in the Palestinian Territory" through "obtaining the support and commitment of the relevant parties, identifying appropriate sponsors and mobilizing the necessary funds".[97]

"The Portland Trust was founded in London in 2003 by Sir Ronald Cohen, founder of the Private Equity firm Apax Partners." Almost all of its founding members are investment bankers, including "Sir Harry Solomon, co-founder and former chairman and CEO of Hillsdown Holdings ... and Lord Freud, former vice chairman of UBS Investment Banking".[98] Soon after it was established in London, the Portland Trust "re-settled" in the area for business. It opened an office in Tel Aviv in 2005, followed by an office in Ramallah in 2006. It is interesting to note, however, that the Tel Aviv's office is directed by Brigadier General Eival Gilady, with a military career spanning three decades, where from 2001 – 2004, or during the re-invasion of the PA areas, he served as Head of IDF's Strategic Planning Division! The head of the Ramallah office is Samir Hulileh, the

97 (http://www.portlandtrust.org/)

98 (Ibid)

CEO of PADICO, and the former Cabinet Secretary of the PA government following the election of Hamas.

It was stated in the first issue of the "Palestine Economic Bulletin" series (October 2006), which is produced in collaboration between the Portland Trust and the Palestine Economic Policy Research Institute, that loans constitute "the highest credit expansion facility" of banks, and "have increased by 0.12%".[99] It was reported, however, that the percentage of bad loans by the banks, at the beginning of 2006, was already at 15.5 percent, and a year later it reached nearly 20 percent.[100]

Increase in bad loans is related, of course, to the state of debt that Palestinian families were under. As an indication, Oxfam International reported in 2007 that "68% of households in Gaza and 53% in the West Bank took on more debt last Year. The average Palestinian household owed $1,750. A third owed more than $2,500. Two in five had been forced to sell off personal assets like jewelry and furniture in order to afford basic services.[101]

We have to remember the overall political context that characterized this time period. Hamas won the legislative council elections in January 2006; a "national unity" government was formed; the national unity government was aborted; a Hamas-run government was formed in its stead; Fateh's attempt to undermine Hamas's government and control of Gaza, which ensued in armed confrontation, which failed; Hamas re-affirmed its control of Gaza; Gaza under complete siege, and all Western aid was redirected to Fateh, the President's Office and the new Western-sanctioned, West Bank government of Salam Fayyad.

During this period, and within this context:

> *The Palestinian Investment Fund (PIF) signed an agreement with the American Overseas Private Investment Corporation (OPIC) and the Wash-*

99 (MAS, 2006)

100 (MAS, 2007, Palestinian Economic Bulletin, issue 4)

101 (MAS, 2007, Palestinian Economic Bulletin, issue 10)

> *ington-based Aspen Institute inaugurating a loan guarantee scheme in the Palestinian Territories. The scheme aims to help small- or medium-sized enterprises (SMEs) by guaranteeing up to 70% of a given loan from a private bank to a Palestinian SME. With funding of $160m – $50m from the PIF, $110m from OPIC – the scheme , will be able to cover almost $230m worth of loans. CHF International, an NGO, will administer the programme. The Portland Trust was closely involved in the development of the scheme.*
>
> *William Phelps, managing director of the programme at CHF, emphasised that the loan guarantee scheme is a Palestinian-driven initiative, praising in particular the PIF's work in setting it up. ... Phelps stressed that the scheme's clients "are the banks, not the borrowers." ... The programme's intent is not only to foster more lending, but to make lending more intelligent by improving the ability of banks to extend credit based not simply on the amount of collateral being put up but on a more refined assessment of the borrower.*[102]

Should we not be very worried about such easy credit access programs, in the light of the fact that their strategists and mentors are Americans, and in the absence of effective regulations? I think these developments are extremely worrisome, and should raise red flags, especially in view of the very detailed and documented American reports delineating the "story of America's mortgage industry", which show the deception, illegality and collusion of the mortgage-extending financial firms that target the unsuspecting citizens.[103]

On another plain, a semi-governmental entity—The Municipal Development and Lending Fund— was formed in 2005 "to support local government [and to] increase munici-

102 (MAS, 2007, Palestinian Economic Bulletin, issue 11)

103 (e.g., Hudson, 2010)

pal transparency and improve coordination of development funding", by extending loans, among other interventions. This was made possible thanks to major funding from the World Bank, the USAID, the EU, and others. By mid-2009, "the MDLF has administered projects with a total value of around $138m".[104]

Availability of micro-credit programs and institutions, as an instrument of economic development, received clearly visible attention from aid agencies, particularly since the launching of the "peace process" in the early nineties of the last century. What concerns us in this analysis is the ease of access to small loans, which micro-credit institutions and programs made available, and which aid agencies supported.

The earliest of these programs is UNRWA's "microfinance" Department, established in 1991, and "aims to alleviate poverty and support economic development in the refugee community by providing capital investment and working capital loans at commercial rates".[105] Palestinian refugees "as well as poor or marginal groups living and working in close proximity to them" are eligible to get these loans.

UNRWA's Microfinance Department (MD) provides a range of loans to various categories of the population "most of whom enjoy no access to formal credit and are vulnerable to shocks". Loans for microenterprises range from $ 300 - $ 8,500. Loans for "groups of women entrepreneurs" range from $400 - $5,000, in order to sustain the microenterprise as well as "household expenditures on education, health, and basic needs". Smaller loans in support of "low-income and working- class family consumption" may range from $150 - $800.

UNRWA claims that its Microfinance Department "remains the largest non-bank financial intermediary in the West Bank and Gaza". The total number of loans it had given, as of March 2009, was 146,600 loans for a total investment of $174.36 million.[106]

104 (MAS, 2009, Palestinian Economic Bulletin, issue 33; http://www.mdlf.org.ps).

105 (http://www.unrwa.org)

106 (Ibid)

The Palestinian Economic Bulletin reported in 2007 about a new push for extending access to credit:

> *The US Agency for International Development (USAID) gave two separate grants worth a combined $2.6m under its Small and Microfinance Assistance for Recovery and Transition (SMART) to fund Palestinian microfinance. One of the grants will go to CHF International's Access to Credit programme and the other to the Microfinance and Microenterprise Department of UNRWA. The grants will run from May to October and* ***will allow the two funded organisations to try out new savings and loan products in the Palestinian market.***[107]

Currently, there are 11 micro-credit institutions operating in the West Bank and Gaza. They are coordinated informally by the Palestinian Network for Small and Microfinance Institutions (*Sharakeh)*, established in 2002. According to a study released in July 2007 by the International Finance Corporation (IFC) and the "Sharakeh", "there are 190,000 potential microfinance borrowers in the West Bank and Gaza Strip". The size of the "microfinance market" was put at $157 million and microfinance institutions cover only 10 percent of it. To remedy this and expand micro-credit facilities, "PlaNet Finance and The Portland Trust, together with the EU, launched a three-year, $1.7m project aimed at removing obstacles to the expansion of this sector.[108]

The Palestinian Network for Small and Microfinance released figures for June 2009 showing that there were nearly 35,000 who benefited from the micro-credit loans offered by these institutions, for a total portfolio of nearly $54 million. The percentage of bad and faltering loans among the main 9 micro-credit institutions, reached 15.6 percent. The average loan size

107 (MAS, 2007, Palestinian Economic Bulletin, issue 9; emphasis added)

108 (MAS, 2007, Palestinian Economic Bulletin, issue 11)

was $2,435. The actual annual interest charged on these loans, however, could reach in excess of 40% annually!

As an illustrative case of these micro-credit institutions, I shall focus on Palestine for Credit and Development "FATEN". "FATEN is an independent Palestinian not for profit corporation, fully dedicated to providing micro-finance services. It emerged out of a microfinance program managed by Save the Children US (SCF). FATEN spun off from Save the Children during March 1999, and became fully responsible for the management of the whole program.[109]

FATEN's market share of all the loans granted by other micro-finance institutions is about 19 percent. Unlike the others, FATEN today is self-sustaining. By the end of 2009, the total number of loans it gave, since it was set up in 1995, reached 82,755, with a total investment of $73,439,961.[110] During my interview with its general manager, more updated information was provided. By September 2010, the total number of loans was around 85,000 of which 10,000 loans were active. Generally, the grace period ranged from 3 -6 months, and the maximum duration of the loan is 48 months. The accrued interest on the loans ranges from 6-12 percent yearly. About 1-2 percent of the loans are failed loans.

Since it became independent of Save the Children (US) and the USAID funding in 1999, it is sustained, on almost a break-even level, by borrowing from local commercial banks at about 7 percent interest. It is always battling the problem of sufficient liquidity. However, since then, and unlike the rest of current micro-credit institutions, it is not dependent on external aid for survival. FATEN claims to provide "a variety of high quality and sustainable financial services, for low income and economically active small scale enterprises and micro entrepreneurs, especially women.[111]

109 (FATEN, 2009)

110 (FATEN, 2010)

111 (Jayyousi, A, 2010)

INDUSTRIAL ZONES (OR INDUSTRIAL ESTATES)

In the context of Israeli occupation of Palestinian lands, the idea of something akin to the industrial zones that is being deliberated today, may be traced back to the time when Moshe Arens was Israel's Minister of Defense in 1989. Arens commissioned then the economist Ezra Sadan, who was the director of the Ministry of Finance, to draw a plan whose aim was to build a domestic industrial base linked to the Israeli economy, which could absorb Palestinian workers. The first example of such a "domestic industrial base" was built at Beit Hanoun (Erez) at the border between Gaza and Israel. The army facilitated the relocation of Israeli industrial enterprises to the designated area, and provided the necessary security for them. Most businesses in that "industrial base" were owned by Israeli Jewish capitalists, and were connected to the military, which facilitated the marketing of their export-products to regional and international markets, especially to Africa.

Thus, the bulk of the businesses was Israeli-owned and managed. The land was occupied Palestinian land, part of Gaza. All workers were Palestinians from Gaza. The aim, then, was not to "integrate" the two economies, but to show the benevolent hand of the occupying army by providing job opportunities to about 4-5 thousand "security-approved" Gaza workers and symbolic Gaza- owned businesses. Then, no illusions were advanced about "economic development" in the occupied areas, other than providing some job opportunities to a selective number of Gaza workers and capitalists to keep them acquiescent to the occupation.

A Gaza businessman saw value in the Erez industrial zone in that:

> *Products from Erez had free access to Israel, so for Palestinians it was very attractive because there was no inspection and subsequent damage to products or delay. Also, people working in Erez could receive Israeli clients. ... There were fac-*

> *tories for plastics and other specialized products that were thus being made in Gaza but according to Israeli standards. ... People learned a lot from these standards, which they applied to Gaza, whether in the form of training or even imitation. Products designed in Israel were imitated and produced in Gaza, raising standards across the board. But once Israel closed its borders with Erez, it became useless and now it is dead.*[112]

Signing of the Oslo Accords in 1993 put a temporary end to this experiment. It was replaced by the idea of planned industrial zones (or Qualified Industrial Zones—QIZ) at various critical border contact points between Israel and the PA areas. The idea of border industrial zones was advocated, pushed and financed by the World Bank, including USAID and EIB (European Investment Bank). The notion is simple and straight forward: in a new environment of "peace", and building on other experiences in the third world countries, the "Zones" will attract international, regional and local (both Palestinian and Israeli) investments. They will provide needed job opportunities for Palestinian workers from the WBG; they will boost the "Oslo" political process and the ensuing PA political elites, by showing that they are providing economic "dividends"; they will help Israel "secure" its vulnerable border points; and they will make it easy to claim a perception of successful economic development. Israel's occupation of Palestinian lands will continue unchallenged; and the main focus will be on profitable economic investments for all parties concerned, as a necessary precondition for a peaceful resolution to the conflict.

The design of the proposed industrial zones was funded by USAID, and was commissioned by contract to the "Technical Services Group", a U.S Virginia-based firm that had designed such industrial zones in a number of countries, including Haiti, the Philippines, and Puerto Rico.

112 (Abu Shahla, 2007)

Before we discuss what is planned now for the next period, let us examine what happened on the ground; what is the "impact" of the first experiment, the Gaza Industrial Zone?

The Gaza Industrial Zone (GIZ) was established in 1995 at the Karni crossing point, from Israel to Gaza. The GIZ was conceived originally "to integrate the occupied Palestinian territory into the Israeli labor market. ... It was quickly promoted as a model for development of the Palestinian economy and a template for its integration into global markets ....".[113] At its peak, before the second intifada in 2000, there were about 200 economic enterprises, about half of which was owned by Palestinian capital and half by Israeli capital. These companies were employing on the average 900 – 1300 Palestinian workers, mostly in low value-added textile jobs, largely subcontracting to Israeli firms.

By the end of 2000, Israeli-owned businesses started leaving, and workers were not given permits to reach the work place. Everything stopped with the Israeli deployment from Gaza in 2005, and the GIZ came to an abrupt halt and total devastation. Karni crossing point, on the other hand, became a fully Israeli controlled crossing point, through which all goods going to Gaza will pass. Subsequently, the entire program of industrial zones was frozen.

However, the same model was applied to the region, as the means to create and strengthen political and economic cooperation between the Arab states and Israel, particularly Egypt and Jordan who signed US-sponsored peace treaties with Israel. Following the signing of the peace agreement between Israel and Jordan in 1995, the US pressed to bolster economic cooperation between the two countries through the proposed concept of the "Qualifying Industrial Zones "(QIZ). "The QIZs are areas designated by the Jordanian and Israeli authorities and approved by the US government whereby products originating

113 (Lagerquist, 2003:5)

in the zones are granted duty-free and quota free access to the US market".[114]

In a recent evaluation of the "impact" of the Jordan-Israel QIZ, the former CEO of the Jordan Agency for Enterprise and Investment Development shows not much difference between the impact of GIZ and the QIZ, with the exception, perhaps, that Jordan is a state. He wrote:

> *Has cooperation between Jordan and Israel improved because of the QIZs? Partially. Jordanian exports to the US market rose to US$1.3 billion in 2006 (with US$1 billion originating from the QIZs alone) from a paltry US$7.9 million in 1998. Israeli components are used in the manufacture of garments and apparel—the bulk of the exports from the QIZs. Several Israelis ... have located in the QIZs. Israeli distributors, relying on the strength of their links with western importers, provide venues for orders and exports to the large chains in the US.*
>
> *On the other hand, two thirds of the labor force in the QIZs is non-Jordanian, mainly from Far Eastern countries. There are virtually no linkages between the QIZs and the rest of the economy. Spillovers in terms of technology and managerial skills transfer are almost non-existent. In addition, cooperation between Israeli and Jordanian businesspersons outside the QIZs remains dismal as indicated by the trade figures between the two economies. In fact, overall economic cooperation outside the QIZs decreased in light of the first and second uprisings in the West Bank and Gaza. ... Furthermore, increasingly, Jordanians are opting to export to the US under the Jordan-US Free Trade Agreement instead of the QIZs.*
>
> *Meanwhile, Palestinians in the occupied territories, who prior to 1996 provided an inexpensive labor source to Israeli manufacturers in the*

114 (Mansour, 2007)

> *manufacture of apparels and garments, which is a labor-intensive industry, and who at the inception of the QIZs voiced concerns that the QIZ agreement with Jordan would transfer jobs across the river, are currently worse off.*
>
> *The upshot is that economic cooperation was not greatly enhanced by the QIZs.*[115]

The current thrust of the PA, Israel, the US and the EU is to revive the whole notion of the Industrial Zones, and to push for their implementation as the means for profitable "economic cooperation" between the PA and Israel, under continued occupation, and as an alternative to reaching a just political solution to ending the colonial occupation of Palestine. This thrust is based on engaging third party countries in supporting the re-invention of these industrial zones.

The first phase of reviving the industrial zones scheme gives priority to the West Bank, since it is considered a "secured" area under the Fayyad government and the Abbas PA. The focus is on three visible such projects: The Jenin Industrial Zone (JIZ), the Tarqumiya Industrial Zone (TIZ), and the Jordan Valley "Corridor for Peace and Prosperity" Zone (CPP). In the meantime, active and diligent contacts and schemes are being deliberated between the PA, Israel and Turkey to revive the Erez Industrial Zone (EIZ).

Let us look in more detail at these four Industrial Zones.

JORDAN VALLEY ZONE: "CORRIDOR FOR PEACE AND PROSPERITY" (CPP)

In July 2006, the prime-minister of Japan declared a "peace plan" under the rubric "corridor for peace and prosperity" (CPP), in which he initiated an agro-industrial zone for processing agricultural produce from the fertile areas of the Jordan Valley. With major investments from Japan and other part-

115 (Ibid)

ners, this is considered one of the largest collaborative projects between Israel, the PA and Jordan.[116]

The concept of focusing on "joint economic development instead of constant struggle over land" was presented by Peres, with great enthusiasm, during his participation in an international conference held in New York in 2006, under the tutelage of former US president, Clinton. To keep the momentum, Japan invited, in March 2007, representatives from Israel, the PA and Japan for a two-day conference in Tokyo. During the same month, the Israeli cabinet adopted the CPP officially. Japan's Foreign Minister reiterated the position that the focus should be on "development first", instead of wasting time on political struggle over the land, and that whatever political entity emerges will abide by the economic conditionalities of the "development first" approach.[117]

> *For centuries the Jordan Valley has been a key agricultural area for Palestinian farmers in the West Bank. But following the occupation of the area in 1967, the Israeli military proceeded to evict many of these farmers, confiscate land, and establish Israeli settlements (first as military-agricultural settlements and then as Israeli agribusiness and civilian settlements). By controlling water, access routes and other resources, the land essentially became an Israeli military zone although scattered Palestinian villages remained in the area.*
>
> *The CPP aims to establish a free trade agricultural zone in the area that will turn the small-scale Palestinian farmers into day-labourers and sub-contractors to large agro-industry controlled by Israeli and regional capital. In other words, not only does the CPP consent to the occupation and expropriation of land that has taken place over the last 40 years in the Jordan Valley, it actually aims to*

116 (Bisan, 2008, and 2010)

117 (Ibid)

> *integrate this occupation into the project itself. The agricultural produce grown as part of the CPP will do nothing to alleviate concerns of food security in the area: the produce is intended for export to Israel and the Gulf states.*[118]

In its monthly "Palestine Economic Bulletin" series, the Portland Trust reported on this agreement in a very upbeat and hopeful tone.

> *Under Japanese sponsorship, Israel, Jordan, and the Palestinian Authority signed an agreement on 14 March (2007) in Tokyo to develop an agro-industrial park near the West Bank city of Jericho. The park is envisioned to become a hub of agricultural processing for the West Bank. Funding for the project will come from Japan, which has assumed an increasingly prominent role in Middle East mediation in the area of economic development. The government intends to send a team to Jericho shortly to survey possible locations for the park, one of a number of ventures that make up the "Peace Valley" vision of former foreign minister Shimon Peres, a vision that comprises a range of regional economic development and integration projects in the Jordan Valley.*[119]

In the Palestine Economic Bulletin issue no. 23 (2008), it was reported further that

> *Japan hosted the third ministerial-level meeting of the four-party consultative unit for the "Corridor for Peace and Prosperity", which plans to start at the beginning of 2009. The "Corridor" will enable collaboration between the Palestinians, Israelis and Jordanians on regional projects. The "Corridor" is*

---

118 (Hanieh, 2008)

119 (MAS, 2007, Palestinian Economic Bulletin, issue 7)

> *expected to provide more than 6000 jobs. The Japan International Cooperation Agency (JICA) will complete its feasibility study by November 2008.The first stage involves exporting fruits and vegetables from the West Bank to the Gulf States via Jordan.*[120]

TARQUMIYA INDUSTRIAL ZONE (TIZ): HEBRON REGION, SOUTH OF THE WEST BANK

This "development" model of Tarqumiya industrial zone was given high importance by the US, Israel and the PA. It was discussed at a top level meeting in Jerusalem, at the end of March 2008, by US Secretary of State then, Condoleezza Rice, the Israeli Defense Minister, Ehud Barak, and the PA Prime Minister Salam Fayyad. Israel agreed at the meeting to facilitate the establishment of the TIZ, and to consider it as a "confidence building" measure. Also, the Quartet promoted it heavily, and Tony Blair, the Quartet envoy, labeled it as one of the four "quick impact" projects tied to the implementation of Fayyad's government PRDP.[121] According to knowledgeable Turkish sources,

> *Turkey will be the major partner and financer of factories in the zone [TIZ] and will control internal security. The PA and Israel will control external security from their respective sides. Turkish sources expect around 200 factories to be established in the zone, employing around 10,000 Palestinians. Turkish business representatives explicitly note that in a global environment of low-cost Chinese goods, zones such as Tarqumiya will assist the relocation of Turkish industry across the region to take advantage of cheap labour. They also intend that the goods produced in the zone would be exported to the US, EU and the Gulf states.*[122]

120 (MAS, 2008, Palestinian Economic Bulletin, issue 23)

121 (Hanieh, 2008)

122 (Sak, 2008), as quoted in (Ibid)

JENIN INDUSTRIAL ZONE (JIZ): NORTH OF THE WEST BANK

The corner stone for the JIZ was laid by the Germans in 2000. The essence of this plan is to create an industrial zone at the seam line between Israel and the PA, where there are plans to erect a "logistics center" and a "medical center", on the Israeli side of the line. These will provide opportunities for advanced technical training and higher education collaboration, etc. Al-Jalameh crossing point will serve as the main path between the two sides, and, most likely, it will be expanded. There is talk about industrial production in textiles, lumber, foods, etc.[123]

In 25 August 1995, the "North Industrial International Company" (*Sharikat al-Shamal*) was registered in Jenin to implement the proposed Jenin Industrial Area. It had an initial capital of $22 million. The primary shareholders, which owned 70 percent of the company, were the Bank of Jordan and the Arab Islamic Bank. Other shareholders included the Jordanian Cigarette Company, Al-Iqbal Company for Investment, and Al-Sanabel Company for Trade and Investment.[124]

The "North Company" embarked in 1996 at purchasing land for this purpose. Today, the company owns 700 dunums (equals 700,000 square meters) inside the proposed area for the Industrial Zone. The "North" Company started since then, with the help of the German KfW Development Bank, in conducting feasibility studies and financial plans, at a cost of DM 600,000. Since the beginning of the idea, the Germans were committed to finance the infrastructure at a cost of $15 million.

The location selected for the Jenin Industrial Zone is an area of fertile agricultural lands. However, it was selected to meet the criterion of being close to the border line between Israel and the PA. Deflecting this criticism, the chairman of the "North" Company reiterated in his interview that "we don't decide on the location. ... But it is convenient location due to its proximity

123 (Bisan, 2008, and 2010)

124 (Al-Aref, 2010)

of crossing points (only 22 KMs from the Haifa seaport and 23 KMs from the Sheikh Hussein Crossing into Jordan)."[125]

All the planning and feasibility studies came to an abrupt halt in 2000. In 2008, with the help of a Jordanian-Palestinian consulting firm, the "North" Company worked on updating and upgrading the plans. However, in 20 December 2009, the PA withdrew from it the franchise and granted it to a Turkish company, claiming that the "North" Company was too slow in implementing the project. Currently, the case is in litigation. The Chairman of the "North" Company was very critical of this move, and alluded that there are other factors at work.

The director of the Israeli-Palestinian research center, Gershon Baskin, expects this JIZ will generate tens of thousands of job opportunities. According to Baskin, developing the plans for the JIZ will proceed if local leaders give the project a chance. Central authorities have simply to facilitate getting all the necessary permits to work, and provide the needed utilities and infrastructure. Plans are ready, and funding is available, he confidently asserted. In conjunction with Konrad Adenouer Foundation, a meeting for local leaders was held at the Foundation's office in Italy.[126]

The JIZ is a clear example how this model of "development" serves to normalize and legitimate the existing structure of the colonial occupation, and to deflect Palestinian concerns from the issue of struggling against continued occupation to the issue of struggling for cheap local employment.

> *In addition to the exploitation of cheap labour, these zones serve to normalize and legitimate the existing structures of the occupation. A clear example of this is shown by the case of the Jenin Industrial Estate (JIE). The land for the JIE has twice been confiscated from Palestinian farmers: in 1998 when the PA first mooted the idea for the industrial zone, and*

125 (Ibid)

126 (Bisan 2008, and 2010)

> *then once again in 2003, when the Israeli military confiscated the land as part of construction for the Apartheid Wall 'buffer-zone.' Indeed, in a striking example of how this model of development is integrated with the structures of the occupation, the Wall will form the northern border of the JIE.*[127]

EREZ INDUSTRIAL ZONE (EIZ): GAZA

The Palestine Economic Bulletin stated in 2007 that

> *After meeting in Washington, DC, a group of Turkish, Israeli, and Palestinian businessmen known as the Ankara Forum announced its intentions to revitalise the industrial estate at Erez. The project, part of the Ankara Forum's Industry for Peace Initiative, will have a budget of about $25m and aims to create 10,000 Palestinian jobs in the industrial zone, which fell into disuse after Israel withdrew from Gaza in September 2005. The World Bank has given its support to the project, which will be modeled on the Organised Industrial Zones (OIZs) that have played a prominent role in the development of the Turkish economy.*[128]

The initiative, however, was rolling soon after the redeployment of the Israseli occupation army from Gaza in 2005. Already in April 2005, capitalists from Turkey, Israel and the PA met in Ankara to launch the idea of revitalizing the EIZ. The initiative came from Turkey's Union of Chambers and Commodity Exchanges (TOBB), an organization representing all 1.2 million Turkish firms. "The idea", as described by the managing director of the Economic Policy Research Foundation of Turkey (TEPAV), "was 'microeconomics' for peace. In other words, it was to use Turkey's economic experience and industrial know-how to make factories and business work again. In practical

127 (Hanieh, 2008)

128 (MAS, 2007, Palestinian Economic Bulletin, issue 8)

terms, the concept is to make the Erez site productive once more under the leadership of a Turkish management company set up by TOBB, and with the cooperation of Turks, Palestinians, and Israelis. The Erez industrial estate ... could serve as a prototype for industrial development and also show how businessmen can cooperate in practical ways to bring peace to the region".[129]

The successful implementation of the project requires "effective coordination and cooperation between Israel and the Palestinian Authority. Recognizing this need for coordination, the Federation of Palestinian Chambers, the Israeli Manufacturers Association and other senior business and political leaders in both nations have given solid backing to the project. Political support has come from all three governments; their foreign ministers signed a memorandum of understanding for the project in January 2006. This is a business venture ... [it] will not work unless it guarantees both security and a return on investments".[130]

This project will be handled and operated by a Turkish company, TOBB-BIS (that stands for "industry for peace". The Turkish firm will handle all aspects of operations, including "land development, logistics services, workforce training, infrastructure regulatory services for the industries in the zone", and primarily "security" considerations. The "security" will be effected according to, what the Turkish firm labels as the "island concept". This security concept

> *Comprises the provision of internal and external security as well as perfectly securing the Erez trucks' loading/unloading area and the short road that connects it to the Erez crossing. This sort of security provision requires* ***effective coordination between the Israeli and Palestinian security forces.*** *However, for the initial stages, third party involvement will be necessary, potentially in the form of an*

129 (Sak, 2007)

130 (Ibid)

> *internationally accredited private security company that will focus on the internal security of the Erez site but also coordinate with Israeli and Palestinian forces on a regular basis.*[131]

However, the "top priority" for the project will aim "at inviting a 'critical mass' of successful companies to invest. ... Many Turkish firms are showing great interest in opening plants at Erez, especially because of tariff-free access to the American market and the Gulf States".[132]

Commenting on the "security aspect", Ephraim Sneh, the retired IDF general, the former military governor of the West Bank, and the former Israeli deputy minister of defense, stated in a recent article.[133]

The Israeli contribution required for the success of these industrial zones is the provision of a fast export channel for the goods manufactured there. Thus, for the new Erez zone we are committed to providing a dedicated export route via the Erez crossing. A two million dollar contribution from USAID and the participation of the Israel Ministry of Defense have facilitated the construction of a dedicated passage for goods from the "Turkish area" to export via Israel.

WHY DOES THIS MODEL OF "DEVELOPMENT" NEGATE "PEOPLE-CENTERED LIBERATIONIST DEVELOPMENT" (PCLD)?

This model of "development", strongly advocated by the US, Israel, the PA, international, regional and local capital, is premised on the following:

1. That available Palestinian labor is a controlled pool of cheap labor with no rights;

131 (Ibid; emphasis added).

132 (Ibid)

133 (Sneh, 2007)

Inside these zones, Palestinian and Israeli labour laws, wage levels, environmental regulations, or other workplace conditions will not apply. Movement in and out of the areas will be controlled by the Israeli military and Palestinian security forces. Presumably, if Israel's typical pattern of movement control applies, workers will need to pass stringent security checks in order to obtain necessary work permissions. In this way, the ability to work becomes dependent upon complying with Israeli military orders (over 11,000 Palestinians are currently held as political prisoners for violating these military orders). The main trade union body in the West Bank and Gaza Strip, the Palestinian General Federation of Trade Unions (PGFTU), has not been given the right to represent workers in the industrial zones.[134]

Although the exact details of these zones have been kept under wraps, institutions involved claim that the initial phase is expected to directly employ around 40,000 workers with a similar number of jobs created 'indirectly' outside the zones. If these plans come to fruition they will have a major impact on the structure of Palestinian labour in the West Bank: just under 20% of jobs in the West Bank will be tied in some way to these industrial zones.[135]

2. The precondition for Palestinian employment in these zones is the submission and acquiescence to the continued colonial occupation (otherwise no permits to cross would be granted by the Israeli occupation structure);

3. Strengthening the role of the PA as the security sub-agent for Israeli security;

Industrial zones are an efficient instrument for creating jobs, increasing employment and advancing economic development in the territories. A variety of practical considerations—particularly available transport, convenient raw materials supply and export channels—render it preferable to establish

134 (Hanieh, 2008)

135 (Ibid)

these industrial zones near the Palestinian border with Israel. The combination of Israeli and Palestinian investors generates a shared interest that ensures stability and creates the basis for normal relations between the two peoples.[136]

As with many other economic initiatives in the territories, it allowed former Israeli security officials-in this instance the erstwhile colonial administrators of the territories-to remarket themselves as private facilitators of Palestinian "development," mediating between official Israeli security apparatuses and the new economic elite that had coalesced around the PA during the Oslo process.[137]

4. Production from "industrial zones" is geared for export to international and regional markets; not for strengthening an independent Palestinian economy;

The institutionalization and frequent tightening of closure remained a critical constraint for many Palestinian enterprises, including the GIE. Resolving such difficulties often became conditional on the mediation of Israeli "partnerships," or agreements with people possessing connections to Israel's government, border bureaucracy, or security establishment. Among other things, these partners moved Palestinian goods through the Israeli export infrastructure as Israeli goods, often securing the necessary intermediary financing as well.[138]

5. Economic activities being planned for these zones do not respond to the needs of Palestinian society under occupation, e.g., providing food security, increasing the productivity of land, developing available water resources, etc;

136 (Sneh, 2007)

137 (Lagerquist, 2003:5).

138 (Ibid:13)

6. Economic activities in these zones are geared primarily towards increasing the profitability of investments of international, regional, and Palestinian capitalists;

7. Industrial zones normalize relations with the colonial occupation structures, legitimize its continued existence, solidify Palestinian dependence on it, and target to benefit only Palestinian capitalists. Its impact on minimizing Palestinian poverty is highly dubious.

Lagerquist argued[139] that "in addition to dubious economics, the scheme [industrial Zones] provided rent-seeking opportunities to Israeli middlemen arbitrating between Israeli security apparatuses and Palestinian economic elites, both rehearsing a wider tendency of development projects to obscure issues of power and control and ultimately itself reinvesting a local colonial genealogy of development as control."

WEST BANK AND GAZA AS A BIG REAL ESTATE PROJECT: AL-RAWABI TOWN AS A CASE IN POINT

Housing construction is the traditional area in which Palestinians invested historically, prior to the onslaught of external Western aid. Building new homes for family members and for close relatives always acquired a certain sacred aura, which buoyed family members and neighbors in participating by volunteering their work, and offering whatever they could to make the endeavor successful. Cost was covered from savings, selling parcels of land, contributions from family members, etc. This was a cultural happening, *par excellence*. This is not what I will be analyzing in this section, however.

My analysis here focuses on the purposeful investments in real estate "development" through housing schemes, which entice the rising technocratic middle class to become mortgaged for generations. The funding for these investments is coming from Palestinian capitalists, either as individuals or through

139 (Ibid:5)

the investment monopolies they created, in conjunction with Western aid agencies, the banking financial institutions, and the Oslo self-rule Authority. Due to the real or putative huge profit margins in these projects, this real estate offensive is generating an unregulated, wide-open involvement of a large number of profit-seeking agents, from inside and outside the Palestinian areas.

Dubious schemes are being planned, prepackaged, and marketed by "professional" consulting firms, aiming at attracting middle-income, mostly on the "public" payroll, financed by the same aid agencies, in the first place. Observe some of the publically-reported housing schemes:

> *The Portland Trust, working closely with the Palestinian private sector and the PA, has developed an initiative to build 15,000 housing units in 6 new communities by 2013 for a total cost of $1bn. The units will have a selling price of $38,000 - $70,000 and will be affordable to Palestinians on a monthly household income of $800 - $1,700.*[140]
>
> *Progress on two sites – one outside Nablus for 1000 homes and another outside Ramallah for 5000 homes – make construction in 2008 a very real possibility. The developers are working with the Palestinian authorities to secure approvals for planning, construction and the provision of essential services to the sites. They are also negotiating directly with the local banking sector to agree the terms of affordable mortgage finance.*[141]
>
> *The Palestine Mortgage and Housing Corporation (PMHC) will provide long-term fixed rate loans for new homes built by the Union Construction and Investment Corporation (UCI). PMHC will be the sole loan provider for an initial 63 units in Etihad (north-west Ramallah) and 29 units in*

140 (MAS, 2008, Palestinian Economic Bulletin, issue 17)

141 (Ibid)

> *the Arkadia Residential Compound (Al Masyoun, Ramallah). House prices range depending on size, from $130,000 a unit to $300,000 for larger villas. 20 year loans with a five year fixed rate of 6.95% will be provided.*[142]
>
> *Residential buildings in Al Jinan will be either $100,000 two-storey, semi-detached villas of 175 square metres, $80,000 three bedroom apartments of 150 square metres or $55,000 two bedroom apartments of 110 square metres. Onsite facilities will include a shopping centre, health clinic, kindergarten, mosque and public spaces.*[143]

To illustrate this further, the analysis focuses on the proposed new town, Al-Rawabi, as a case in point.

If allowed to be completed, Al-Rawabi project would be the first Palestinian town, designed from scratch, for middle and upper classes. It is, as the *Washington Post* described it, "specifically designed for upwardly mobile families of a sort that in the United States might gravitate to places such as Reston, VA."[144] It is the flagship project of the Fayyad's government, which intends to show that Palestinians under occupation are building their future state institutions, irrespective of all obstacles imposed by the occupation. Without saying, however, that the successful completion of this project, like many others being flaunted by the Fayyad Government, is totally contingent on the cooperation of the colonial occupation structure. This is a real estate project that is intended to be a magnet for corporate investment, locally, regionally and globally.

Al-Rawabi is to be erected at a location about 10 kilometers north of Ramallah, close to the Palestinian village of Atara and the Zionist colony of Ateret. It is a town designed to accommodate up to 40,000 residents. As described by Maher Sawalha,

142 (MAS, 2009, Palestinian Economic Bulletin, issue 36)

143 (MAS, 2009, Palestinian Economic Bulletin, issue 38)

144 Quoted in (Lunat, 2010)

the site engineer, the new town will have "retail stores, hotels, a cultural centre, restaurants, a theater and a cinema, and an open-air theatre." [145]

The master plan for the 5000 housing-unit project was approved by the PA in January 2009. It was prepared by a consortium of Bayti Real Estate (Rawabi's developer), EDAW, the British subsidiary of the international firm AECOM, and local experts from Al-Najah and Birzeit universities. The new town will cost over $500 million to build. The new town

> *Will offer more than 5,000 affordable housing units for up to 40,000 Palestinians, as well as employment opportunities, schools, healthcare provision and a commercial hub for businesses and service providers. Amir Dajani, Deputy General Manager of Bayti, explained that the public-private partnership with the PA stipulates that the PA will financially support the offsite infrastructure and public services in Rawabi, in line with the Palestinian Reform and Development Plan (PRDP). Bayti will follow an "economic growth strategy" for Rawabi and hopes to create 8,000-10,000 jobs during construction and as many as 5,000 long-term employment opportunities once construction is complete. Bayti is committed to attracting foreign investment.*[146]

Actual construction started during January 2010. The full amount of infrastructure funding is still to be secured, as well as Israeli approvals for the main access road, which crosses through Area C. It was reported in April 2010 that

> *The US Trade and Development Agency (USTDA) will support two technical assistance projects for Rawabi. ... A $413,000 grant will enable the*

145 (Lynfield, 2010)

146 (MAS, 2009, Palestinian Economic Bulletin, issue 29)

> *development of an ICT masterplan to provide the residents of Rawabi with cost-effective and essential communications services and infrastructure. USTDA will also finance a feasibility study, at a cost of $274,000, to assess potential wastewater treatment technologies in Rawabi and the surrounding area.*[147]

The "Bayti Real Estate and Investment Company" is overseeing the development of the new town. It is a Palestinian-Qatari investment company. Bashar al-Masri, the Managing Director of Bayti, boasts that the new town "will have a lot of Western components and a lot of Palestinian components … a purely Western town will not sell here". Al-Masri, who is a native of Nablus and studied in the US, admits that "we are for profit, that's for sure, but taking the risk is motivated by the fact that I'm Palestinian and we need to build this nation … Most residents will be middle-income. … Every residential building will have underground parking … everything from kindergartens to electricity will be meticulously planned".[148] To emphasize, further, how meticulously planned Al-Rawabi will be, Shirene Nazer, the project's architect, adds that the design will evoke the old city of Nablus and Jerusalem, "with narrow alleys made of stone or brick, for pedestrians only. … The town will be divided into 23 neighborhoods that will feature 'semi-private pocket gardens' so that residents will meet, and relationships will be forged and reinforced", invoking the concept of the traditional "hara".[149]

In the same breath, and in the same interview, the General Manager of Bayti Investment Company scuttled his earlier statement about his willingness to take an investment risk because of his patriotic commitment to "build this nation" if the investment is hampered by Israel. "If the access road [between Ramallah and Al-Rawabi] is not built", he said, "at some point

147 (MAS, 2010, Palestinian Economic Bulletin, issue 43)

148 (Ibid)

149 (Ibid)

a decision will be taken to scrap the town. ... It would be stupid to continue until it is totally completed if the road is not approved".[150] As mentioned earlier, the success of the project is at the mercy of Israel, i.e., the colonial occupation structure and the Zionist colonists. Although Israeli press alluded, during May 2010, that Israel will "facilitate the opening of the roads between Ramallah and Al-Rawabi"[151], barely a month later reports appeared in Israeli press that Zionist colonists in the area are ready to mount a campaign against opening the road between Al-Rawabi and Ramallah.

The Spokesman for the Palestinian Government, Ghassan Khatib, indicated in no uncertain terms that the PA is "strongly backing the project". The justification, he advanced, was based on the false claim of 'housing shortage'. "It is very important for the Palestinians because we have a housing shortage and very high demand on housing that the cities are not capable of dealing with".[152] The PA public justification is false considering the fact that, on the one hand, currently in Ramallah alone there stand thousands of empty residential units, and, on the other, the new town is targeting middle and upper income classes. Al-Rawabi is not designed to offer affordable housing to the poor or to the lower income working class; capitalists, on the other hand, are not in need of subsidized housing, and they have access to numerous options. For the middle class to be eligible to benefit from this housing opportunity, it has to buy into the "mortgage structure" that is being pushed by the US and the USAID funded "corporate" NGOs.

Such a real estate project is "relying on another American import, the home mortgage, including creation of a Fannie Mae-style institution for the West Bank. ... USAID is funneling funds through NGOs for the promotion of a mortgage culture in Palestine to support these initiatives from bottom-up. One such example is CHF International, a corporate-led develop-

150 (Ibid)

151 (Maan, 2010, May 18)

152 (Ibid)

ment NGO, which is organizing community level focus groups and technical training as part of their 'Homebuyer Education' program." [153]

A major question that needs verification related to the question of land. How was the land for this new town acquired? Where did "Bayti Real Estate and Investment Company", which was set up specifically for this project, get funds to acquire these lands? Whose town is it that is being proposed?

COLLABORATIVE INITIATIVES BY ZIONIST AND PALESTINIAN CAPITALISTS AND THE OSLO POLITICAL ELITES IN SUSTAINING THE OCCUPATION UNDER THE GUISE OF "ECONOMIC DEVELOPMENT" AND "INDEPENDENT STATE INSTITUTION BUILDING"

One of the objectives of the Fayyad Government's Program, dubbed "Ending the Occupation, Establishing the State", is:

> *To achieve economic independence and national prosperity" by "liberating the Palestinian national economy from external hegemony and control, and reversing its dependence on the Israeli economy", since recognizing "that sustainable development cannot be attained under the occupation, it is our national duty to do all that we can to pull our economy out of the cycle of dependence and marginalization. ... Accomplishment of this goal is essential to resisting the measures imposed by the occupation regime and ending the occupation itself. Achieving economic growth is a necessity so that we can promote our people's ability to persevere and remain on their homeland by alleviating the poverty and unemployment generated by the continued occupation. It will also promote the contri-*

153 (Lunat, 2010)

> *bution of all segments of our society in the struggle to build an independent and self-sufficient state.*[154]

These are lofty and laudable nationalistic objectives. In reality, however, as the various maneuvers and initiatives analyzed in this chapter are showing, this is not happening on the ground. What is happening, actually, is the reverse. All indications are pointing to an increase in the dependence of the Palestinian economy on Israeli economy and "donor" funds; dependent and unequal collaboration between Palestinian and Israeli-Zionist capitalists; and total acquiescence to a continued and more brutal and intrusive colonialist occupation. Actually, the collaborative initiatives by capitalists and ruling political elites on both sides seem to emphasize not an end to occupation, but a more entrenched Palestinian economic dependence and dissolution. Albeit the emphasis is casted in terms of "economic integration" as a necessary precondition for "peaceful co-existence"!

Consider, for example, some of the "collaborative" public initiatives, which, I am certain, they represent only the tip of the iceberg of what is really going on behind closed doors. All these initiatives point to an economic normalization of two unequal sides, where capitalists and political elites on both sides play a very active role in ensuring their sustainability. The clear message on the Palestinian side to the Israeli side is that there is a clear separation between the political effects of the prevailing colonial context (my term not theirs!) and economic normalization and collaboration. We are ready and anxious to get involved in the second. Succeeding in the second, therefore, has more priority than struggling to free ourselves from the first. And succeeding in the second would ensure normal relations, and may ease the harsh political effects of the first. It is a position of a subservient and acquiescent slave.

This collaborationist economic normalization escalated visibly since Hamas won the legislative elections in January

154 (PNA, 2009)

2006. Since, moves towards normalization were rushed and facilitated by Palestinian capitalists, Zionist capitalists, whether they were in Israel or in the West, and by major Western aid agencies and institutions.

1. During the World Economic Forum, held in Jordan in May 2007, which brought together selected Palestinian, Israeli, Arab, and international capitalists, under the watchful eye of centers of Western capital and transnational finance agencies, a "Council of Palestinian-Israeli Businessmen" emerged. The new Council claimed in its declaration that "it will endeavor to strengthen the relations between Palestinian and Israeli business sectors, and it will support the efforts seeking to achieve peace and co-existence".[155] The Declaration promised, further, that "the new group will urge the economic sectors in both Palestinian and Israeli societies **to develop an agenda that calls for rationalism and dialogue in support of reconstruction and economic reform in the region ...".**[156]
2. Among the Palestinian capitalists and aspiring capitalists participating in the Forum and in the Joint Businessmen Council, were: Munib Al-Masri, Abdul-Malek Al-Jaber, Samir Huleileh, Hassan Abu-Libdeh, Walid Al-Najjab, and Odeh Shehadeh. Walid al-Najjab, the Palestinian co-chairman of the new Council emphasized: "We are not in the business of offering political solutions, but we constituted a group that is capable of providing a direction, which will help in solving the critical issues that affect our region." In parallel, almost well-rehearsed terms, Amos Shapira, the Israeli co-chairman, reiterated the emphasis that "we don't deal with political issues, nor do we seek to find solutions for them. Notwithstanding our cognizance of the past, we are more concerned with the future".[157]

155 (Al-Quds Daily, 19 May 2007)

156 (Ibid.; emphasis added)

157 (Ibid)

3. The Peres Center, in cooperation with the Federation of Israeli Bi-National Chambers of Commerce and the Portland Trust was instrumental in establishing the Israeli-Palestinian Chamber of Commerce (IPCC). "The Chamber will work to foster and strengthen economic and trade relations between Israelis and Palestinians". IPCC was officially launched in May 2009. It promotes business opportunities, trade and cooperation between Israelis and Palestinians. Ofir Gendelman, the Israeli Ministry of Foreign Affairs spokesman, was appointed as its CEO. Eival Gilady, who heads the Portland Trust's Israel's Office is its chairman. The IPCC held its first meeting in February 2009. "60 Israeli and Palestinian business people met to discuss ways of improving imports and exports. Representatives from the Ashdod Port Company, Israeli Customs and the Israeli Civil Administration also took part in the meeting".[158]
4. IPCC held its Second Annual Gala Dinner on 9 June 2010 in Tel Aviv with 320 guests. Approximately 50 top Palestinian business people attended the event with the Israeli business community, Ambassadors, representatives from international organisations and government officials. In its first year of operation a number of events have been held, a Breakfast Club has been launched for its members to meet prominent Palestinian business people, Palestinian business opportunities have been studied and links have been made with other business chambers around the world. The importance of economic cooperation between the business communities was highlighted at the event, as well as the vital role that the economy can play in paving the way for and supporting political progress.[159]

5. In an article on 1 May 2007, Simon Clark[160] reported on various initiatives by top Jewish Israeli capitalists to explore

158 (MAS, 2009, Palestinian Economic Bulletin, issue 31).

159 (MAS, 2010, Palestinian Economic Bulletin, issue 46).

160 (http:// www.bloomberg.com)

joint business ventures with Palestinian capitalists, with the encouragement of official political elites on both sides (the Israeli and the Palestinian), under the rubric of "business deals … foster peace." It was revealed that in January 2005, Idan Ofer, the chairman of Israel Corp, a huge Israeli conglomerate, visited Ramallah "wanting to meet Palestinian businessmen". That he did. One of the businessmen he met was Talal Nasereddin, chairman of Birzeit Pharmaceutical Co. Following the meeting, Nasereddin stated: "Our best business could be with the Israelis. … [Idan] has a common interest in peace on a business level. … This is a good thing."

One of the other Palestinian businessmen he met was Abdul Malek Al-Jaber, the CEO of Paltel. Following the meeting, Al-Jaber stated: "The business community shouldn't wait until the politicians set and talk. … We should start investing now to create joint interests. If people have interests in common, they will be willing to compromise." In the meantime, Idan Ofer concluded: "Economic progress for the Palestinians would go a long way toward making a better solution for the neighborhood."

Idan Ofer is the co-chairman, with Samer Khouri, of the Middle East Strategy Group of the Aspen Institute. Samer Khouri is a current member of PIF's BOD, a current member of WA Board of Trustees, and a current member of the BOT of MAS, as well as the son of Said Khouri, a Palestinian capitalist tycoon from Safad, who established and owns, with Hasib Sabbagh (his brother-in-law), one of the biggest construction companies in the Middle East (CCC). Like the late Sabbagh, he is one of the founding fathers of WA.

6. An internet startup company called G.ho.st (Global Hosted Operating System) is a joint venture between Palestinian and Zionist capital, with headquarters in the colonial settlement of Modi'in and an office in Ramallah. The Ramallah office employs about 35 software developers, and a much

smaller Israeli team in Modi'in.[161] Its Ramallah office was set-up by Tareq Maayah, a Palestinian technologist-capitalist. The CEO of the new company is Dr. Zvi Schreiber, a 41 year-old Israeli-British capitalist. In an article on 29 May 2008, he said that "... it was time to merge his technological and commercial ambitions with his social ones and create business with Palestinians".[162] While he tried to emphasize that this is not a simple case of outsourcing, he reiterated in the same breath that "employing Palestinians means the money goes farther; salaries for Palestinian programmers are about a third of what they are in Israel." So, he tapped into a pool of cheap Palestinian technological labor!

The company has a "philanthropic" component, a foundation headed by Noa Rothman, Rabin's granddaughter. The "foundation" aims to establish computer center in Ramallah, and in "mixed Jewish-Arab towns in Israel."

The new start-up company, which was launched in the Bethlehem area in mid-July 2009, started with US$2.5 million investment from major US venture capital firm Benchmark Capital. Benchmark Capital is headquartered in California, USA, with an Israeli office in Herzliya. Dr. Zvi Schreiber, the brainchild of the project, told the Bulletin he saw 'great potential in the project. While there is currently more business experience in Israel, Palestine has great talent, cost competitiveness and some growing experience too.' There are already around 200,000 users for the 'virtual computer'.[163] A friend IT management consultant indicated to me recently that "Ghost" has since closed.

7. A news website in Nazareth[164] reported that on 7 April 2010, Tzim Israeli maritime company, which is owned by Hahivra Liyisrael, a subsidiary company of Israel Corp, the

161 (http://www.jewschool.com)

162 (Ibid)

163 (MAS, 2009, Palestinian Economic Bulletin, issue 35)

164 (http://www.bokra.net, report by Hanan Amarah, 9 April 2010)

Ofer group of companies, held a meeting for its "clients" at Grand Park Hotel in Ramallah (in which the PA owns much more than quarter of its shares through PIF). Present from the Israeli side were billionaire Idan Ofer, president of Hahivra Liyisrael and chairman of Israel Corp, the president of Tzim, the director general of Hahivra Liyisrael, Nir Gilad, the general director of Tzim, Rafi Danieli, and others.

On the Palestinian side, it was reported that 150 Palestinian businessmen participated in the meeting. They listened to a talk by Idan Ofer , titled "peace through economics" in which he claimed that "peace would be realized much sooner if the Palestinian economic situation improves really." In this context, Ofer praised the economic policy of Salam Fayyad. It was further revealed that a month earlier, Ofer had invited Fayyad to his house in Northern Tel Aviv, and arranged for him meetings with important Israeli capitalists, including Shai Agassi, the owner of Better Place Israel company (BPI), in which Idan Ofer is one of its largest investors, the president of Bank Hapoalim , Ehud Olmert, the former prime-minister, Dov Weissesglass, the former director general of Sharon's office, and other important businessmen.

In his talk, Idan Ofer listed a number of possibilities for economic cooperation with the PA. He alluded that he sensed that the PA is interested in the Chinese "electric car project", in which Hahivra Liyisrael is a partner. He indicated further that a profitable area for future mutual economic cooperation could be in importing Chinese electric cars.

One of the participants at the Ramallah meeting commented that Tzim Israel maritime company is interested in strengthening economic commercial cooperation with the PA, and, to show its seriousness, it presented the Palestinian participants with information and graphic illustration of its maritime lines, and its Arabic website. According to this participant, Palestinian businessmen expressed a special interest in Tzim's new line connecting Asia with Northern Europe through Israel.

Furthermore, it was revealed by a leading Israeli newspaper[165] that recently the same Idan Ofer visited secretly, with a group of Israeli capitalists and entrepreneurs, the Kurdish areas in Iraq to explore opportunities for investment in oil.

8. In a recent expose by the co-founder of the *Electronic Intifada*, Ali Abunimah,[166] about Better Place Israel (BPI) company, he revealed that James Wolfensohn, the former World Bank President and former Middle East Quartet envoy, is an investor in Better Place (BP), the mother company of BPI. Other investors include the Morgan Stanley Investment Bank. BPI (Better Place Israel) is a company founded by Israeli capitalist Shai Agassi, and Idan Ofer is "one of its largest investors". BPI's CEO is former IDF general Moshe Kaplinski who commanded Israeli forces during the second intifada and the re-invasion of the West Bank, and who was the deputy Chief of Staff of Israel's army during its war on Lebanon in 2006.

   "Better Place's goal is to bring fully-electric vehicles and the infrastructure to support them to the mass market—starting with Israel. It also has pilot projects as far afield as Denmark, Canada, California, Australia and Japan. Specially-built electric cars, due to be available to the public in Israel next year, are manufactured by French-Japanese conglomerate Renault-Nissan under an agreement with Better Place. Better Place had also recently signed a memorandum of understanding with Chinese car manufacturer Chery, to jointly develop electric car technology for the Chinese market."

   To ensure that it provides full service to its electric cars, BPI is establishing a network of thousands of charging spots on all major road networks in Israel and the Jewish

165 (Maariv, 25 June 2010)

166 (Abunimah, 2010)

colonies in the West Bank. Dor-Alon, the huge energy group and largest oil refinery in Israel, which is owned by the Ofer Group, and which holds the monopoly to provide petroleum to the PA, is to provide the "charging spots" for the new electric cars, in its gas stations along the road networks. This is the context that framed Ofer's visit to Ramallah in January 2005 (mentioned above), and Tzim's meeting with Palestinian capitalists and PA political bureaucracy at Grand Park Hotel in Ramallah in April 2010. Both of these exploratory contacts (plus, perhaps, many other undisclosed contacts) clearly aim, at first instance, to normalize economic relations with the Zionist apartheid regime in Israel, enlarge the economic market of the Ofer empire, and attract Palestinian investments. The economic motive here is not very convincing, however, due to its miniscule nature. But the political economy of these moves is more convincing. Imagine the resulting economic-political integration and normalization by opening the mini-market of the West Bank to electric cars manufactured in Israel, which have to be serviced by "charging spots" on the Palestinian road networks of the West Bank, alongside the apartheid road networks that serve the Zionist Jewish colonists in the occupied areas, and Israel. What's wrong with little profits on the side!

BPI is a company fully supported by Israeli political establishment, from Peres down. In an interview with CNN, Agassi, BPI chairman, stated "I would not be doing this today were it not for Peres."[167]

9. Another case of normalization in economic cooperation, between Palestinian capitalists in the PA areas and Jewish Israeli capitalists, is in the field of solar energy. Recently, a group of Palestinian capitalists signed a Memorandum of Understanding (MOU) with an Israeli company, Shahar Energia, to build solar energy stations to generate electric power in the West Bank. The investment will be about

167 (CNN, 19 April 2010)

USD 20 million. The solar systems for the production of electric power were produced by the Chinese company ET Solar. The plan is to produce around 5 Megawatts of electricity which will be sold to the Jerusalem District Electric Company. Ze'ev Peretz, the director general of the Israeli company revealed that the solar systems will be financed from European sources, which invest in joint Israeli-Palestinian projects "whose aim is to solidify economic relations between the two peoples as a bridge for peace."[168]

10. Another economic collaborative effort between Israel, the PA, and Jordan is in the field of agriculture. This agricultural project ("biological campaign to combat citrus fruit flies") in the Jordan Valley is funded by the International Agency for Atomic Energy, and was approved since 2003, but the implementation was delayed, and is being currently implemented between the Israeli and Palestinian ministries of agriculture. In this context, the Israeli minister of agriculture (Shalom Simhoni) declared that "agriculture is the bridge to peace".[169]

11. A very recent brief news item in Israeli press revealed that tens of PA police participated in a training session in Yaffa, with Israeli police, thanks to funding by the EU. It was reported also that the Israeli police arranged for their visitors from Ramallah a tour in the "ethnically cleansed" city of Yaffa, and a visit to the "Peres Center for Peace".[170]

This is only a sample of the publically reported capitalists' initiatives in normalizing economic relations with the political-economic structure that imposes and maintains a colonial occupation of our people, with the direct support and

168 (Maan Developmental Center, 2010)

169 (Ibid)

170 (http://www.arabs48.com, 25 May 2010)

facilitation of the political elite on both sides. Unless the PA government has a divergent perception of "ending the occupation" and "minimizing" dependence of Palestinian economy on Israeli and Western capital, clearly this sample of initiatives points to an increasing dependence of Palestinian economy and society, and to relegating the struggle against the continuous occupation and the system of colonial apartheid to a very secondary and minor place. This brings into high relief the disingenuousness of the public claims being toted in the Fayyad's government program, as well as the "patriotic" assertions and concerns about "peace" and "an independent state" advanced by the capitalists themselves. This approach has been dubbed already as "Fayyadism"—as if it is an innovative theory in the political economy of the occupied![171]

Furthermore, taken comprehensively, these various initiatives lend credence to assertions made by a number of analysts that "the current Palestinian government is a government of capital ... with wide-open channels to it", where, simultaneously, capital is "investing in politics"; and coalescing and collaborating towards building a political base to strengthen its influence.[172]

Although the Fayyad Government's program and its flagship—the PRDP—generated a flurry of economic activities, it clearly did not generate "economic development", and most certainly, not a PCLD environment. For example, in a recent editorial in British press, an engaged, honest, Palestinian economic activist and practitioner commented on some aspects of "Fayyadism", as follows:

> *Economic activity, in which I am involved (and of which I am proud), is happening [but] ... it should ... not be toted as economic development. ... Economic development and growth which is worthy of building toward an economy of a future*

171 (see Friedman, 2010)

172 (see, for example, Samara, 2007, Mitnick, 2007)

> *state is nowhere to be found. How could it be? All key aspects of a true economy are squarely in the hands of Israel, our occupier. Israel, alone, holds the levers to our water, movement, access, all borders, airspace, electricity, electromagnetic spectrum, just to name a few. A new building in Ramallah, or 100 for that matter, make for good ribbon-cutting ceremonies, but are as far from economic state building as is wrong is from right".*[173]

The "Fayyadism" approach, propagated by Salam Fayyad, the Ramallah PA Prime-Minister, and the "economic peace", propagated by Netanyahu, through his Deputy Prime- Minister, Silvan Shalom, are two sides of the same coin. This unitary (dual) approach entails normalization with continued occupation and hegemonic control; sustained flows of international aid; and, in effect, declaring the small piece of the West Bank, the 17 percent that is called "Area A", as an economic project for sale!

The platform of "economic peace" on which Netanyahu was elected, contended "that developing the Palestinian economy, by providing Palestinians with jobs and a better living stands, would render the 'problems' between Israelis and Palestinians 'more accessible for solutions'.[174]

At the Bethlehem Investment Conference, Gordon Brown, the then British Prime-Minister, dangled in front of his British corporations and investors an economic prize, namely the creation of a Palestinian equity market. "The Palestine Investment Fund (PIF), the body leading such effort, expects to deliver an annual return of 15 percent. PIF plans to use cash deposits in local banks as well as money from investors to encourage growth in consumer spending".[175]

173 (Bahour, 2010)

174 (Lunat, 2010)

175 (Ibid)

Assessing the Netanyahu-Fayyad economic peace approach a year later, one observer noted:

> *A year on, the cost of the Netanyahu-Fayyad plan is becoming clear. Low-income Palestinian families and small business are being encouraged to borrow to fuel a high-risk economy. Israel has proven time again that it won't hesitate to strike a blow against Palestinian infrastructure should they dissent from the current consensus in its favor. Families are risking their possessions as collateral for their debts. Corporations responsible for the global financial collapse are applying their failed models in Palestine. Abraaj Capital, a Dubai-based investment fund that recently sparked fears for debt default, announced a $50 million private equity fund dedicated to "raising standards of living," mirroring the predatory behavior that led to the collapse of the sub-prime mortgage system in the US".*[176]

On the other hand, a very sympathetic and supportive observer of the Fayyad's approach, dubbed it as "a real Palestinian revolution".

> *It is a revolution based on building Palestinian capacity and institutions* ***not just resisting Israeli occupation,*** *on the theory that if the Palestinians can build a real economy, a professional security force and an effective, transparent government bureaucracy it will eventually become impossible for Israel to deny the Palestinians a state in the West Bank and Arab neighborhoods of East Jerusalem.* [177]

176 (Ibid)

177 (Friedman, 2010); emphasis added

Of course, such an approach is fully backed by Palestinian capital. They see it as a good and profitable alternative to the real and more demanding and engaging revolutionary struggle. PADICO's CEO expressed it clearly.

> *I have to admit, we, the private sector, have changed. ... The mood used to be all the time to complain and say there is nothing we can do. And then the politicians were trying to create this atmosphere of resistance — resistance meant no development under occupation. ... Now the mood is that improving the Palestinian economy is what will enable you to resist and be steadfast. Fayyad said to us: 'You, the business community, are not responsible for ending occupation. You are responsible for employing people and getting ready for the state. And that means you have to be part of the global world, to export and import, so when the state will come you will not have a garbage yard. You will be ready.'* [178]

CONCLUDING REMARKS

I analyzed in the previous pages the nature of the Palestinian capitalist class and its role in impeding the creation of a People-Centered Liberationist Development (PCLD). Although it may appear that the capitalist class and PCLD are two conceptually different categories, the thrust of this chapter was on showing that Palestinian capitalists' investments, under the guise of "developing" the society and economy, are thwarting the necessary conditions for a PCLD environment. To provide indications to this assertion, the analysis focused on capitalists' alliances with the Oslo-generated political elites, and their collaboration with Israeli-Zionist capitalists to establish and maintain control over specific monopolies for major essential services, general consumption projects, real estate and housing, financial institutions, border industrial zones, and occupation-controlled and privatized work opportunities. It is clear from

178 Ibid

the analysis that no capitalist investments were made in major production projects, and no emphasis on alleviating the roots of poverty. On the contrary, by investing capital in creating easily accessible credit schemes, capitalists' investments are setting the stage for increasing the indebtedness of the average person, entire households, and the society at large. Furthermore, the analysis points to indications that profits from these investments are siphoned off outside Palestine, without being re-invested in people-controlled and protected development projects.

Chapter Three

PALESTINIAN NGOS AND TRANSNATIONAL "AID" AGENCIES: THEIR ROLE IN IMPEDING PCLD APPRAOCH

"There can be no meaningful mass movement when dissent is generously funded by those same corporate interests which are the target of the protest movement."[1]

INTRODUCTION

In this chapter I shall analyze the role of Palestinian and transnational NGOs in thwarting or undermining the process of "People-Centered Liberationist Development" (PCLD). I aim to show, through detailed micro-analysis, how the confluence between the newly-emerging group of Palestinian "developmental" NGOs [2] in the context of supporting and legitimiz-

1 (Chossudovsky, 2010)

2 The label "developmental" is a self-claim and self-definition of this category of NGOs. It is intended, primarily, to distinguish themselves from traditional service providers and care givers "charitable societies". The self-acclaimed label, furthermore, was intended to embody a certain "positive" value-laden message, namely that their work is more advanced, more professional, more in tune with how and where the society should be going, and more appealing to the concerns and programs of international funding agencies.

ing the "Oslo process", in the aftermath of the invention of the PA, and the transnational Western NGOs, is leading to a state that is antithetical to the emergence of a PCLD environment. I shall argue, further, that this confluence is purposeful; and is cemented, pre-shaped, and sustained by the flow of international political aid, in general, and Western international political aid, in particular. The problem at hand is that since the beginning of the Oslo process and the influx of nearly 18 billion US dollars, a new category of "developmental" NGOs was created, at the expense of political-social grassroots movements, and for the purpose of serving as footholds for transnational aid agencies. By doing so, "developmental" NGOs removed themselves from grassroots constituents, and became closer to the central authority; became overtly depoliticized, and totally dependent, for their survival, on the flow of international political aid.

Available literature is replete with theoretical discussions and analyses about the concept of civil society; its scope and historical evolution; its connection to the process of "democratization"; and its relationship with the development of human societies, worldwide. Consequently, and due to the wealth of available literature, we shall not dwell in this chapter on any of these aspects. Our concern here is very specific and limited in scope.

Cognizant of the various deliberations and theoretical analyses about what the concept of civil society encompasses,[3] we shall limit our discussion, on the Palestinian side, only to non-governmental organizations (NGOs), and particularly, to those dubbed, or self-perceived, as "developmental" organizations. This is irrespective of the local vernacular used, which shifts simultaneously between "*munathamat Ghayr Hukumiyya"(NGOs), or "munathamat ahliyya"(communal or civic organizations), or "mu'assasat al-mujtama' al-madani"(CSOs), or "Jam'iyyat Khayriyyah"* (charitable societies), *etc.*[4] To circumscribe and

3 Please refer to the extensive list of sources at the end of the book.

4 See my earlier work on this subject (Nakhleh, 1991)

contextualize our current analysis, therefore, we shall focus on the category of the so-called "developmental" NGOs.[5]

INDIGENOUS "DEVELOPMENTAL" NGOS

NGOs in this category share, by and large, the following characteristics:

1. They emerged mostly over the last 25 – 30 years, proliferated, and became more visible and assertive, most specifically, since the beginning of the "Oslo peace process";
2. They transformed themselves, and shifted their approach and methods of work, through their aid-prescribed relations with Transnational Western NGOs (TNGOs). Thanks to TNGOs sustained financial support and training, these "developmental" NGOs shifted away from their grassroots base and constituencies, their politically-left

---

5 In his detailed analysis on "Palestinian Civil Society", Challand (2009:69 and 2010) stated:

> *Two hundred NGOs constitute the professional developmentalist sub-type. They are the secular NGOs active in health, agriculture, education, advocacy and community service, as well as research organizations. Although many were historically linked to political parties, political affiliation has become very loose, to the point that they can sometimes be considered as independent. They are the most visible organizations for the international donors, even though they represent the smallest sub-type (14 percent of all the NGOs at the time of the establishment of the PNA.*

In a recent "literature review" article on Palestinian civil society organizations, Hilal (2010:24) commented on "developmental NGOs", and complemented Challand's categorization, above, as follows:

> *Steady relations with the international NGOs and assistance from partner organizations in Europe and elsewhere, as well as the type of experience borne of their former political experience sets these organizations apart from other NGOs in terms of their capacity, scope of services and potential to impact the community. This type of organization has also been at the forefront of establishing the Palestinian Nongovernmental Organizations Network (PNGO) as it foresaw a need to create a lobby in order to safeguard the right of NGOs to operate independently of government intervention.*

leaning ideological thought and connections, to becoming "professionalized", managerially run entities, and proudly following Western standards;

3. "Developmental" NGOs specialize primarily in advocacy functions, knowledge production and dissemination, civic and civil education and principles, consciousness-raising, "democratization", human rights and good governance, women's rights, etc, and not, particularly, in service delivery;
4. They constitute the primary ingredients of the main general NGO umbrella network organization, the "Palestinian NGO Network" (PNGO), as well as the issue-specialized coalitions, e.g., the Coalition of Accountability and Integrity "AMAN";
5. Although it is difficult to determine precisely what is the percentage of this category of NGOs from the total number of NGOs, it is safe to maintain that it does not exceed about 20 percent;
6. "Developmental" NGOs, however, receive probably the lion share of Western international aid directed to NGOs.

My analysis here applies particularly to the category of active research centers and "think tanks", major human rights and good governance organizations, major organizations active in civic education, women's rights, workers rights, cross cultural and multi-cultural dialogues, political participation, active organizations in water and the environment, as well as those umbrella organizations that were created specifically to enhance coordination among "like-minded" organizations, and other organizations whose mission is to train, and indoctrinate on behalf of Western aid agencies, smaller, inexperienced, or recently established NGOs, in capacity building and professionalization, which Challand labels "multiplicator" NGOs.[6]

6 (Challand, 2009:189)

I maintain that in the Palestinian context these "intermediary" or "sub-agents" NGOs, like, for example, The Palestinian NGO Network (PNGO), The Palestinian Coalition for Integrity and Accountability (AMAN), The NGO Development Center (NDC), etc., play a pernicious role on behalf of their Western funders. They are funded to reinterpret, re-package, and disseminate the political and anti-developmental messages of their political Western funders, under the guise and claim of national and patriotic concerns of strengthening Palestinian civil society, through, essentially, a well-oiled process of cultural re-engineering of a new crop of depoliticized and managerial NGOs, under the rubric of "capacity building".

Since the focus of this study is the "development" of the occupied current Palestinian society over the last twenty years, I am targeting only "developmental" NGOs in order to examine to what extent "people", on the one hand, and "liberation", on the other, figure into the work of those NGOs that claim to be "developmental". By this focus, I am not claiming, necessarily, that the work of these NGOs is more effective or less effective than that of charitable societies or other service NGOs. I am claiming, however, that these self-proclaimed "developmental" NGOs, by and large, like the capitalist class, are hindering, in concert with other forces, the evolution of a PCLD environment. Let us keep in mind that these NGOs have their counterparts in the private sector, under the guise of "economic development" and "employment generation" (e.g., Massar International).

To go into depth, my analysis will be anchored in certain selected case studies that fuse indigenous "developmental" NGOs with Western Transnational NGOs, through the channel of Western "aid", be it labeled "development" or "humanitarian". I shall focus in this chapter on case studies highlighting the role of, first, "knowledge producing and disseminating" NGOs, where three cases will be analyzed: PASSIA, MUWATIN and MAS. The second category of case studies will highlight the role of the "umbrella" coalitions NGOs, whereas the third category of case studies will focus on the role of an intermediary and "sub-agent" NGO, the "NGO Development Center"

(NDC). However, its analysis will be expanded in the context of its "mother" NGO (the Welfare Association), which will be addressed in depth later in this chapter. The fourth category will focus on the overall issue of "harmonization and alignment" of aid, by presenting a detailed micro-analysis of a specific case in point, initiated by Western international "donors", and where I had a leading role to play in it.

Following the analysis of the case studies, I present a discussion of the interplay between transnational NGOs and Palestinian indigenous "developmental" NGOs. The chapter will be concluded with remarks on NGOs, governments, donors, and people, with a stress on the changing relationships as a basis for heightened control and dependency.

CASE STUDY 1: KNOWLEDGE PRODUCING AND DISSEMINATING NGOS

This category of "developmental" NGOs refers primarily, but not exclusively, to specific research centers, which were created, on the whole, since the Oslo Process began, "to cater for the social and economic planning needs of the PA".[7] Basically, we are talking about couple of dozens of such institutions. In its updated "mapping" study in 2007, MAS lists 19 research centers.[8] Others[9] listed a higher number. But, these numbers are not necessarily accurate, because of the encompassing typologies, and the actual number is not important for our analysis. What is important is to know that a significant majority of these NGOs (over 60%) was created since the process of "political settlement" to the conflict started rolling towards the end of the *intifada* in the early nineties of the last century, and that there is almost total dependency on external (primarily Western) sources of aid for their survival.

We are interested in this analysis in those "developmental" NGOs who were set-up with the specific aim of producing

7 (Hilal, 2010:25)

8 (MAS, 2007)

9 E.g., (Challand , 2009:108)

"knowledge", and "disseminating" it to a wider audience, supported, primarily, with political funds largely originating from Western governments and official agencies, for the purpose of impacting, or informing, PA policy. This phenomenon raises a number of critical questions: What "knowledge", and for what? To which audiences it is being disseminated? What evidence, if any, that this body of generated "knowledge" is having an impact on PA planning, strategy and policy? And, more importantly, since the PA is a creation of a political process, crafted and financed by major Western forces, the US and Europe, to the satisfaction of Israel, and shaped and controlled by the outside, isn't it a grand delusion to expect that such "knowledge" can have an impact on PA strategic planning and policy? If that is the case, then why Western sources of aid are still sustaining these organizations?

To shed some light on these questions, the analysis focuses in detail on three such organizations, namely, (1) The Palestinian Academic Society for the Study of International Affairs (PASSIA), (2) The Palestinian Institute for the Study of Democracy (MUWATIN), and (3) The Palestine Economic Policy Research Institute (MAS).

PASSIA

PASSIA, The Palestinian Academic Society for the Study of International Affairs, was founded in 1987 in Jerusalem by Dr. Mahdi Abdul Hadi and a group of Palestinian academics and intellectuals. Dr. Abdul Hadi remains until this day, or 23 years later, PASSIA's Head and the Chairman of its Board of Trustees.

PASSIA defines itself as an independent, Arab non-profit institution, which is not affiliated with any government or political party. "It seeks to present the Palestinian Question in its national, Arab and international contexts through academic research, dialogue and publication, [and it] endeavors that research undertaken under its auspices be specialized, scientific and objective and that its symposia and workshops, whether international or intra-Palestinian, be open, self-critical and conducted in a spirit of harmony and cooperation". While it endeavors "to ensure a wider understanding of Palestinian issues", it does that by "providing a forum for the free expression and analysis of a plurality of Palestinian perspectives and methodology," and by developing and clarifying "its own and others' understanding of international relations as they affect the Palestinian struggle for justice and peace".[10]

In addition to its general, and somewhat eclectic, focus on the connection between "international relations" and "the Palestine question", PASSIA prides itself, correctly, of being genuinely engaged in the question of Jerusalem. In support of this engagement, it has published, since it was established, at least 21 titles, whose focus is the multilayered aspects of current and historical Jerusalem. Topics ranged from Israel's annexation of Jerusalem, to US foreign policy towards Jerusalem, to applicable UN resolutions, to religious aspects, to social and spatial history, to Israeli settlement policy in Jerusalem, to planning, and negotiations, etc.

PASSIA has a vibrant Research Studies Program with multiple components including, in addition to Jerusalem, an "Information Papers" series, a "Dialogue" series, a "Religious Studies" series, a "Seminars" series, a "Palestine Facts and Figures and Maps" series, and an annual "Passia Diary" series. By my account, PASSIA has published around 140 titles on a huge diversity of subjects relating to the Palestine question. PASSIA asserts that it "intends to continue its efforts to provide background information, theoretical material and in-depth studies on relevant issues, and thus, to assist academics and professionals to develop and exchange their ideas as well as to contribute to the enrichment of the Palestinian library".[11]

One is forced to ponder: What is the purpose of these studies? Who benefits from them? And what's the rationale of funding a new NGO, in the context of the "Peace Process", to produce such mélange of studies when some of the existing uni-

10 (http://www.passia.org)

11 (Ibid)

versities may be empowered to do the same? To answer some of these questions, partially, PASSIA maintained that its studies "are widely distributed both locally and internationally and aim at providing a better understanding of Palestinian affairs, perspectives and aspirations. In the light of the current stage in Palestinian and regional history, it is becoming even more crucial that reliable and informative data be dispersed throughout the local and wider communities. PASSIA's research studies are a reference source for academics, diplomats, professionals, libraries and anyone with an interest in the Palestinian issue, the field of international affairs, and the developments in the Middle East".[12] It is also known that Mahdi, PASSIA's Head, gives briefings to diplomats, politicians, etc, almost daily. He does it, however, personally, without any presence to PASSIA, as an institution, unless, of course, PASSIA is embodied in him. This, indeed, raises questions about the nature of these NGO institutions. Perhaps, as a friend suggested in personal communication with me, that they should be called "non-for profit private companies".

Analysis of the "information papers" (22 titles all together) reveals two aspects of this "knowledge producing" NGO process: one, there is non-coherence in the selected topics for research and publication, and their connectivity with the main objective of PASSIA, and, two, the only way to explain this non-coherence is through the funds available for it. In a way of illustration, the topics of the "information papers", for example, ranged widely from Dutch development policy towards the Middle East, to Australian press and Palestine, to the German unification and the EU, to Islam in Germany, to Swedish foreign policy, to an Arabic translation of Orwell's 1984, etc. I am totally at loss to understand the qualitative addition from these publications! At the same time, PASSIA made it clear that its funding came primarily from the German Friedrich Ebert Stiftung (FES), the Finnish Representative Office, the Rockefeller Foundation, USAID, the Ford Foundation, the Dutch Representative Office,

12 (Ibid)

the Canadian Embassy and Canada Fund, Germany, the Open Society Institute, and the Welfare Association.

Another puzzling aspect of PASSIA's activities is the "Seminars" series. Simply put, it does not fit within PASSIA's core activities. The "seminars" series seem to be an example of donors' outsourcing through NGOs. For a period of 5 years, 2005 – 2009, PASSIA conducted a total of 25 seminars most of which were held in the first two years, 2005 and 2006, i.e. the election year for the PLC, and the year following Hamas's election. The subjects of the seminars encompassed training and imparting skills in two areas. One area may be called the art of diplomacy, political discourse, and the "preferential" approach to conflict resolution, while the other area encompasses skills in project design, planning and financial management. Training sessions in the first area focused on such topics as, leadership, political parties, party development, civics and citizenship, conflict resolution, public policy, negotiation skills, community development, governance, human rights, democratization and reform, detecting and fighting fraud, etc. Training in the second area focused on project monitoring and evaluation, strategic planning, financial management, project design, proposal writing, fundraising, etc.

It is compelling, in the light of the above, to reiterate and sharpen the question, raised earlier: what kind of knowledge PASSIA, as a "knowledge producing and disseminating NGO", is producing at this political juncture, for whose interest, and why? And a corollary to this question: is PASSIA transforming itself from an active and credible independent research institution, focusing on the "Palestinian Question in its national, Arab and international contexts through academic research, dialogue and publication," to an effective outsourcing NGO on behalf of Western donors? Surely, the "Info. Papers" and "Seminars", that have been produced, were possible only thanks to external funding received mainly from the German FES, the Canadians, the Dutch, the British, the US, and others.

The larger question, which requires further investigation, and which is not specific to PASSIA, is this: How do "knowledge producing" NGOs decide on the subjects for research, study and publication, at a certain point in time, and what is the connection between that and the availability of donor funds in support of these subjects, and their self-perception of their changing roles? Put more directly and bluntly, are Palestinian indigenous "developmental" NGOs, specializing in "knowledge production", the ones who decide what topic to fund for study and dissemination, and at what time, or that decisions filter down from interested donors, and get reinterpreted, or "nationalized" by the NGOs themselves? This is a legitimate question to raise since, to my knowledge, most if not all, "knowledge producing" NGOs—like the rest of "developmental" NGOs—have no financial endowment to sustain their programs, nor do they have reliable and sizeable funds from self-generating income. And consequently, if their relationships with their traditional funding sources are shaken, or broken, their research and publication programs will come to a complete halt! Such a precarious situation would endow any suggestion, or indicative ideas, coming from these traditional (friendly) funding sources, for a seminar, conference, publication, etc., with bigger weight, and with qualitative importance.

From my actual and intimate experience with these types of issues, I can think of numerous cases to that effect. Having said that, however, the relationship that governs the indigenous "knowledge producing" NGOs, with whom I am familiar, with their donors, is more complex and far from being horizontal. It is imbued with, what intellectuals and academics, love to define as "a higher sense of rationality", an "intense morality", and a keen "awareness of the public and national good". Thus, there is an essential psychological dimension to this relationship, which is required to qualify to what degree "committed", "nationalist", "public" intellectuals can "whore" for funds, without flagrant contradiction and dissonance? The emergent discourse, therefore, is a camouflage, an acceptable cover, which shrouds the entire interaction in a complex web of iterations and reiterations and an encompassing deep sense of "justifiable" self-discipline.

Challand alluded to this phenomenon in his work on "Palestinian civil society". He stated that "the NGOs are intellectual policemen who define 'acceptable' research, distribute research funds and filter out topics and perspectives that project a class analysis and struggle perspective.[13]

The second "knowledge producing" NGO we are analyzing in this section claims to produce and disseminate a more specialized and purposeful body of knowledge, in the aim of influencing official policy.

MUWATIN

Muwatin (which means "citizen" in Arabic), The Palestinian Institute for the Study of Democracy, was founded in 1992 in Ramallah, by a group of scholars and academics "to promote the study and development of democracy in Palestine and in the region". Further, Muwatin viewed itself to have been established "at a critical juncture when, for the first time in their history, Palestinians were able to govern themselves [?] while seeking to establish an independent and sovereign state. Muwatin is committed to playing a clear and effective role in the process of democratic transformation in Palestine". It was established at the cusp of the "Oslo Process", following the Madrid Conference, buoyed by the context of the emerging public euphoria of an imminent negotiated settlement, as a prelude for an independent Palestinian political system.

Muwatin was established with a specific focus on the "issues of democracy". It saw itself as contributing "to the process of democratic transformation in Palestinian society in particular and, in Arab society in general", through "networking and activism, research and publication, preparation of educational material and its dissemination to schools and the general public, training workshops, symposia, seminars, and conferences".[14]

13 (Challand, 2009: 137)

14 (http://www.muwatin.org)

It delineates the aims of its research and studies program in a number of points. I shall focus below on those points that are directly pertinent to this analysis, as follows:

In addition to initiating "a full and wide ranging debate on democratic issues and options", it seeks to:

1. "actively intervene in the reform of the Palestinian political system through **policy directed research** and public education campaigns on governance issues such as reform of legislation, the separation of powers, reform of political parties, and issues concerning transparency and accountability (emphasis added).
2. To help build a strong research community in Palestine that will produce original research including **policy oriented research**, thus building a knowledge base on the processes that affect democratic transformation in Palestine, and that **can influence policy formation at the highest level".**[15] Although Muwatin's program consists of a number of core activities, including research, publications, reform and governance, seminar and conferences, resource library, networking, our analysis here will focus on the type of knowledge produced through the research and publications program. Furthermore, we shall try to assess which aspects of this produced knowledge is "policy oriented", and how much influence, if any, it had on "policy formation at the highest level". The underpinning premise of this analysis is that "knowledge producing" NGOs, that were established as a part and parcel of the package of the Oslo Process, and who depend for the survival and continuity of their research program on sustained funding by Western aid agencies, are not positioned to influence official policy; nor were they created for that purpose. A research organization, who is completely dependent on the same Western funding sources that are primarily responsible for the creation of the Oslo-invented authority, and for

15 (Ibid; emphasis added)

> its financial sustenance, is deeply deluding itself if it claims that the research it conducts and disseminates, will be permitted to influence official policy. Similarly, the same Western funding sources who sustain the Oslo-invented PA, will be inherently self-contradicting if their funds were to produce studies and knowledge that propose divergent policies from the planned political agenda of the Oslo Process. Thus, at the bottom line, serious questions have to be raised about the original underpinning assumptions, and the type of "policy oriented research", and the degree and level of "influence" it may, or could, have on decision makers.

Since 1993, Muwatin produced over 100 titles under the various components of its research and studies program, in addition to a bi-monthly newsletter, circulated under the title of "Parliamentary Horizons". These titles addressed the issue of democratization and democratic governance in Palestinian society, broadly, through the examination of its historical, sociological, political and intellectual dimensions. The range of topics spanned the Palestinian political system, Palestinian elite, education, NGOs, Islam, Palestinian society under occupation, Palestinian development, elections, student movement, political parties, Palestinian left, Palestinian civil society, intellectuals, etc. With very few exceptions, all the titles were produced in Arabic, and disseminated locally.

The bulk of these studies, especially over the last ten years or so, was made possible through a longer term cooperation agreement with the Norwegian Chr. Michelsen Institute. It was indicated to me, however, that most certainly this cooperation agreement will be terminated by the year 2012.[16] The Chr. Michelsen Institute is a Norwegian academic research institute, specializing in democratic transformation and development, and funded by the Norwegian government through NORAD. Earlier publications were funded by other donor organizations,

16 (Jayyousi, M. 2010)

e.g., the US Ford Foundation, the German Buntstift e.V. Foundation (the precursor of the Heinrich-Boell Foundation), etc. However, it is not clear who funded Muwatin's first publication, "*On the Democratic Option: Critical Studies*", which came out a month after the signing of the Oslo Accords[17], as well as a few publications during 1995 on "Palestinian democracy", "civil society and democratic transformation in Palestine", etc.

Deliberations on ideas raised in the research and publications, and on other relevant issues, take place, generally, in the context of small internal seminars that get attended on the average by 10-15 people, who are specifically invited to attend and participate in the discussions. These seminars are slated to "examine various issues that can facilitate or hinder democratization processes, developments in the political process in Palestine and Israel, as well as address the need to explore different possible strategies in the struggle for democratization".[18]

To get an idea about the type of information deliberated, a review of the seminars held over a period of four years (2004-2007) is instructive. It shows that more than one-third of these seminars focused on the Palestinian political system and Palestine, the Western powers and Israel. The second biggest focus was on the elections, the electoral system and the media. This sample reveals more of an intellectual and academic diagnosis of the political and historical developments, rather than a clear focus on the "different possible strategies in the struggle for democratization". The question is why? Is a small group of Oslo-engaged, somewhat like-minded intellectuals/political analysts on the left, or with a leftist background, able and willing to discuss and produce such possible strategies, as these seminars formally anticipated? Then, is it realistic for an NGO, such as Muwatin, to claim and expect that the kind of knowledge it generates is capable of, or even permitted to influence official policy?

17 (Giacaman, Bishara, Ghalioun, and Zeidani, 1993)

18 (http://www.muwatin.org)

In an honest reflection and assessment by Muwatin itself on the possible impact of its knowledge production and dissemination over the last seventeen years, it was claimed that their most impact was in the area of legislative reform. They credit themselves with influencing the reformulation of certain laws passed by the PLC, e.g., election law, the proposed social security law, etc. At the academic research level, they are convinced that their research and publication program contributed to creating a new research culture, and filling important gaps in the Arabic library on the issue of democratic transformation. On the other hand, there is a realization that the value and effectiveness of the small internal seminars are questionable at best.[19]

MAS

To a certain degree, this is a different "knowledge producing and disseminating" institution than the two NGOs, previously analyzed. It is different in its evolutionary history, its identity and organizational structure, and its evolving funding base. We will discuss these points in the following sections.

In its website, it is claimed that "The Palestine Economic Policy Research Institute (MAS) was founded in Jerusalem in 1994 as an **independent** non-profit institution to contribute to the policy-making process by conducting economic and social policy research."[20] The fact of the matter is, MAS was established as a "PLO institution' by "presidential decree" at the time when the signing of the Declaration of Principles of the Oslo Accords was eminent. In preparation for the return of the Fateh PLO leadership to establish the self-rule authority in the West Bank and Gaza, potential Western sources of aid, under the umbrella of the World Bank, insisted that the PLO would set-up two PLO agencies to coordinate and protect donors' funds. Thus, under the World Bank tutelage, PECDAR, The Palestinian Economic Council for Development and Reconstruction, was set up while the PLO was still in Tunis, as the official aid coordination and

19 (Jayyousi, M. 2010))

20 (http://www.mas.ps; emphasis added).

streamlining institution. Immediately, Arafat put himself as its head, until donors complained, and thus, under pressure, he replaced himself with Farouq Qaddoumi, the PLO Head of the Political Department. Concomitantly, and under the same tutelage of the World Bank, MAS, The Palestine Economic Policy Research Institute was set-up, as a PLO agency, for the purpose of conducting social and economic policy studies that would provide ideas for the newly established self-rule authority for implementation.

On 1 August 1994, the then Head of PECDAR's Council of Governors (no other than Farouq Qaddoumi, the PLO's foreign minister) ratified the bylaws. Since then, a number of top Oslo political and economic elites have been in control of MAS through a structure of re-circulation of Board of Trustees' membership and the Directors-General. A cursory look at the list of membership of MAS's Boards and Directors-General reveals the recurrent inclusion of former ministers, deputy ministers, Governor of the Monetary Authority, CEO's in Oslo monopolies, etc. Some of the same people have occupied the position of MAS's Director- General twice or three times, since it was set-up.

Like MAS, PECDAR, too, identifies itself "as an **independent** institution". It states in its website that it is an institution "in full cooperation and coordination with the donor community to Palestine in support of the peace process". After the PLO approved its bylaws on Oct. 1993, "PECDAR's mandate was endorsed by the general meeting of the donors which was held in Washington D.C. under the chairmanship of former U. S. Secretary of State Warren Christopher and The World Bank. The mandate covers a wide range of responsibilities including aid coordination, **economic policy**, project management, coordination with NGO's and UN specialized agencies, technical assistance and training as well as IT".[21]

In its declared mission, MAS stated that it is " dedicated to producing sound and innovative policy research, relevant to the

21 (http://www.pecdar.ps; emphasis added)

economic and social development in Palestine, with the aim of assisting policy-makers and fostering public participation in the formulation of economic and social policies." [22]

MAS lists six declared "strategic objectives" revolving, as it may be concluded from the list below, around two foci: The first focus is informing and influencing official economic and social policy through conducting research, deliberations of the results, and publication and dissemination of those studies. The second focus is empowering and strengthening an economic and social policy research culture and capabilities. The formal "strategic objectives" are the following:

1. "Promoting knowledge-based policy formulation by conducting economic and social policy research in accordance with the expressed priorities and needs of decision-makers.
2. Evaluating economic and social policies and their impact at different levels for correction and review of existing policies.
3. Providing a forum for free, open and democratic public debate among all stakeholders on the socio-economic policy-making process.
4. Disseminating up-to-date social and economic information and research results.
5. Providing technical and expert advice to PNA bodies, the private sector, and NGO's to enhance their engagement and participation in policy formulation.
6. Strengthening economic and social policy research capabilities and resources in Palestine."[23]

KNOWLEDGE PRODUCED

Since it was established, MAS produced in excess of 180 published studies. These are specific studies, which are conducted with the aim of "assisting policy-makers in designing effective

22 (http://www.mas.ps)

23 (Ibid)

strategies and policies to overcome economic and social problems and to promote sustainable development. Research activities in 2009 are comprised of studies that aim to develop the competitiveness of the Palestinian economy, improve the status of food security, develop policies capable of promoting human resources and Palestinian social capital and foster the development of small and medium enterprises".[24] The studies encompassed reviews of proposed draft laws of banking, labor, agriculture, industrial, commercial agents, etc), as well as an assessment of various economic sectors, including garment industry, tanning and leather industry, footwear industry, pharmaceutical industry, etc. Furthermore, the published studies addressed trade policy, the banking system, infrastructure, employment, internal migration, water and food security, vocational training, brain drain, poverty, NGOs, development, etc. Thus, the knowledge produced covered an entire gamut of social and economic issues and concerns in the West Bank and Gaza, but primarily in the West Bank.

PRELIMINARY ASSESSMENT OF IMPACT DURING THE FIRST TEN YEARS

At its ten year anniversary (in 2004), MAS conducted its first assessment in order to gauge its effectiveness and efficiency, its relevance, and its sustainability potential.[25] This assessment report reflected the perceptions of all government ministries and agencies that were reviewed, as well as selected PLC committees, some civil society organizations, and some funding sources. The main conclusions showed that, in general, that the performance of MAS, in so far as identifying national priorities and conducting studies that are coherent with official priorities, was modest. Cooperation between MAS and governmental institutions was weak. Furthermore, translation of studies into implementable policies was not perceived to be the case.

24 (MAS Annual Report 2009:4)

25 (MAS, 2004)

According to the current Director-General,[26] the impact of MAS's studies on policy-making is improving. For example, some ministries or governmental agencies approach them to conduct certain study or analysis on, what they consider a pressing issue. Dr. Abdullah claims, further, that their analysis of certain draft laws led to some amelioration in some of the laws that were passed. Also, MAS had a visible contribution to the "developmental vision" of the Fayyad Government, claims the Director-General.

FUNDING

Unlike the previous two cases, the funding that established MAS came from the Technical Assistance Trust Fund (TATF), from the World Bank through PECDAR. That covered its establishment phase. Based on that, they were enabled to attract funds from SIDA, Ford Foundation, FES, IDRC, NORAD, UNDP, the World Bank's Economic Development Institute (EDI), the Canadian Fund (CF), the EU and Amideast. Additionally, MAS, with the help of the Arab Fund for Social and Economic Development in Kuwait, was able to start a very modest endowment for its programs, which, at its current level, cannot sustain its research and publication program, and, consequently, it has to rely on receiving funds for specific commissioned studies, project by project, and from day to day.

But, very much like the previous two cases, MAS depends in operating its research program on funds it receives from European, American, and UN aid agencies, for commissioned research on certain topics of concern. Also, MAS receives funds from Arab and Islamic regional funding agencies, as well as from individual Palestinian capitalists. In addition to the above, MAS's "Annual Report 2009" lists the Korean International Cooperation Agency (for building their current headquarters), among others, including some Palestinian capitalists who are members of the Board, the Palestinian Ministry of Finance, The Portland Trust, and PADICO (whose CEO's is on the Board).

26 (Abdullah, 2010)

ON THE RELATIONSHIP BETWEEN KNOWLEDGE, POLICY AND INDEPENDENT NGOs

It must be stated clearly at the outset that this is not an assessment of the technical or academic quality of these studies, and the knowledge produced, or its usefulness. I, like many others, find that many of the studies the three NGOs produce provide a very useful reference for researchers and academics in these areas of concern. But our concern in this analysis, however, is to examine if these studies can have an impact on post-Oslo official policy and strategy, and what kind of impact; and if not, why not.

More importantly, it is my assumption that the claim that these "knowledge producing" NGOs advance uncritically, that the knowledge they produce can have an impact on official policies and strategies, is dubious, at best, if not deceiving. In a situation where, at one level, the source of these policies and strategies (i.e., the PA) is far from being sovereign, it renders the resulting policies and strategies externally controlled and prescribed. Thus, influencing them, through research and published studies, is an illusory exercise in futility, or self-deception. On a second level, the potential influence of the knowledge produced by these NGOs remains in the realm of wishful thinking, in so far as these NGOs themselves are not independent, politically and economically, both from the central authority and from Western, and Western-influenced, sources of aid. The reality is, as we have observed from these 3 cases, "knowledge producing" NGOs are totally dependent on the same Western sources of aid that have been propping up the Oslo-invented PA, since its idea was conceived.

There is moot and general underlying assumption that there is an objective relationship between knowledge and policy, on the grounds that political and economic decision-makers seek academically-produced knowledge to make their decisions. This may be the case when the political and economic elites really emerge from the people, in a transparent participatory process, and committed to articulate and respond to their people's needs.

In reality, however, the assumption itself is dubious. How many legitimate decision-makers, regardless of whether they are in "established democracies", "transitional democracies", or "fake democracies", etc, allow "think tank" studies to inform their decisions? Unless, of course, the specific "think tank" ideology is coherent with theirs, and with their overall plans of sustained control and dominance.

In the current Palestinian situation, this process is compounded. At one level, there is actually no struggle of opposing ideas. Major ideas that are generated and circulated by "knowledge producing" NGOs remain confined basically to the prevailing paradigm. And, on another level, the formation of these elites came about as a result of acquiescence to an externally imposed political and economic agenda that imbue them, somehow, with the notion that they are the legitimate inheritors of this piece of Palestine, including its people and resources. To translate this into action, they operated as if it is their legitimate right to horde privilege, political and economic resources, to be corrupt and corrupt others, etc, through a system of clientelism, exploitation, unequal opportunities, exclusive monopolies, etc, all under the guise of developing "the national homeland"!

Reflecting on the recent study, conducted and published by MAS, on the gap between research and policy making in the "Palestinian Territories",[27] brings into relief some interesting and relevant points about this discussion. The research and publication were financed by the German Foundation, Friedrich Ebert Stiftung (FES), and were conducted and published by MAS. The analysis relied on information gathered through interviews with selected "stakeholders", and an entire chapter was devoted to "identifying the gap" between research and policy.[28]

This eleven-page chapter presented, what might be described, an abstract, un-insightful, and un-enlightening discussion of what causes this "gap" to exist. It focused mainly on institutional and bureaucratic incapacities to produce quality

27 (DeVoir and Tartir, 2009)

28 (Ibid: 27-38)

research, and to make it accessible to decision-makers in a potentially usable form. Thus, it concluded that there is "lack of capacity in the policy making arena," as well as "lack of capacity in the research sector", and a negative impact of "international aid on domestic research". Basically, I have no disagreement with this type of diagnosis, and I agree with most of the points made. The problem, however, is that this type of research remains within the confines of the overarching paradigm. It does not once allude to the question of how truncated the policies are, and is it possible for this type of research and knowledge production to "un-truncate" them, and how much? And if so, what are the other types of constraints that extend beyond local institutional incapacities. Furthermore, and surpassing the notion that almost all "knowledge production" institutes are totally dependent on external aid, no question was raised as to the important and ubiquitous connection between the overall ideological interests of sources of aid and the type of research domains they are willing to fund.

In the light of the above, and after reading this study, I began to wonder seriously about its value, in terms of encouraging, or facilitating the connection between knowledge and policy-making, and who, possibly, could have benefited from it. FES, the German funding foundation, is known to be interested in "social democracy", "democratic education" for the purpose of encouraging and enhancing "international understanding and cooperation". Is that what they were hoping for here? This study proposed in its conclusions, projects (e.g., electronic "knowledge bank") that are foreseen to prepare Palestinian decision-making bodies to benefit from the produced knowledge. Of course, the study did not allude to the fact that these decision-making bodies are not the primary ones, and they come at a secondary or tertiary level at best, after Israeli decision-making bodies. Will this kind of study really enhance and strengthen "social democracy"? I seriously doubt that.

As for "think tanks", the original idea was to create an environment of unhampered, free and creative thinking able to respond to the needs of the Western military capitalist center in enhancing its grip and continued exploitation of the rest of the world. The term started surfacing since the 1950s. A 2009 study[29] found that there is a total of 5,465 think tanks worldwide. About one-third of which is based in the US, and about 20 percent of that are in its capital, Washington, D.C.

The idea of think tanks was to afford a group of independent academics, thinkers, planners, strategists, the needed opportunity to generate the cutting edge in scientific knowledge and ideas, through research, thinking and deliberation, and to apply the new information and ideas to policy programs. For this to happen, total and complete independence was required. On the whole, this idea of independent think tanks has been corrupted and co-opted world-wide. Now, think tanks are beholden to a specific political party, a specific ideological orientation, a specific capitalist corporation, a specific industry, etc. Our situation, albeit, at a very miniscule scale, is not different from this global trend.

Therefore, an NGO does not become independent just because it lists itself as such in its bylaws, or on its website. The "independence" of the three NGOs, discussed above, is questionable, at best. As of this writing, and from available evidence, they are heavily dependent on external funding sources to sustain their research programs, and they are embedded to the core, but in varying degrees, in the post-Oslo produced culture, and in their relationship with the non-sovereign and dependent PA. Consider, for example, the specific case of MAS. It is amply clear that neither MAS nor, similarly, PECDAR, can claim to be independent, based on their historical evolution. On the other hand, the term may refer to having separate bylaws and an independent organizational structure. Or, it may refer to the notion that the institute abides by Western empirical and quantitative research methodology, with the delusion of "scientific objectivity". Thus, the circulated, and publically made claim, that these "knowledge producing" NGOs can influence

29 (Bergsten, 2009)

PA policy, or propose new and different policies to be adopted, falls in the realm of self-delusion and public deception.

CASE STUDY 2: NGO COALITION UMBRELLAS FOR COORDINATION?

With the exception of the Union of Charitable Societies, which was established under Jordanian law in 1958, as the coordinating body for all Palestinian charitable societies in the West Bank, no other umbrella coordination bodies existed then. However, soon after the signing of the Oslo Accords in 1993, the door opened for a plethora of such NGO coalition umbrellas. Leading this trend, was the "Palestinian NGO Network" (PNGO), an umbrella organization whose membership includes most of the existing "developmental" NGOs, with leftist background or leanings. It was established in November 1993.

The formation of other specialized NGO coalitions followed, and, as expected, memberships overlapped. The Coalition for Integrity and Accountability (AMAN) was established in 2000 "upon the initiative by a number of Palestinian civil society organizations working in the fields of democracy, human rights, and good governance". There were six founding NGOs, 4 in the West Bank and 2 in Gaza. AMAN's core program funding comes primarily from the Norwegian and Dutch governments through their corresponding representative offices in Ramallah.[30] By now, AMAN itself has become a registered NGO. In 2007 it generated another coalition network of Palestinian NGOs, under its own umbrella, tantamount to a daughter "company". It is known as "NGOs against Corruption", "who pledged to join forces in the fight against corruption in the Palestinian society".[31]

In 2005, "The Civic Coalition for Defending the Palestinians' Rights in Jerusalem" (CCDPRJ) was established as a "nongovernmental nonprofit coalition of institutions, societies,

30 (http://www.aman-palestine.org)

31 (Ibid)

associations and individuals with experience and mandate of working in the different fields of human rights".[32] Currently, the coalition has a membership of 25 Jerusalem institutions. The justification given for the need to establish such a coalition was that since the PA was not playing any effective role in responding to the needs of the Jerusalemites, the Jerusalem NGOs had to take the lead. The stated mission of the Coalition, therefore, is to "mobilize efforts, capacities and resources to protect the political, civil, economic, social and cultural rights of Palestinians in Jerusalem based on the international law and human rights law".[33]

The Palestinian NGO Network (PNGO) is the broader umbrella coalition network encompassing 132 "developmental" NGOs. It identifies itself as "a civil and democratic body, which seeks to support, consolidate and strengthen the Palestinian civil society on the basis of the principles of democracy, social justice and sustainable development".[34] In this process, PNGO's mission may be condensed to two areas. One area focuses at the level of the society at large, through advocating for democratization, social justice, respect for human rights, rule of law, exposing Palestinian human rights' violations under occupation, etc. The second area focuses at the level of its NGO members. The primary emphasis here is on "coordination and networking" and "capacity building". What concerns us in this analysis is the second area of activities, if we are to gauge the value-added impact, if any, of this umbrella structure within the current political context, in terms of our proposed PCLD development.

The first area of activities, although important in and of itself, it does not concern this analysis because it is bound by the Oslo ceiling, and its derivatives, i.e., government agencies and ministries, PLC, etc. In other words, it operates within the imposed parameters of Oslo, and acquiesces to them. For example, at the

32 (http://www.ccdprj.ps)

33 (Ibid)

34 (http://www.pngo.net)

level of coordination and networking, PNGO formally claims that it "promotes coordination, cooperation and consultation not only among Palestinian NGOs but also between the Palestinian NGO sector and the different bodies of the Palestinian National Authority. In addition, PNGO facilitates the exchange of information and experience between NGOs at the local, regional and international levels".[35]

The second area of activities is more revealing. It focuses on enhancing the organizational, managerial and professional capacities of its NGO members, in order to ameliorate and expand the level and quality of articulation between them and Western aid agencies. The net result, presumably, may be summarized as follows: the NGOs will become more professional, more "business-like", more depoliticized, more acceptable to Western funding sources, and, consequently, more amenable to attract external funds and to sustain themselves.

Based on all the statements and documents I read, and my own intimate observations and participation in this type of work, I cannot detect, in this process, not one indication about, what I consider, much more pressing and urgent "capacity building", namely, enhancing the capacities of NGO members to go back to their grassroots constituencies; to return and become re-embedded in their community base and become active organizers and local planners; and to spring from their bosoms new, politically engaged, people-concerned active and productive mass social movements. To do that, however, PNGO would be advocating a process of, what might be called, a "reverse NGO transformation", which would render the contradictions between it, as the umbrella, and its NGO members, on one side, and the PA and Western donors, on the other, patently glaring.

On the contrary, PNGO's capacity building activities, for which it becomes eligible to receive Western aid, are summarized in the following. "PNGO holds regular meetings with member organizations to discuss matters of concern, it organizes meetings with international NGOs, diplomatic missions, parliamen-

35 (Ibid)

tarians and international governmental organizations, it holds coordination meetings with Palestinian governmental bodies and it participates in local and international events which aim at strengthening coordination and cooperation among civil society organizations worldwide (such as the World Social Forum and regional Social Forums, UN conferences and events organized by the bodies of the EU, national governments or NGOs)".[36] Additionally, it organizes and involves its NGO members in a variety of organizational enhancement in finance and administration, including training courses and workshops in "conflict resolution, media and communication, advocacy and networking, project planning, proposal writing, fundraising and project management".[37]

To shed more light on the "value" of PNGO's coordination role, I chose to analyze a particular activity in which I participated.

On 24-25 September 2008, PNGO sponsored a "national workshop" on "The European Neighborhood Policy (ENP): towards a full partnership". PNGO was sub-contracted by two European NGOs, EUROstep and ACSUR, who in turn were sub-contracted by the European Commission to "market" the idea of the ENP in the Palestinian areas. The workshop was held in a hotel in Ramallah. At the beginning of the workshop, PNGO presented the purpose of the workshop, which was followed then by a representative from the EUROstep network. The second session concentrated on the ENP and the mechanisms used to implement the policy and the European partnership, at the governmental level. During this "governmental partnership" session, the head of the Social Affairs division at the EC office in Jerusalem elaborated, blow by blow, on the ENP: what is it, why is the EU offering it at this time, how will it benefit the PA, mechanisms for implementation, available funds for it, etc. This was a heavy dose of redundant and screaming European information, coming at the heels of the presentation of the

36 (Ibid)

37 (Ibid)

EUROstep representative, which had covered basically all the information repeated here. The last speaker in this session was the Palestinian Deputy Minister of Foreign Affairs, who reaffirmed what the PA expects of the EU, and that the EU should play a more active political—not only economic—role in this situation.

The focus of the third session was on "program planning" at the EU. Presentations were made again by the EUROstep representative, on the European side, the Deputy Director General of "aid coordination and management" at the Palestinian Ministry of Planning, and a leading member of PNGO Steering Committee, on the Palestinian side. Except for the last presentation, which raised some critical questions, albeit within the same dominant paradigm, about problems in ENP planning process and assumptions, the first two presentations were a direct heavy sell for EU programs and available budgets, worldwide and regionally, and EU contributions to the PA.

The fourth session focused on "the impact of EU policy on sustainable development, and its support to PA priorities". This was a Palestinian session in which small groups discussed the main topic by discussing in detail six themes: democratic governance, socio-economic reforms and trade, energy and environment, gender, the rule of law, and social and health services. Each of these focus groups elaborated on the needs in each "sector", the type of EU intervention in the "sector", and priority areas for EU funding.

The fifth and last session, before summarizing the recommendations, targeted again EU financial support to Palestinian areas: modalities, transparency and accountability. Two presentations were made by two EU representatives highlighting different aspects of the PEGASE funding mechanism, which builds on the so called Temporary International Mechanism (TIM) experience, and which lends strong support to the PA's Palestinian Reform and Development Program (PRDP).

The official view of the EU is that the ENP and its related action plan (AP), which was signed with the PA in 2004, is "a part of the EU's response to the new Palestinian Authority's political and economic era". This era is characterized by the agenda of "peace-building, security restoration, reform and economic recovery. The formulation of the Caretaker Government in mid 2007 headed by Dr. Salam Fayyad marked the beginning of this era. And the resumption of international aid thereafter has lent credibility and substance to the peace, reform and reconstruction objectives, all of which coincide with those of the ENP process." [38] What can be learnt from this case? PNGO, the Palestinian umbrella coalition of leftist leaning "developmental" NGOs consented to be the sub-sub agent for European transnational NGOs to mediate in marketing the fictitious developmental role of the EU and its agencies. PNGO justified its involvement in seizing the chance to express the views of Palestinian civil society organizations in a new program with funding potential. By accepting to do this, PNGO distanced itself from the grassroots constituencies, and brought itself in proximity to the EU, as a source of aid, and to the central authority (the PA government), as the facilitator of this aid.

The "Arab Thought Forum" (ATF) NGO, which is a member of the three umbrella networks mentioned above (PNGO, AMAN, and the Jerusalem Coalition), initiated in Ramallah on 11 February 2008 a seminar to review the NGOs' coalition experiences. The title of the summary report of deliberations[39] reflects their concern. As an involved member in these coalitions, ATF was concerned whether these NGO coalition experiments are progressing, or standing still, or regressing. Each coalition was invited to make a presentation about their experience, followed by active deliberations. I was invited to comment on the different presentations. It was clear from the deliberations that there was an expressed dissatisfaction with the results of these coalitionist networking experiments. In their self-assessment, PNGO, for example, admitted that it failed so far in influencing official decisions. A major concern that was reiterated, however,

38 (PNGO, 2008, ENP Workshop)

39 (ATF, 2008)

revolved around two points. The first relates to the recognition that available funding from donors to individual NGO members was not enhanced, or expanded, as promised or anticipated. The second point dwelt, with consternation, on the noticeable trend that once the coalitions are formed, and become successful, they turn around and register as an NGO themselves, which means that they start competing with their own members, but on a firmer ground because of their broad NGO constituency and mastery of the funding solicitation game.

Before concluding this section, the above discussion forces us to raise an important question about the qualitative value added from these umbrella coalitions to the work of "developmental" NGOs, and its contextualization. A number of corollary questions have to be raised, regarding the real purpose of establishing these coalitionist networks in a society under occupation. Are these umbrella coalitions set up to become an intermediary bureaucratic layer, a broker, or a sub-agent, if you will, between their professional NGO constituency, on the one hand, and official Western transnational funding agencies and the PA and its agencies, on the other? In this hierarchical set-up of depoliticized NGOs, totally dependent on governmental Western sources of funds, and the consent and approval of the PA to access those funds, within a formal umbrella framework that claims to speak for them, the clear result is impeding and negating the PCLD developmental approach.

It is worth remembering that prior to the existence of these coalitionist networks, and the consequent availability of foreign funding, local committed political groups and grassroots movements played a more effective role in mobilizing people to resist occupation. They were sustained by their own indigenous energies and resources.

CASE STUDY 3: "INTERMEDIARY" OR "SUB-AGENT" NGOS

The reference here is to NGOs whose actual role is to intermediate between donors and local indigenous NGOs, to convey to the local level, training, information, managerial skills and values, on behalf of the donors that fund them. In this way, they become sub-agents for the donors, and intermediary bureaucratic layer between the transnational and the national.

I maintain that in the Palestinian context, these "intermediary" or "sub-agents" NGOs play, inadvertently, a pernicious role on behalf of their Western funders. They are funded to reinterpret, re-package, and disseminate the political and anti-developmental messages of their political Western funders, under the guise and claim of national and patriotic concerns of strengthening Palestinian civil society, through, essentially, a well-oiled process of cultural re-engineering of a new crop of depoliticized and "professional" NGOs, under the rubric of "capacity building".

As a case in point, we focus below on relevant functions of the "NGO Development Center" (NDC), while remarking that it will be discussed in more detail in case study 5 that addresses the evolution of Welfare Association into an intermediate agent for international aid.

BACKGROUND

NDC represents the third phase in the World Bank emphasis on the Palestinian "NGO sector". This emphasis started with a World Bank initiative following the establishment of the PA in 1995 within the context of the Oslo Process. The approach adopted by the World Bank in pushing this initiative was to entice all major NGO umbrella and coalition networks in a framework that cooperates and collaborates as much as possible with the PA. All this was done under the guise of strengthening and empowering the Palestinian "NGO sector". The result of this type of approach, however, was to bring NGOs to cooperate as closely as possible with PA agencies, and to dilute and depoliticize, somehow, this new political authority that was invented by the Oslo Process.

World Bank's consultations regarding the formulation of this initiative culminated in an international tender to support Palestinian "NGO sector". The tender was for USD 14 million, for three years (1997 – 1999). Submitting for this tender, the Welfare Association formed a consortium with 2 British institutions (the British Council and the Charities Aid Foundation). This consortium, which became known as the "Welfare Consortium" was successful in winning this tender. Later, this phase was dubbed as PNGO I, and was managed by a technical Project Management Organization (PMO).

After a positive assessment of PNGOI, the World Bank committed additional funding for a second phase (PNGOII) to be implemented by the WA Consortium. The Consortium was successful in investing USD 42 million during both phases (PNGOI/II) "into the Palestinian NGO sector".[40]

The first phase (1997-2000) was approved on 10 July 1997 and formally closed on 31 December 2003. It had a total budget of USD 16.5 million, which was financed by the World Bank, the Saudi Government, the Italian Government, and WA. The second phase, which lasted until 30 June 2006, is actually an extension of the first phase, but under the rubric of PNGO II. PNGO II had a budget of USD 33 million, which was financed by the World Bank, the Canadian International Development Agency (CIDA), the Italian Government, DFID, IDB (through PECDAR), the French International Agency for Development, and the Swiss Agency for Development.[41]

In the World Bank "Completion Report" of PNGO II, it was assessed that "outcomes have been so impacted by forces external to the project ... that assessment of the project's achievements and shortcomings is complicated and clear findings are hard to substantiate."[42] With the completion of PNGO II in 2006, however, extensive discussions among the consortium partners, the PA, and the "NGO sector" were undertaken, regarding the future of the PNGO II framework. It was decided, as a result of these consultations, to establish an independent NGO entity

40 (http://www.ndc.ps)

41 (WB, 1997 "Project Appraisal Document"; WB, 2007 "Completion Report, PNGO II")

42 (WB, 2007:10)

to continue the work of PNGO II, "under the umbrella of WA". NDC was registered in March 2006 as an independent entity (i.e., an NGO, according to Palestinian Law of 2000), with the major funding and support coming from the World Bank.[43]

NDC stated in its latest "Strategic Report" [44] that "the successes of PNGO I and PNGO II led the PNA, in 2005, to request that the World Bank support a third Palestinian NGO project. ... This process led to the formulation of the Strategy for the Development of the Palestinian NGO Sector. The Strategy proposed a set of strategic directives for the NGO sector, and also identified the resources and institutional arrangements that would be needed to implement them.

The World Bank report[45] emphasized further that NDC is "the implementer of PNGO III. ... Clearly, the maintenance and establishment of NDC provide the institution with the accompanying technical and financial know-how setting to ensure effective project continuity. Due to the timely initiative of the Supervisory Board, the skills, experience and institutional set-up of the PMO have been embedded as the executive arm in the new NDC." The members of the "Supervisory Board" of the WA Consortium became the "Founding members" of NDC, and it was decided by the BOD (in its meeting of 19.4.2008) that they will be permanent members of NDC's General Assembly. The members were increased from 13 to current 25.[46]

After having been set-up, NDC attracted more funds from the French. Additionally, in 2008, it was selected by a group of "like-minded" donors (Switzerland, Denmark, Sweden and the Netherlands) for the management of the "Human Rights and Good Governance Secretariat in the OPT", whose precursor was *Mu'assasat,* discussed in case study 4, below.

43 Other WB relevant reports and author's interview with NDC's director (Kassabreh, 2010)

44 (NDC, 2010: 8)

45 (WB, 1997:10)

46 (Kassabreh, 2010)

SELF-DEFINITION, VISION AND OBJECTIVES

In its most recent "Strategic Plan", NDC defined itself as "a non-profit nongovernmental organization established in response to the need of having a sustainable Palestinian mechanism for providing support to the NGOs sector. Through providing technical and financial support, NDC works on developing the capacities of Palestinian NGOs ... on enhancing their self-reliance, and on empowering them to be more sustainable. At the same time, NDC contributes towards the development of the **NGOs sector** as a whole by facilitating sharing and exchange of information and experience, by supporting research and policy development, and by strengthening NGOs relationships with development partners.[47]

The crux of NDC's mission "is to build the capacity of civil society institutions and increase their self-reliance and sustainability; and to develop participation and cooperation levels among institutions, networks and unions. It also strives to provide accurate, comprehensive studies and information that will be available for all, on civil society, its programs and activities".[48] To realize this mission, NDC works on three tracks: **grant making**, sector development and **capacity building.**[49]

In identifying its strengths, NDC claimed that it "has established good foundations for securing funding from diverse sources: Over a short period of time, NDC has established itself as a **professional**, accountable, **and reliable agency that is trusted by donors for effective channeling of funds and assistance to Palestinian NGOs. ...** Through this, NDC's annual cash flow has risen from around 2.5 million dollars, in 2007, to more than 10 million dollars, in 2008. In the first half of 2009, NDC was able to solicit new grants amounting to 4.85 millions. As mentioned earlier, the pool of donor partners is

47 (NDC, 2010:15); emphasis added

48 (http://www.ndc.ps)

49 (NDC, 2010:10); emphasis added

expanding to include - in addition to the World Bank and the Welfare Association - new donors such as: the European Commission (EC), Swiss Agency for Development and Cooperation (SDC), Arab Fund for Economic and Social Development (through Welfare Association), the Netherlands, Germany, AFD, and others. ... The successes of NDC, its track record, and **professionalism**, combined with PNGO I & II legacy, render it **credible and trustworthy** for further channeling of funds to Palestinian NGOs.[50]

Weary of the image it is creating, NDC concluded in its self-assessment and strategic planning exercise that "diversification of funding would enhance NDC's independence and image, [in order to] reinforce its identity as a Palestinian institution working for the benefit of Palestinian NGOs, and the Palestinian population at large, rather than being a project or tool of any donor".[51]

Basically, what we have seen is a successful and an effective Palestinian intermediary NGO. Through its "professionalism", "credibility" and "trustworthiness", it has marketed itself as a "reliable agency that is trusted by the donors for effective channeling of funds and assistance to Palestinian NGOs". The more it performed this function, the more funds it received from Western aid agencies. It is a reliable "sub-agent" on behalf of the donors for assisting in the invention and re-invention of a new professional NGO culture under the ceiling of the "Oslo Process".

CASE STUDY 4: HARMONIZATION AND ALIGNMENT OF AID

Aid "harmonization" and "alignment": Background and conceptualization

As a rationale for the need to harmonize donors' aid, and as a prelude to the Rome High-Level Forum on Harmonization, held in February 2003, it was stated:

50 (NDC, 2010:11-13); emphasis added

51 (Ibid)

> *Donors fund more than 60,000 development aid projects around the world. The demands on recipient capacity are overwhelming: some developing countries receive as many as 800 new projects a year, host more than 1,000 missions to monitor the work, and have to present 2,400 quarterly reports on progress. Meanwhile, as aid funds shrink, donors themselves are realizing that their many processes and procedures tend to detract from development impact and are asking, are there ways to use resources more efficiently?*[52]

It was re-affirmed, further, that:

> *Harmonization has the potential to not only reduce the costs of aid, but to increase the benefits of aid, indeed to increase the impact of all government expenditures. The cumulative effect could change the way development business gets done in the 21st century.*[53]

In February 2003, leaders of the major multilateral development banks and international and bilateral organizations, and donor and recipient country representatives gathered in Rome for the High-Level Forum on Harmonization (Rome-HLF). They **committed** to take action to improve the management and effectiveness of aid and to take stock of concrete progress before meeting again in Paris, February 2005.[54]

Thus, in the ensuing "Rome Declaration on Harmonization" (25 February 2003), the participants reaffirmed their "commitment to eradicating poverty, achieving sustainable economic growth, and promoting sustainable development ...". It was stated also that "the key element that will guide this work is a country-based approach that emphasizes country ownership

52 (http://www.aidharmonization.org)

53 (Ibid)

54 (Ibid)

…". This was elaborated through the participants' commitment to ensure "that development assistance is delivered in accordance with partner country priorities … and that harmonization efforts are adapted to the country context."[55]

The Paris High-Level Forum that followed was hosted by the French Government on 28 February – 2 March 2005. It was attended by "development officials and ministers from ninety one countries, twenty six donor organizations, representatives of civil society organizations and the private sector. In the concluding document - **the Paris Declaration on Aid Effectiveness**, the participants committed their countries and institutions to "far-reaching actions to significantly increase aid effectiveness." They reaffirmed, *inter alia*, their commitment to:

- Increasing alignment of aid with partner countries' priorities … and helping strengthen their capacities,
- Eliminating duplication of efforts and rationalizing donor activities to make them as cost-effective as possible,
- Reforming and simplifying donor policies and procedures,
- Respecting partner country leadership and help strengthen their capacity to exercise it,
- Implementing, where feasible, common arrangements at country level for planning, funding, disbursement, monitoring, evaluating and reporting,
- Harmonizing their monitoring and reporting requirements.

They committed themselves, further, to addressing the remaining challenges, including:

- Donors' failure to provide "more predictable and multi-year commitments on aid flows to committed partner countries",
- "Insufficient delegation of authority to donors' field staff",

55 (Ibid)

- "Corruption and lack of transparency".[56]

I maintain, however, that all of the above is in the realm of official declarative and palliative statements. I maintain, further, that these claims about commitments to "harmonize" aid is nothing more than a camouflage for actual widening of donors' control on the ground, and accelerating and tightening Third World dependency on Western international aid. The micro-analysis of the following experiment, in which I was directly involved, is a case in point.

THE CASE OF "THE SECRETARIAT FOR PROGRAM MANAGEMENT OF HUMAN RIGHTS AND GOOD GOVERNANCE NGOS IN THE WEST BANK AND GAZA" (MU'ASSASAT)

Directed by this background, and prompted by the spirit, and desired results, imbued in the Rome and Paris Declarations, a group of European donors embarked on this aid harmonization experiment in Palestine.

A group of self-defined "like-minded" donors in Jerusalem and Ramallah, composed initially of Sweden, Switzerland, The Netherlands, EU Commission, Norway and Denmark, conducted consultations, in March 2004, on ways and means of harmonizing their procedures, particularly within the Palestinian NGO sector, and regarding specifically the support they had been extending to activities in human rights and democratic governance (good governance). In effect, however, this move was prompted, primarily, by the embarrassing "LAW" case[57] of mismanagement and/or misappropriation of funds received from some of the donors themselves, and of which they were aware, but they took no action. These donors claimed that

56 (Paris Declaration on Aid Effectiveness, 28 February – 2 March 2005).

57 The case refers to a Palestinian human rights NGO (LAW) that collapsed due to mismanagement and/or misappropriation of donors' funds, where large amounts of donors' funds are still unaccounted for, and where litigation processes are still ongoing.

they embarked on this move in order to examine the complex problem on the ground. They characterized this problem by: a low capacity among indigenous NGOs to absorb their aid; a tendency to receive funding from different sources simultaneously; overlapping and redundant activities; and that many, if not most, activities these donors were funding are not sustainable, and have dubious impact.

The donors suspected that they, themselves, could have been contributing to the corruption affecting civil society organizations, and that they were not encouraging serious strategic thinking and planning processes among the NGOs they were supporting. They decided that a more professionally-grounded, and comprehensive approach was needed. Hence, a group of European representative offices to the Palestinian Authority, mainly Sweden (through its Consulate General), Switzerland, The Netherlands, Norway and Denmark began by commissioning a feasibility study, with very specific terms of reference. The study was finalized in September 2004.

In the meantime, the donors also commissioned a Mapping Study of Palestinian NGOs working in the field of human rights (HR) and good governance (GG), in order to show that they were operating on the basis of an empirically accurate base-line. This study was concluded early 2005. Thus, based on this study, four of the original group of European governmental donors, Austria, Denmark, Swedish International Development Cooperation Agency (Sida) and the Swiss Agency for Development and Cooperation (SDC), decided to "harmonize" and "rationalize" their financial assistance to NGOs working on human rights and good governance in the West Bank and Gaza. They decided to pool their funds earmarked for this sector (according to prescribed percentages per each) , and to establish a Secretariat, as the Program Management Unit, to ensure the channeling of their funds, according to their procedures. Formally, the four donors had the overall objective of "improving human rights and good governance in the West Bank and Gaza", and the immediate objective of "increasing the impact of NGOs promoting human rights and good governance". The terms of reference (TOR) of the Program Management Unit stipulated:

1. Strengthening the performance, outcomes and strategic outreach of programs implemented by human rights and good governance NGOs,
2. Improving coordination among NGOs and avoiding duplications of efforts,
3. Reducing transaction costs to NGOs and donors through harmonizing donor procedures, and
4. Improving internal performance in terms of accountability and organizational performance.

A Danish consulting firm (Copenhagen Development Consulting—CDC, currently, according to our information, is defunct) won the bid to manage the Secretariat. On 8 November 2005, Denmark, on behalf of the donors, signed a Service Contract with CDC for the provision and management of the Secretariat. The Service Contract included three phases for a period of 4 years, with the first two years (1.12.2005 – 30.11.2007) as binding, and the next two years as optional one-year extensions. Thus, the potential duration of this Program was 1.12.2005 – 30.11.2009. But this meant, further, that financial commitments could be made for two years maximum.

To formalize the harmonization effectively, i.e. to oversee the smooth channeling of donor funds to indigenous NGOs, and to the Danish consulting firm (the Consultant), according to the formal share to be contributed by each donor, a total of six separate agreements had to be drafted, reviewed, commented on, finalized and signed. A bilateral agreement was signed between each of the donors and the Consultant (4 in total); another agreement had to be signed between the consortium of donors and the Consultant (1 agreement); and another agreement had to be signed by the four donors themselves, specifying procedures and size of commitment of each (1 agreement). Finalizing these agreements, from the initial drafting stage until final signature, took nearly 6 months. Thus, the first 6 months of the first two years of the "harmonization project" were wasted on management procedures, and no decisions to allocate funds to local NGOs were taken.

ORGANIZATIONAL STRUCTURE

The organizational structure was devised to have three levels.[58] Clearly, the decision-making authority was retained by the donors, exclusively, as it is described below:

1. **The Program Steering Committee (PSC)** is the decision-making body for this Consortium. It is composed of representatives of the three "founding" donors (Denmark, Sweden, and Switzerland), and the team leader (ex-officio). Austria, with the miniscule share of contribution was considered a "silent" PSC member, i.e. it did not attend meetings but was kept informed.

As the decision-making body, the PSC "decides on the overall policies of the Programme". It was foreseen to have regular quarterly meetings, unless the implementation of the program warranted differently. The Team Leader convenes the PSC, after consultations, and drafts minutes of the meetings and submits them for approval. Twelve PSC meetings were held during the first two years.

2. The **Consultant (Copenhagen Development Consulting—CDC)** won the contract to manage the Secretariat. It was to be "fully accountable and responsible for the implementation of the Programme and for the management of the financial contributions of the donors."

CDC marketed itself as "one of Scandinavia's leading development consultancy companies… It operates within a frame of intercultural appreciation and respect of cultural diversity with a special obligation to support the socially and economically

58 Based on the terms of the signed "Service Contract" (8 November 2005), and the subsequently drafted by the Team Leader and approved document about "Division of Roles" (4 July 2006).

disadvantaged groups ...". Further, it defined its mission "to provide high quality consulting services in support of sustainable economic and social development within a framework of democratic governance." [59]

During the first meeting between the donors of the Secretariat and the human rights and good governance NGOs, held in Ramallah on 14 December 2005, to introduce the Secretariat to the potential "partners", CDC presented a high sales pitch for the company. It emphasized its potentially value-added role in the success of the Secretariat. It presented a list of clients it serviced, ranging from the European Commission to the World Bank, as well as it emphasized its ability to carry out its overall contractual responsibility, by highlighting the expertise of the Team Leader and the Human Rights Specialist, and by providing project management back stopping, quality assurance, and short-term technical assistance from home office.[60]

However, CDC had no prior direct experience in the management of such a human rights secretariat, nor did it have any experience in Palestine or in any other Arab country.

3. The **Secretariat (Mu'assasat)** represents CDC on the ground, and "has the full decision making authority for day to day operations of the Programme", specifically, planning, administration, financial management, monitoring, reporting and implementation of financial and technical support to HR and GG NGOs on behalf of the donors.[61]

59 (http://www.copenhagendc.com)

60 Project Director's power point presentation, meeting with NGOs in Ramallah, 14 December 2005).

61 I served as the Team Leader of Mu'assasat since its beginning until it was terminated in October 2007. In this capacity, I was responsible for setting up the Secretariat in Ramallah; for overseeing and reviewing requests for funding from indigenous "human rights and good governance" NGOs; for managing a financial commitment of nearly $ 8 million for 24 NGOs, and for initiating strategic discussions with active NGOs in the "sector".

ACHIEVEMENTS

Mu'assasat launched the first call for proposals one month after it was established; it assessed 43 applications for funding, and signed agreements, in June 2006, with 16 NGOs (about 37%) for core funding for a two-year period (guaranteed), and in some cases for a three-year period (contingent). A second call for proposals was launched in November 2006, which resulted in the assessment of 59 applications. Agreements with 8 (about 14%) additional NGOs for core funding for one year were signed in February-March 2007.

Mu'assasat was also given additional responsibilities to promote consolidation, enhancement and networking within the human rights and good governance sector in the West Bank and Gaza, and to facilitate dialogue between donors and NGOs. Consequently, Mu'assasat called for, and held, on 21 September 2006, a "strategic seminar" to discuss issues and challenges facing the Palestinian human rights and good governance sector, as identified and discussed by the 83 NGOs which attended.

Based on the above deliberative "strategic seminar", Mu'assasat prepared, in January 2007, the first "HR/GG Sector Status Report, 2006", as stipulated by its terms of reference, in which it identified the main activities/initiatives undertaken by HR/GG NGOs. Further, it analyzed the major issues and challenges facing the sector, from the point of view of the indigenous active organizations. The report was circulated, simultaneously, to the specific donors and to all attending HR/GG NGOs. It was also posted, as a public document, on Mu'assasat's website. The donors (the PSC members) reacted with consternation that the Report was circulated to the active NGOs before the donors approved it! However, it became clear later that the main reason for their consternation was that they disagreed with the analysis, and with what was being advocated in the Report, and they characterized it as "political" and "academic"!

In May 2007, about 18 months since the start of this process, the donors initiated an external review of Mu'assasat. The Review Team recommended, *inter alia*, that:

> *Mu'assasat should be equipped and supported to take on functions that CDC has fulfilled until now. Those functions include overall responsibility for the administrative functions of the secretariat, accountability for the implementation of the program and for the management of the financial contributions of the donors, responsibility for the planning, administration, procurement, financial management and implementation of the program, maintenance of the financial system, maintenance of the program monitoring system and responsibility for the timely submission of the annual budget, work plans, reports and audits.*[62]

Furthermore, the Review Team recommended strongly that the donors should "democratize and indigenize" Mu'assasat, by re-establishing it as "a local foundation … with three functions: grant making, capacity building, and strategic development… governed by an independent board."[63]

MOMENTUM INTERRUPTED

At the height of this momentum, and totally unknown to the donors, and to us—the locally established CDC office for implementation—the management of the CDC company embarked on a possible "reconstruction" of the company, as part of a bankruptcy procedure, initiated on 30 July 2007. Immediately, I, as the Team Leader, was informed by "home office" that I was not allowed to make any payments from the project's accounts, and I was requested to notify them of existing balances. On 31 July 2007, we received a letter from a Danish law firm, in which it stated: "I am sorry to inform you that the above company (CDC) went into bankruptcy 30 July 2007. I am handling the estate. In that capacity, I hereby terminate your employment.

62 (Sidoti, 2007: 14)

63 (Ibid: 32)

You must not continue working as the bankruptcy estate is without funds".[64]

So far, no direct contact between CDC and the donors regarding this development; the donors received their first communication about this from me. When pressed, Mu'assasat's donors claimed that they, too, were caught completely off guard. All of a sudden, through bureaucratic and legal procedures, according to Danish law, to which we were not privy, we were placed in a complete quandary, vis-à-vis formal financial commitments we made to Palestinian NGOs less than four months earlier. This move rendered all our earlier discussions about strategy, etc., with indigenous human rights NGOs, whom we were making serious efforts at convincing that they were our actual "partners", totally meaningless and superfluous. This concern did not seem to matter at all to "our" donors. Their reiterated concern was how to be very cautious as they proceeded to rectify the situation. They accelerated their consultations with their home capitals and their respective legal departments. Their main and immediate concern, it seemed, was how to contain this mess, utilizing the most internationally appropriate legal and administrative procedures. Whereas, in the meantime, no concern was voiced about the promised "longer term commitment" to the "human rights sector"!

Our immediate concern, however, was about available funds in the local Mu'assasat accounts, and whether or not we could meet our immediate, and formally signed, financial commitments towards our NGO partners. Last outstanding transfers from two of the donors for the year, earmarked to meet our outstanding commitments to 10 NGOs, were interrupted on the way. The amounts were returned to source, as donors claimed that they were not very certain that the NGO account was not subject to the bankruptcy procedures. In the meantime, formal communication with Copenhagen was sparse.

On their part, the donors decided to commission an international audit firm (with offices in Ramallah) to close this phase,

64 (Letter from Lund Elmer Sandager Law firm, 31 July 2007 (Ref. 801068)

by meeting all outstanding commitments to locally-hired staff and to NGOs. Thus, an extensive inventory was conducted of all physical acquisitions and outstanding bills, and the office of *Mu'assasat* was formally closed on 23 October 2007. No formal communication about this development was initiated with our NGO partners. Rumors of varying degrees of veracity were abounding.

Even though, before this happened, the donors were in agreement with the major recommendation of the Review Team, namely, the "indigenization and democratization" of *Mu'assasat,* they adopted a very cautious approach of how to proceed, and decided on a "temporary" halt of the entire program. Their preoccupation was how to cut their losses, and not to fall in the same trap again. In the meantime, all staff were released.

During November 2007, the month following the closure of the office, the donors initiated meetings with the partner NGOs to inform them, formally, about what happened, and to get their views on how to proceed. Most, especially the smaller and not well-established NGOs, saw value in the structure and approach that was established locally, and as implemented over the last two years. They preferred to have it continue in one way or another. However, the bigger and more established human rights NGOs, which had developed deep and reliable connections with Western donors and transnational NGOs, expressed their desire to return to having unilateral, direct contacts with individual donors, as was the case before the setting-up of *Mu'assasat.* They saw in that an unchallenged and guaranteed funding.

As a result of all of the above, the donors (who became now Sweden, Switzerland, Denmark, the Netherlands) selected, through local bidding, the NGO Development Center (NDC) to manage the "Human Rights and Good Governance Secretariat in the OPT". NDC was discussed under a separate section in this chapter.

HARMONIZATION OF WESTERN INTERNATIONAL AID: THE REAL OBJECTIVE?

The micro-analysis of the failed Mu'assasat experiment uncovers a number of factors that reveal the real objectives of the visibly flaunted "harmonization" and "alignment" of aid by the donors. The objective was never clear from the start, nor was it transparent. Although, as mentioned earlier, the overall objective to which the four donors agreed formally was "improving human rights and good governance in the Occupied Palestinian Territory of the West Bank and Gaza". Their actual and immediate concern, however, focused primarily on reducing their transaction costs, through harmonizing donor procedures, improving internal performance of NGOs, improving coordination among them, and by avoiding duplication of efforts. If achieved, all would reflect positively on them and their funds. The inexplicit driving force, in this case, was to do everything possible to avoid repeating a "corrupt and mismanaged" situation, similar to that of the defunct "LAW" case, in which the reputation and credibility of some of the donors were tarnished, and where some of them were engaged in a corrupting role, by knowing and not doing anything about it when it happened.

On the other hand, the long-term objective of "strengthening the performance, outcomes and strategic outreach of programs implemented by human rights and good governance NGOs", active in the Occupied Palestinian Territory, was given only a lip service. Every time the local Palestinian team insisted on giving centrality to this issue, through internal reports and memos initiated as a basis for structured discussions, it was never fully supported, or the support was reluctant, at best. Discussion of which was often deferred as being "academic" and/or "political", and not of pressing concern! On the contrary, the main thrust was pushing for more and more external financial audits, to avert the perceived "rampant" corruption that plagues the Third World, and, by extension, Palestine. When it came to that, no consideration of the very high cost was ever raised, or even contemplated. Whenever the issue of extravagant costs allocated, without any question, for "international" consultants, external auditors, Western monitors or evaluators (generally academics from Western universities), etc, was raised on our part, it was always countered by the claim that we had to abide by international best practices, and by the international market rates for these services.

Clearly, conflict of interest was the driving force here. The Project Director from the "home office" (Copenhagen), with whom I constantly argued about the extravagant costs allocated for these consultants, was very keen to submit the highest rates possible for consultants, irrespective of the potential added value from their work, because the higher the rates, the higher they were able to charge the donors for overhead. This, absolutely, had nothing to do with the quality of work, or the "development" of the "human rights sector" in Palestine.

In real practice, the essence of the "aid harmonization" approach remains unchanged from the traditional approach of allocating formal aid by Western donor agencies (on behalf of their governments) to projects in the 3rd World. The change was only in the narrative—the proclamations—not in the substance; nor did it reflect itself in the level of commitment. It is based on the prevalent Western condescending approach to the non-Western recipients of aid, whether governments or non-governmental organizations. It is clearly evident that the so-called "harmonization" of aid, as it is applied in reality on the ground, is nothing more but a camouflage for widening control, and accelerating Third World dependency on Western official aid.

In our case, for example, the dissonance between the public narrative and action on the ground, was clearly deceptive and terribly embarrassing for us. We went to great lengths from the outset in explaining that the added value of the new initiative of this "aid harmonizing" experiment with human rights NGOs (AKA *Mu'assasat)* is anchored in our commitment to fund core-programs of active NGOs, and sustained for longer time periods. However, in the first call for proposals, real donor funding commitments were made only for 2 years, with contingent funding for a third year, with a vague promise that the process would be ongoing. In the second call for proposals, the reversal in our "sustainability" premise had already become evident, at the insistence of the donors, that funding commitment could be promised for one year only.

On another plain, it was taken for granted, from the outset, that the responsibility to "manage"(read: control) the locally-established mechanism for this "aid harmonization" experiment should be placed in an international "body. The underpinning unquestioned, and racist, assumption was that the "international" body would be more objective; it would draw on rich and diverse "international" experience; it would instill a solid basis of transparent and responsible management system; and it would provide an automatic check on perceived (and anticipated) local corruption and mismanagement. All of that was readily assumed from the start of the process. So, it was clear that the basis for granting the bid to the Copenhagen consulting firm did not even consider examining the "solidity" track record of this company, in terms of its own possible internal corruption, mismanagement, internal incoherence and conflict, ignorance of conditions in Palestine under occupation, etc., which led, in part, to its demise in the middle of the road, and to the failure of this experiment. I am certain, on the other hand, that bidding non-Western firms would have been subjected, without any reluctance whatsoever, to a much harsher assessment.

Furthermore, by selecting this Danish company, the donors did not consider the most cost effective management arrangement; nor did they contemplate seriously the value-added role this foreign company could provide. Consequently, and based on the actual experience, and intimate knowledge of the first nearly two years, the management could have been carried out much more efficiently, much more cost effectively, much more streamlined and "harmonized", and much more responsive, credible, and sensitive to local needs, and with much higher commitment to encourage local participation of partner NGOs.

On top of that, objective assessment shows that the value-added input of the Danish firm diminished substantially after the establishment phase of the first 6-8 months, where procedural mechanisms had to be established. Since that period, the input of the Copenhagen firm became obstructive, cumbersome, expensive, and without utility, the more the Project Director insisted on micro-managing the project by remote control, from Copenhagen, and, in person, through repeated and costly unnecessary visits to the field.

It is instructive to look at some of the main conclusions arrived at in the mid-term review of Mu'assasat [65]:

1. "The assessments of narrative reports indicated that Mu'assasat took its responsibilities very seriously. Reports ... were meticulously read and a thoughtful and concise commentary provided for each organisation. Reports were shared with partners and discussions took place ... about report form and content. The partners noted that this type of feedback was in their experience unique to Mu'assasat. They were provided good advice on monitoring and reporting that was helpful in building their capacity."
2. "It was stated by one NGO that Mu'assasat support was invaluable in bringing attention to bear on topical issues, in drawing attention to new approaches, networking and ensuring that there was a division of labour between the NGOs. All these features represent a form of low-cost coordination in that organisations are not involved in bureaucratic/ administrative coordination procedures nor do they have to spend time going to coordination meetings. ... These forms of informal coordination represent a good example of Mu'assasat's value added that has been recognised and appreciated by partner organisations. These efforts are not reported on by Mu'assasat, yet their impact is substantial."

65 (Saltmarshe, 2007)

3. "Mu'assasat staff are highly respected by partner organisations and are professionally delivering services to the organisation's mandate. It is evident that within the short time it has been operational Mu'assasat has created a sound operational base."

CASE STUDY 5: "AID" BROKERS: IMAGINED AND REIFIED "DEVELOPMENT"

INTRODUCTION

Analysis in this case study focuses on highlighting the evolution and subsequent entrenchment of the initial and continuous interplay between Palestinian "shatat" (expatriate) capitalists and politics, starting in Lebanon and threading itself through different stations until it landed in Ramallah, in the institutional framework of the Palestinian Welfare Association, or better known in Arabic as "*Mu'assasat al-Ta'awun*". This pernicious process of interplay of imposing pressures and wielding influence, between leading Palestinian "shatat" capitalists and the leading political faction (Fateh), commenced—overtly at least—in the aftermath of the Israeli army invasion of Lebanon, in 1982, and continued—covertly or implicitly—after it landed in Ramallah.

This Israeli invasion aimed, and succeeded, at destroying Palestinian institutions in Lebanon, and expelling the PLO as an influential quasi-political and military force in Lebanese, Arab and Palestinian political configurations. Eventually, this interplay process of capital and politics succeeded in embedding itself, with the massive political and financial support of the enemies of Palestinian liberation and freedom, in the heart of official Palestinian politics, propped up by the parameters of the "Oslo Surrender Process". The beginning of this process was contextualized and matured in the Palestinian Welfare Association (WA), which ended up relocating to the Palestinian areas under the jurisdiction of the Palestinian Authority.

In an attempt at, what might be referred to as, an institutional self-assessment, the WA decided in 2008 to commemorate its 25th anniversary by producing an uncritical, self-laudatory assessment of its accomplishments.[66] A Palestinian literary writer was commissioned to write a special public "Document" highlighting the particular conditions that led to the establishment of WA. The document flaunted WA pioneering achievements in protecting and strengthening Palestinian institutions and cultural and national identity. The unstated purpose of this "inventory" document was to put in high relief the generous, genuine, and nationalist commitment of leading expatriate (shatat) Palestinian capitalists in saving Palestinian institutions and national identity from total collapse and disintegration. The idea was to show how a select number of wealthy capitalists, who succeeded in accumulating their considerable wealth through finance capital, construction and services, by accepting and adopting the dominant political programs and approaches at the time, of the PLO in Lebanon and the Arab ruling dynasties in Kuwait, Jordan, Saudi Arabia, the rest of the Gulf areas, etc., took an unprecedented initiative in investing some of their money in the establishment of WA, and how each invested one million dollars to create an endowment that ensured the sustainability of the new organization.

The leading initiative was accredited to 4 Palestinian capitalist tycoons (namely, Munib al-Masri, Hasib Sabbagh, Abdel-Majeed Shoman, and Abdel-Mohsen Qattan) who, following the Israeli military invasion of Lebanon in 1982 and the devastation of the PLO institutions and the organizational base in Lebanon (and their base of economic operations!), sprung into action, out of deep patriotic commitment, and emotional attachment, to save Palestine. They huddled in London in 1983, in the aftermath of the shock that reverberated from the Israeli occupation of an Arab capital—Beirut—and the expulsion of the PLO from it, to reflect on the idea of setting-up a new Palestinian organization for the purpose of "supporting and strengthening the steadfastness (sumoud) of the Palestinian people in all its places of existence".

66 (WA, 2008)

The Welfare Association (WA) was invented by the "shatat" capitalists as the public 'development' institution or association, outside Palestine, prior to the establishment of the Palestinian Authority. However, it aspired, all along, to become a Palestinian national institution operating physically from the actual land of Palestine. This aspiration materialized following 1994, thanks to the "Oslo Surrender Process", in which a number of its key and influential founders were involved and instrumental in urging Arafat to accept the American-Israeli imposed political and economic agenda, i.e. surrender (as discussed in Part II, earlier). Welfare Association combines within it, through its own evolution, and its current actual presence and work on the ground, a number of key elements analyzed in this book. This justifies using it as a detailed case study.

Since it was formally established as a Palestinian "development" assistance organization in Switzerland in 1983 by expatriate ("shatat") Palestinian capitalists, Welfare Association continues to do its "developmental" mission based on its accumulated $75 million endowment fund. In addition, today it functions primarily as a broker of aid for 25-30 transnational aid agencies. (It, however, prefers to label this role as "leveraging international donor agencies"). These agencies can be lumped, for ease of reference, in five categories: (1) official agencies of Western governments, including the US, Canada, EU, Britain, France, Italy, Switzerland, and Austria. The second category includes the corporate transnational agencies, namely the Ford Foundation and the World Bank. The third category encompasses major Arab and Islamic regional and transnational agencies: the Arab Fund for Social and Economic Development, the Kuwait Fund, the Islamic Development Bank, The Arab Monetary Fund, the Arab Gulf Program for UN Development Organizations (AGFUND), the Arab Bank for Economic Development in Africa (BADEA), and the OPEC Fund in Vienna. The fourth category encompasses some UK charities, including, *inter alia*, Karim Rida Said Foundation, Princess Diana Memorial Fund, and others. The fifth category encompasses UN agencies, including UNESCO, ESCWA, and UNRWA.[67]

WA operates on different levels, all strengthening the entrenchment and reification of the myth that it is feasible to effect independent "development" under occupation in a dependent, non-sovereign entity called "Palestinian Authority". It operates with the underpinning premise that seed capital from Palestinian capitalists, leveraged three to five folds from official Western, Arab and Islamic funding agencies, can alleviate poverty and "develop" the fragmented and occupied Palestinian society in the context of imaginary "self-rule".

Thus, in addition to being a funding channel for official governmental, regional, and transnational funding agencies of Western, Arab and Islamic governments, it is clearly a funding agency for some Palestinian capitalists' funds, specifically utilized for 'soft' social-economic "development" that acts to endow its capitalist members with an image of social responsibility and patriotic nationalist commitment. In the meantime, these same Palestinian capitalists, who are responsible for founding the WA, channel their serious economic investments into their own companies, which they were determined to establish as monopolies with permeating proliferations of subsidiaries. It is clear, as analyzed in part II above, that the PA encouraged them, and colluded with them, to set-up these monopolies following 1994. For some of its Palestinian capitalists' members, the WA could be viewed as tantamount to the tax-exempt foundations and charities set-up by American corporate capital, e.g., Ford, Rockefeller, Soros' OSI, etc, which help deflect the concerns of how those accumulations were made in the first place, and under what "national sell-out positions"! The possible difference between this case and that of the Ford or Rockefeller foundations, for example, may be limited only to scope, where the WA's original remit was limited to segments of the Palestinian people in the PA areas, the 1948 areas (Israel), and the refugee

67 (http://www.welfareassociation.org)

camps in Lebanon. In this sense, WA is a specialized Palestinian aid agency.

The fundamental question underlying this discussion is this: is the current WA, which still perceives itself as an independent Palestinian development assistance organization, because it was set-up by non-official Palestinian funds from the "shatat" capitalists, different from other current funding agencies operating in the Palestinian areas? If so, in what way, and if not, what actual role is it really playing in solidifying the Oslo political-economic agenda, i.e. the "surrender process"? What is the impact of the "aid-brokering" function that it so proudly claims to play, as a Palestinian organization, on the necessary entrenchment of a People-Centered Liberationist Development (PCLD) environment in a free and unified Palestine?

On the Oslo road and beyond: The transformation

To illustrate the transformative nature of WA, the analysis will focus on three phases that will cover fairly and comprehensively WA's overt transformation. As it will be shown below, the "transformation" was not in the direction of radicalizing the WA in favor of the Palestinian people. It was motivated, however, by some key founding capitalist members to preserve their economic accumulation base by getting closer to the relevant prevailing political powers, whether it was Kuwait during the Gulf War, or Arafat/Fateh following 1988 and continuing through the establishment of his authority in the West Bank and Gaza following 1994. This transformation merely consolidated the various positions within the leadership of the WA into one major prevalent position, with close proximity to the newly set-up PA, and legitimizing the subservience of its key capitalists' members to the political agenda of the Oslo self-rule government as they enhance their own economic opportunities.

Phase 1: 1983 – 1993, The Preparatory phase

The first ten years of the life of the WA were hemmed, on the one side, by the Israeli invasion of Lebanon, the occupation of the first Arab capital, Beirut, and the expulsion of the PLO from Lebanon in 1982. And on the other, by the negotiated Oslo Accords, which sanctioned the establishment of a PLO self-rule in the West Bank and Gaza following the PLO's recognition of Israel. It was the surrender agenda. The WA channeled during this phase, either from its own resources or brokered through external sources, a total of $43 million.[68] Four pertinent developments occurred during this time period, which exposed two important latent trends in the approach of the WA to the "development" of Palestinian society, which have direct bearing on our analysis. The first trend is the active brokering of external aid for emergency needs. The second trend revealed the true partisan (in the factional sense) nature of the WA key founding capitalists. These trends began to take a clearer and more defined shape as WA relocated to the PA areas in Ramallah. These four developments are analyzed below. [69]

Brokering of aid from external resources for emergency needs

With the eruption of the first intifada, at the end of 1987 and the beginning of 1988, the WA founding capitalists were urged by the PLO leadership in Tunis to secure financial sources in support of the rising serious and pressing emergency needs of the people in the West Bank and Gaza. The WA obliged. It established in 1988 a special fund, referred to as "Intifada Fund" (IF) to receive specific contributions earmarked for that purpose. The contributions came mainly from Arab Gulf governments and organizations, and some individuals. The total accumulations in the IF account reached $6.56 million, and were disbursed completely to organizations in the West Bank and Gaza, as long as there was 'no objection' from the PLO.

Simultaneously, and based on its modest and brief experience in the extension of small, interest free loans to very small economic enterprises, WA began to coordinate with the then

68 (WA, 2008)

69 For more details, refer to my earlier work (Nakhleh 2004:52-62)

Jordanian Ministry of the Occupied Territories in Amman, and, later, with the Kuwaiti Arab Fund for Economic and Social Development, to establish and finance a "credit fund". In retrospect, this did not prove very successful. The coordination with the (now defunct) Jordanian Ministry of the Occupied Territories was possible because the then minister, the Palestinian economist Taher Kanaan, was a member of the Board of Trustees of WA.

It should be noted that 51 percent of all commitments in 1990 came from external sources. At the same time, about one-third of total commitments that year went to emergency needs. This marks a double shift: more focus on giving aid to emergency needs, as a politically safer option, and seeking to cover this from external funding sources, where WA becomes a mere channel for these funds.

With the Iraqi invasion of Kuwait and the ensuing Gulf War in 1991, the revenue base of the WA was eroded. That led to three noticeable results: (1) conscious decision and subsequent planning by WA's decision making bodies to actively seek and mobilize external sources of funds; (2) behind the scene attempts to placate the Kuwaiti regime, without incurring the wrath of the Arafat leadership, and in covert consultation with it; and (3) the surfacing of latent "cliques" among the capitalist members of the WA executive committee. Two well known Kuwaiti-connected executive committee members (namely, Abdel Mohsen Qattan and Said Khoury) were active in smoothing the relationship with the Kuwaiti regime, based on behind the scenes consultations with Arafat and the PLO leadership.

Underpinning the preoccupation with the issue of "*tanmiyat al-mawarid*" (resource development) during this phase, I commented in my previous book that

> *there were the unspoken internal jockeying of power games, increasing competition over turf, and the fight to gain control of the real say in terms of deciding how much to spend on what. Behind the scenes lurked cliques: the 'Amman group', the 'London*

> *group', the 'Kuwait group' ... These were not necessarily mutually exclusive cliques, nor were they distinguished by differing political ideologies, even though different opinions surfaced, once in a while, about the Iraqi invasion of Kuwait, the maneuvers of the PLO, etc. Somehow, it became clear ... that these cliques were positioning themselves for the day after in a way that would lead them to maximize their benefits—money, prestige, credibility, proximity to the emerging political leadership, etc—from the evolving political settlement".*[70]

Each clique was identified with key figures in the executive committee, according to their primary place of residence, but more so, according to their connections with certain Arab political regimes and the PLO leadership. For example, the reference to the 'Amman clique' was always associated with the names of the late Abdul Majeed Shoman, the president of the Arab Bank whose main headquarters are in Amman, Munib al-Masri, who was well connected to the Jordanian regime and to Arafat, simultaneously, and other smaller capitalists who revolved in their financial and political sphere. The 'Kuwait clique', on the other hand, was always associated with the names of Abdel-Mohsen Qattan, Said Khoury, and younger capitalists, e.g., Nabil Qaddoumi, among others, who lived in Kuwait, acquired Kuwaiti citizenship and had joint capitalist ventures with Kuwaitis. They constituted Arafat's channel to mollify the Kuwaiti regime after the PLO's position in support of Saddam Hussein in the Gulf War. The 'London clique' was always associated with the names of some members of the executive committee who lived primarily in London, e.g., Zain al-Abideen Mayyasi, Ramzi Dalloul, etc. These sought to provide a counter-weight for the other two, while insisting on keeping all their investment options open, and untied to any political regime.

Although brokering of external funds for emergency needs started in this phase, as a result of the increased and ruth-

70 (Nakhleh 2004:57-8)

less Israeli oppression during the first intifada, WA made it its mandate to continue this process of aid brokering for emergency as confrontations escalated since 2000. For example, in its three-year strategic plan (2008-2010), the proposed budget for "emergency and humanitarian aid was $3,600,000, only 20 percent of which was to come from the self resources of the WA, and the rest to be brokered from external resources.

Seeking to ingratiate themselves with Arafat (i.e. the PLO and Fateh)

The key capitalists' founders of the WA spread the notion from the outset that they were perceived by Arafat and his closest clique that their active coalescing role in WA, as the 'association of nationalist capitalists', constituted a threat to Arafat's authority. Although I was inclined to believe it then, I am more convinced now, in a retrospective reflection, that this was invented to justify their push to re-direct the WA, in an overt manner, to become under Arafat's PLO, and more accepted by it. This was more profitable for them, considering that the bulk of financial support the WA will allocate to Palestine, later, will be from external sources. Their own resources will be used to leverage support from other transnational aid agencies, and this cannot be effective unless they put their organization (WA), informally, under the PLO umbrella.

During this phase which represents the first ten years of its life, there were three (known to me, at least) incidents that provided a clear indication of my claim. The first incident is what became known as the "War of the Camps", in the refugee camps surrounding Beirut, in 1985. The second is the split within the DFLP (Democratic Front for the Liberation of Palestine) in 1990. The third is the PLO-inspired configuration of the so-called 'higher councils' in Palestine in the early nineties, following the intifada. I shall analyze each separately, based on my direct involvement in each in my capacity as the then director of programs of WA.

1. During the 'War of the Camps', the Shi'ite AMAL forces, in collaboration with the Fateh splinter group (that split from Arafat), defeated the mainstream Arafat-Fateh forces, and were able to control the Palestinian refugee camps around Beirut. The active, broad-based, popular committees in the camps were operating in tandem with the Fateh splinter group. They requested emergency support from WA to respond to immediate humanitarian needs of the Palestinian refugees in these camps. The request, which I verified then in a specifically designed field visit, was discussed during WA executive committee meeting on 26 June 1985. Based on assessment of emergency needs, following field visits, it was recommended that the WA executive committee would allocate $100,000 for immediate emergency support, to be channeled through these active popular committees in the camps.

   In the meantime, it became clear that top political leaders of mainstream Fateh (i.e. Arafat) contacted key WA executive committee members and expressed their consternation and disapproval of cooperating with those popular committees. During the said meeting, Hasib Sabbagh proposed that a $1 million emergency fund for refugees in Lebanon be established, under the supervision of the WA, from additional individual contributions, and that the allocation from this fund be based on the recommendations of select local Palestinian and Lebanese personalities acceptable to the PLO leadership. In other words, leading capitalists' members of the WA decision making body consented to grant a veto power to Arafat on the issue of allocations of emergency needs for Palestinian refugees in the camps in Lebanon. However, and fortunately, the proposed $1 million emergency fund did not materialize, in part because some major individual Palestinian capitalists declined to contribute when approached by leading WA members.[71]

71 For example, Omar Al-Aggad, who was visited by a delegation from WA executive committee members in his house in London, especially for this purpose, declined. As a director of programs, I took part in that visit. It

2. In 1990 a split occurred within the DFLP (the Democratic Front for the Liberation of Palestine) enticed by Arafat. The resulting splinter faction was labeled 'Fida'. The actual head of this faction, Yasser Abed Rabbo, was very close to Arafat and was in his immediate inner circle. He came back with him in the context of Oslo as the Secretary General of the PLO Executive Committee; and continues in this post until this day! Even though the split occurred outside Palestine, DFLP projects in Palestine were also split, including, of course, those funded by WA. To sort out the situation from Geneva, a decision was taken to freeze all WA commitments for those projects. To influence this decision, Zahira Kamal, who was the leading personality of the new faction in Palestine, used the Abed Rabbo channel in Tunis, to intercede on her behalf at Welfare Association. Abed Rabbo contacted members of the WA executive committee on 17 June 1991 to pressure for the release of funds for their projects. Consequently, an influential member of WA executive committee, with close and open channels with Arafat (Basel Aqel), interceded in favor of Yasser Abed Rabbo. We should recall that Basel Aqel was instrumental with Hasib Sabbagh in convincing Arafat to accept the American conditions for surrender, which led to the Oslo Process.

3. The period before and after the Madrid Conference in 1991 witnessed an escalation in public maneuvers and preparations for political compromise and surrender, characterized by the visible involvement of the PLO and their people on the ground. In that atmosphere, specifically during 1992, the executive staff of WA was given clear instructions by the executive committee to coordinate with the "higher councils", before recommending any project for funding. Those "higher councils" were established under the direct supervision of the PLO, and specifically, with the direct

---

should be remembered that Al-Aggad group succeeded in establishing the Arab Palestinian Investment Company as a holding company in the PA areas soon after the PA was established, as discussed in part II.

involvement of Ahmad Qrai (Abu Ala'). Abu Ala' was then the head of the PLO Economic Department, and, as is well known, he became later the chief negotiator of the Oslo Accords, and the king-pin of the direct negotiating process with the Israelis that followed. He was maintained in that capacity until very recently.

PHASE 2: 1994 – 2006, IMMERSION IN THE OSLO "SELF-RULE" PA AND CLEARER ROLE OF BROKERING TRANSNATIONAL AID

The founders of WA emphasized that their role during this phase was to "participate in state building",[72] as they physically shifted the location of the Association from Geneva to Jerusalem to Amman and, finally, to Ramallah. Although WA activities were re-clustered into three program areas: institutional development, human resource development, and culture and identity, our analysis of this phase will focus particularly on two primary programs that repositioned WA as a strong contender for brokering transnational aid. One program focused on the Old City of Jerusalem, and the other on NGOs. About 75 – 80 percent of total allocations for this phase were leveraged from transnational aid agencies. Below, I shall analyze in detail these two program areas and provide some explanation for the WA role of brokering external funds, and the impact that may have had on Palestinian "development" under occupation.

The Jerusalem Focus...

At the beginning of this phase, a new program of "reconstruction and rehabilitation of the Old City of Jerusalem" was launched thanks to a grant from the Arab Fund for Social and Economic Development in Kuwait, as a result of the influence of one key WA capitalist (Qattan) who sat as the "Palestine Governor" at the Fund's Board, and who is the primary WA's connection with Kuwait. The claimed objective of this program

72 (WA, 2008)

was to "preserve the Arab-Islamic identity of the city", and to maintain Arab presence in it as a countermeasure for the escalating process of the city's Zionization.

The initial funding from the Arab Fund for this program, through WA, was $3 million. Later on, the EU and UNESCO allocated funds for the same program, for setting up a training center for conservation engineers. All in all, more than $29 million were brokered and spent on this program until 2008. "These funds could not have been materialized", stated Abdel Mohsen Qattan, "had it not been for the high professionalism, transparency, independence, and strong internal control that boosted the position of the WA with international and Arab donor countries."[73] This, as we shall see later, is pure self-deception and effective marketing!

On the other hand, it is clear that Jerusalem was used as a focus only, or a magnet to draw Arab and Islamic funds around it, while endowing WA with nationalist and patriotic credibility, vis-à-vis the newly established PA. Had the WA capitalists been genuinely committed to preserving the Arab character of Jerusalem, they would have responded positively by investing from their own wealth, as early as 1986, when an initial plan for action was proposed to them at that time. Purchasing and rehabilitating Arab premises in the old city, which were threatened by Zionist colonization, were proposed much earlier, but no action was taken then. It was not perceived then that the time was opportune for investing in safeguarding Jerusalem. So waiting for minimal Kuwaiti or Saudi funds in order to claim achieving this goal, in the shadow of an emaciated self-rule authority which they were instrumental in establishing, is symbolic at best, and downright hypocritical.

The WA focus on Jerusalem is maintained until this day. In its meeting in Amman, Jordan, on 17 November 2007, WA Board of Trustees (BOT) took a decision to make a special and serious effort in mustering serious funds for the support of Jerusalem. A "Jerusalem Committee" (JC) was established. The

73 (Ibid)

Committee became known as "Lajnat al-Quds—Wikalat Beit Mal al-Quds al-Sharif". Munib al-Masri became the Head of "al-Quds Support C'ttee".

The legal advisor for the JC (attorney Mazin al-Qubty) was requested to prepare a background paper on "the legal impediments for work and investment in the city of Jerusalem". Pursuant to that, a full-fledged "Jerusalem Document" was drafted. Initial (internal) comments on the draft from the JC members were highlighted in the following points:

- "Avoid political slogans and make it sound factual, humanitarian and cultural. Essentially remove sentiments, stick to key facts and focus on activities";
- "WA will just manage";
- "Build an Advisory Group with international and European stature personalities to provide legal protection" (the name of Tony Blair was reiterated often);
- "Establish an Advisory Board from key donors (which should be kept primarily Arab);
- "We need endorsement from Abu Mazin [the PA president] who will write to Arab leaders in support of the WA initiative";
- "Ensure that the PA is neutral in this."

Consequently, the Jerusalem Document (JD) was approved in January 2008. The "Document" is a 5-year plan with a proposed total budget of $1.3 billion. The expected financing of this Plan was to be secured from a number of sources, primary among them are Arab and Islamic sources, the EU and its member states (particularly, the Italian Cooperation, the Spanish and Danish Representations, etc), Beit al-Mal, the Islamic Development Bank, and the PA. In a meeting at WA offices in Ramallah, on 13 March 2008, the JC recommended that WA will contribute to the JD, over the five years, $ 25-50 million from its own resources.

The marketing of the Plan was discussed during a "JD consultative meeting" in Amman, on 16 February 2008. It was agreed that a "WA Delegation" will be formed, and it was hoped that it would be led by the PA President, or his representative (Dr. Rafiq al-Husseini), plus the following members from WA: Abdel Mohsin Qattan, Said Khouri, Munib al-Masri, Nabil Qaddoumi, and Tafeeda Jirbawi (the then director of research and planning) . It was decided, further, that the Delegation will target first Arab kings and heads of states, starting with Saudi Arabia, and to "adjust the contents of the document to be acceptable to them". In a follow-up JC meeting, on 22 April 2008, the composition of the "WA Delegation" was firmed up, as proposed. In the meantime, Munib al-Masri, the Head of the JC, acknowledged that he met with Abu Mazin in Sharm al-Sheikh during the first half of May 2008, and they agreed that he would be involved in the fundraising effort for al-Quds (Jerusalem).

In a subsequent meeting of the JC at WA offices in Ramallah on 28 May 2008, in which Ahmad Ruweidi, the Head of Al-Quds Unit at the President's office, participated, the Committee decided "to unify efforts between WA and the President's Office in preparation to support Jerusalem, starting with sharing the JD with Ahmad, for comments and possible revisions."

Concurrently with the preparation of the JD process, however, another similar initiative was launched by Mazin Sinoqrot, a known and respected indigenous Jerusalem capitalist, and the former PA Minister of National Economy. This initiative started by convening a 2-day workshop in Jericho in February 2008, in which at least 100 businessmen, activists, experts on Jerusalem participated, in order to "plan strategically" for Jerusalem.[74] None of the WA capitalists involved in the "WA Jerusalem Document" was present, although a person from the President's Office (who works closely with Dr. Rafiq Husseini) attended and participated actively. Also present was the CEO of the Palestine Investment Fund (PIF). It seems odd that no reference to either initiative was made by either group! As if, each

74 I was invited to participate in this meeting, and was active in subsequent meetings to prepare the "education focus" in the Plan.

group of Palestinian capitalists has their own Jerusalem, for the sake of their own private investment and nationalist credibility?

As if to complete the above two initiatives, during the Palestine Investment Conference (PIC) held in Bethlehem, in June 2008, where it was declared openly that "Palestine is open for business", the same Munib al-Masri of WA launched, in his capacity as the chairman of PADICO, "Al Quds Investment Fund". Al-Masri confirmed

> *that the fund will have initial capital of $100m, $25m provided by PADICO. It will be governed by an investment advisory board that will be responsible for making investment decisions. The fund is intended to finance small and large projects, concentrating particularly on housing projects in East Jerusalem as well as commercial buildings, entertainment centres, tourism and economic projects. It hopes to achieve above average returns. Munib Al Masri said that there are ongoing talks with the Ministry of Waqf and Religious Affairs, as well as with the local Church Authorities, in order to build housing units on land they own".*[75]

Likewise, following his 2-day strategic planning workshop on Jerusalem, held in Jericho, Mazen Sinoqrot, a former PA minister of national economy, was not late in announcing publically about the establishment of "Al-Quds Holding", on 31 August 2010[76] he declared further:

> *The city contains a big potential for growth in tourism, education and other services ... It includes unique and important opportunities for investment... The new company is a nucleus for big investments for businessmen from inside and outside... It looks to invest in four comfortable and profitable*

75 (MAS, 2008, Palestinian Economic Bulletin, Issue 22)

76 (Maan, 2010; http://alqudsholding.com/)

> *main sectors ... We are talking here about economic concepts, away from emotions; and we emphasize that the rate of profit is high in Jerusalem.*

This shows what is really happening. Jerusalem was marketed as a promising profitable investment axis bearing no significant relationship to the WA's initial claim of "preserving its Arab-Islamic identity"! WA is used by its capitalist founders as a legitimate and credible channel for brokering external funds to enhance their own corporate investments. This open investment process is done with the tacit agreement of both the PA and Israel.

The NGO Focus...

The focus on the Palestinian "NGO Sector" in the West Bank and Gaza started with the initiative of the World Bank following the formation of the PA government in 1995. In a sympathetic report by a consultant to the World Bank on its Palestinian NGO Project, it was stated:

> *As the Bank was designing this project with the aim of supporting the PNGO community, the PA under Yasser Arafat was considering legislation that would severely restrict PNGO activities. ... The Bank recognized this tension ... and determined that the PNGO project could be utilized to improve NGO-PA relations. Indeed, it determined that without such an improved relationship the primary objectives would not be achievable or sustainable. In this context, the Bank decided that the most important objectives for this project are:*
>
> 1. *To deliver services to the poor and marginalized in Palestinian society, using NGOs as the delivery mechanism;*
> 2. *To improve the institutional capacities of NGOs receiving grants under the project; and*
> 3. *To support efforts by the PA and the Palestinian NGO sector to strengthen their working*

> *relationship.[77] Based on these prioritized objectives, listed above, the Bank received the approval of all the relevant parties, i.e., the PA, PNGOs and Israel. The Bank made it very clear that "support to Palestinians in Jerusalem could not be done with Bank funds." Thus, the actual Saudi and Italian contributions to this Project, which totaled $5 million, were used as a cover for funding Jerusalem NGOs from this project, and the funds were channeled through the Project Management Organization (PMO).[78]*

After formulating the necessary documents, the World Bank launched the Project for international bidding. The bid was for USD 14 million, for three years (1997 – 1999). Together with "over 30 NGOs and NGO consortia" submitting formal "expressions of interest" (EOI), WA submitted an EOI as a consortium with 2 British institutions (the British Council and Charities Aid Foundation). The Welfare Association Consortium (WAC) was shortlisted as one of five competitors.[79] It was successful in winning this bid. The WA contributed from its own resources $300,000 to the NGO Project. It was designated as the PMO [Project Management Organization] for the project for a period of three years (phase I). However, hiring WAC for three years only out of the Bank's 6-year commitment to this Project generated some "consternation ... on the part of WAC." [80]

This process of selection begs a deeper analysis that transcends the mechanical quantitative process of evaluation of the

77 (Sullivan, 2001:19-20)

78 (Ibid: 21)

79 The five competitors were: (1) CARE, (2) CIBG Consortium (Christian Aid, ICCO, Bisan Center, the Galilee Society), (3) Save the Children Federation (US), Save the Children Fund (UK), and Birzeit University, (4) The Welfare Association Consortium, and (5) World Learning (US) and Amideast. (Ibid: 26).

80 (Ibid: 27)

short-listed bids, especially if we consider carefully comments made in this regard by Nigel Roberts, the Bank's representative in Jerusalem, and who was the official most responsible for this project. He stated in an interview:

> *This [project] is the first of its kind—the first time the World Bank works directly with NGOs and not with the government. Running the operation will require a great deal of trust in us from both the NGOs and the PA. The PA will be kept informed, fully, of what we're doing. But they will not sit on the board governing the disbursal of funds.*[81]

If this is so, let us examine what type of PMO would be the most logical, expedient and effective manager for this project, to ensure the required political control acceptable to the Bank for the success of this new initiative that would reflect positively on the Bank. Clearly the important and real concerns here are neither for the poor, nor for nurturing and sustaining resilient Palestinian civil society organizations under colonial occupation. Improving "the institutional capacities of NGOs receiving grants under the project" is a coded concept for creating, through external aid, a class of professional and managerial NGOs, removed and insulated from the needs and pressures of broad-based grassroots constituencies. For this to be effective in the post-Oslo Palestinian context, this improvised and "aid-created" NGO class has to internalize, accept and operate under the Oslo umbrella; It has to ignore the notion that it operates under a structure of occupation; it has not to be concerned with prevailing Israeli policies; and it has to embed itself in the PA subservient mental set. Furthermore, in this case, the management of the project, i.e. the PMO (Project Management Organization) has to be accepted by Fateh, or, better yet, managed and run by a Fateh-affiliated person, as this was the case during the first two phases (PNGO I and II).

81 Quoted in (Ibid: 21)

Of the five short-listed bidders, two were full-fledged US NGOs with activities in the Palestinian areas; one was a consortium of two European church-based NGOs and two Palestinian development NGOs; one was a consortium of US and UK Save the Children federations with a Palestinian university; and one was the Welfare Association Consortium. Although this Consortium was embellished by the addition of two UK charities, the critical partner, in terms of this project and the Bank's anticipation from it, was clearly the Welfare Association. The WA was the only "unique" Palestinian NGO whose track record shows the active involvement of its Palestinian capitalists' founders with Arafat, and their deep immersion with the Oslo regime, as well as the capitalist structure in Israel, under the guise of "developing" Palestine through investment. The others, with certain differences, could have been even stronger in delivering "services to the poor and marginalized in Palestinian society", based on their transnational experience and track record. But, the WAC was unmatched in delivering objective (3), namely supporting "efforts by the Palestinian Authority (PA) and the Palestinian NGO sector to strengthen their working relationship." No wonder, then, that WAC was selected as the Project's PMO!

This case provides an obvious manifestation of how WA groomed itself, with the support of others, to become a favorite broker for transnational aid agencies. Its gradual transformation to accept a comfortable position within the lap of the Oslo-invented PA structure, without contradiction, is to be viewed as a net asset in this context.

Following what was hailed and perceived as great success, a WA former Director General commented in the 25th anniversary document, "WA moved from a local organization to an organization working on a respected and elevated international level".[82] Of course, he would not elaborate on the notion of "respected"; by whom, and for what?

82 (WA, 2008, 25 Year Doc.)

In fulfillment of its function, the PMO conducted, in 1997, a broad needs assessment, specifying the three areas: the West Bank, Jerusalem, and Gaza. The identified needs that required interventions were comprehensive, and specified by region, as follows:

1. **The West Bank:** Land reclamation, development of NGOs, income generation, housing, youth services, rehabilitation, early childhood education, and "programs to oppose confiscation of land";
2. **Jerusalem:** Legal services, development of NGOs, schools, youth services, housing, early childhood education, community empowerment, income generation and production, school health, and management training;
3. **Gaza:** Primary health care, early childhood education, adult education, vocational training for the disabled, credit programs for the poor, and medical financial assistance to the poor.

However, under the claim of "focusing" these needs, the Bank conducted a "Supervision Mission" in February 1988. On that basis, the Mission Aid-Memoire by the Bank's Task Manager re-identified and contracted the priorities, to the following:

1. **The West Bank:** Informal education, primary health care, and "agricultural intensification"[?];
2. **Jerusalem:** Legal advisory services, informal education, and schools;
3. **Gaza:** Informal education, rehabilitation for the disabled, and primary health care. [83]

83 (Sullivan, 2001: 30-1)

It is evidently clear, based on the above, that the Bank did not merely shorten, or re-focus the list, but, in effect, it emasculated the identified needs and squeezed them into a very de-politicized frame, skirting potential empowerment interventions, and friction with the Israeli occupation, such as land reclamation, income generation, housing, programs targeting the poor, etc. With the Bank retaining, ultimately, the "no objection" card, or final say, the PMO gets reduced, in reality, to merely a politically acceptable manager and aid-broker, performing the Bank's expectation, and ensuring to sustain the project because of self-vested interest. This is the function of aid-brokers, in general, and particularly those with self-delusion that such a process empowers them sufficiently to do their people enough good, and just enough to permit them to claim national credit for it.

The World Bank PNGO project is continuing, and it is currently in its 3rd phase, with slight modifications, as we shall see below. After a positive assessment of PNGOI, the World Bank committed additional funding for a second phase (PNGOII) to be implemented by the WA Consortium. The WAC was successful in brokering $49.5 million during the first two phases (PNGOI/II), for the period 1997 - 2006. The transnational aid agencies contributing to these two phases were: the World Bank, the Saudi Government, the Italian Government, the Canadian International Development Agency (CIDA), the Italian Government, DFID, IDB (through PECDAR), the French International Agency for Development, and the Swiss Agency for Development. [84]

The second phase of the Project (PNGO II) formally ended on 30 June 2006. In assessing the Project, the World Bank stated: "The governance of the project through the WA Board still has to address a number of significant shortcomings". [85] It

84 Refer to http://www.ndc.ps, Minutes of the first meeting of WA Programs and Projects Committee, 6-7 March, Amman, Jordan; World Bank Report "The Palestinian NGO Project: Project Appraisal Document, 19 June 1997, and World Bank Report "Completion Report, PNGO II, 3 April 2007

85 (WB, 2007:9)

commented further that "outcomes have been so impacted by forces external to the project … that assessment of the project's achievements and shortcomings is complicated and clear findings are hard to substantiate."[86] This is clearly a facile "exit strategy" for being involved in a project, which was sold with a promised illusory impact, while knowing fully-well in advance that all such, so-called "development" projects under occupation, are affected by "external forces", notable among them is the World Bank itself! Be that as it may, the Bank, for whatever reason, had apparently decided to replace one "aid-brokering" horse with another.

In preparation for that shift, the PMO acknowledged in its appended "Completion Report" that "members of the Supervisory Board (SB) encouraged the development of the SB into a Palestinian NGO Foundation …". Simultaneously, the Bank affirmed that the NGO Development Center (NDC) is

> *the implementer of PNGO III. ... Clearly, the maintenance and establishment of NDC provide the institution with the accompanying technical and financial know-how setting to ensure effective project continuity. Due to the timely initiative of the Supervisory Board, the skills, experience and institutional set-up of the PMO have been embedded as the executive arm in the new NDC.*[87]

The two "horses", so to speak, came from the same stable. NDC was a project of the WA; it was funded by it, and WA sits on its Board. However, about 3 months prior to the official termination of PNGO II, in March 2006, NDC registered as a separate NGO with the PA (according to the 2000 Law; see Part II). In August 2006, the World Bank "financed the feasibility studies and other assessments for the establishment of NDC" under PNGO III. WAC was officially closed on 31 October

86 (Ibid:10)

87 (Ibid)

2006, and NDC started its operations on 1 November 2006. This shift was described by NDC, on its website, as follows:

> *The assets, systems, and staff of the Consortium [WAC] were transferred to NDC, capturing nearly ten years of valuable experience and knowledge in the new permanent Palestinian organization. Ongoing programs of PNGO II were also transferred to NDC. ... The WA contributes towards NDC's management costs, and allocates an endowment to cover the Center's running costs. Additionally,* ***the Welfare Association will utilize the services of NDC to channel donated funds it receives for purposes of grant-making to NGOs.*** *The Welfare Association is also active on the governing board of NDC, which also includes representatives of Palestinian NGOs, unions and networks, international donors, the private sector, government, and academia."*[88]

The emerging but oscillating relationship between WA and NDC in the context of the World Bank NGO Project is not crystal clear. But, I tried to understand this shift from one Palestinian "aid-broker" agency to another, in the context of the current analysis of the need to rely on local aid-brokers by Western transnational aid agencies, and the ensuing benefits to them.[89]

It can be observed that the relationship between WA and NDC became unclear from the moment the decision was taken to transform the PNGO Project (the WA Consortium) from a WA-led Consortium to an independent entity (NGO) with WA partial funding, but without a prominent representation of WA

88 (http:// www.ndc.ps); emphasis added.

89 In addition to the above references used for this discussion, I relied on a personal interview with NDC's director (Kassabreh, 2010), on WA's PPC Meeting minutes, 28-29 September 2007, and NDC's BOD Meeting, 8 December 2007.

on the NDC's Board. The question of the role of WA in NDC and its "control" of it was not clear. It seems to vary from one document to the next. During the WA's PPC meeting on 28-29 September 2007 in Amman, there was a discussion of "the current role of WA in NDC, and a stress was voiced on the necessity of influencing [NDC's] decisions to render them coherent with WA objectives. ... Some members suggested that NDC's Director should be invited to participate in the Committee's meetings for the sake of coordination." [90]

About two months later, NDC, in its Board of Directors (BOD) meeting in Jerusalem (on 8 December 2007), "rejected in principle receiving funds from USAID [to avoid having to sign the "Anti-Terrorist Clause" (ATC), and to explore receiving US funds through other channels. Furthermore, during the same meeting, NDC's BOD assessed critically the PA's Palestinian Reform and Development Plan (PRDP) of 2008-2010, from the perspective that "it expresses mainly the view of the Ministry of Planning (MOP), and does not take into consideration the Palestinian public good, and that civil society organizations (CSO's) were not consulted."[91]

Thus, there has been a clear shift in the locus of power and control in the relationship between WA and NDC, on the one hand, and that of WA as an aid-broker with the World Bank, on the other. During the first ten- year history, the precursor to its establishment as an independent organization, NDC was a project of WA, funded by it and through it, and under its full control. Since 2006 when the WA Consortium was urged and encouraged, largely by its major creator and funder—the World Bank—to develop into a separate and registered "independent" entity, theoretically it had the potential of competing with WA, at all levels, in vision, programming focus, access to funds, local credibility, etc. The potential was present for the eruption of conflictful relationship between parent and offspring. If so, how

90 (WA, 2007)

91 (NDC, 2007)

did this potential manifest itself? And what impact did it have on Palestinian NGO development?

If the underpinning assumption used here, namely, that this shift occurred by a pre-meditated design on the part of the World Bank, is correct, the question is why was there a need to replace one local aid-broker with another? What's the added value that NDC provides, and why was it being marketed as a more credible professional alternative to connect and mediate with indigenous NGOs on behalf of the Bank? The former PMO director, known to have been affiliated with Fateh, was replaced by a new PMO director, the director of a PA-registered NDC, who shows no factional color. The chairman of the BOD of the new NGO (NDC) is a "shatat" capitalist coming from the US to invest in the PA areas through the Coca Cola monopoly. In this, he is not distinguishable from the other "shatat" capitalists who control the Board of WA.

The puzzling and unclear question is this: why did the World Bank push for the establishment of a new, redundant, NGO to manage the continuation of its NGO Project, after a ten-year experience with another, fairly successful, PMO? And why did it entice other transnational funding agencies to utilize this improvised NGO as their aid-broker, as was the case with the four European "like-minded donor" countries (Switzerland, Denmark, Sweden and the Netherlands) who established a joint fund in support of human rights and good governance of Palestinian and Israeli NGOs?

Clearly, NDC could not have been created, most probably, had it not been for the World Bank and its NGO project. Unlike WA, it is a specialized aid-broker with a focus on "NGO development". It carries none of the historical "baggage" of WA, and could provide a sparkly clean image as a professional NGO "godfather", with no political color, or direct connection with the ruling PA faction. It seems that it was marketed by the World Bank as such. As NDC experienced "rapid growth and solid credibility", and attracted more funds, its director felt that there are current moves by WA to "separate themselves from NDC", which he could not explain. Although he sensed that it could be due to jealousy of their successful aid-brokering role, about which they are very open. "NDC creates a platform for leveraging funds from other international donors ... In addition, NDC will engage in fundraising from institutional and individual donors, especially regional Arab and Palestinian donors." [92]

PHASE 3, 2007 — 2010: FOCUS ON EMERGENCY AND HUMANITARIAN AID AS PERCEIVED BY TRANSNATIONAL AID AGENCIES

The third phase whose declared focus was on "emergency and reconstruction" was identified to have three specific foci, namely, "supporting NGOs", "diversification of sources of funds," and providing "emergency and humanitarian aid". It must be recalled that the starting point of this phase is the attempt to erase militarily Hamas's electoral legitimacy after winning a majority in the PLC elections, and to undermine its government. This led to a forced separation between Gaza and the West Bank; to besieging Gaza by Israeli forces; to declare the Hamas political movement, its "sympathizers" and "supporters", by the Ramallah PA, as illegal, and to subject them to physical elimination, imprisonment and torture; and to freeze any aid from Western transnational agencies to Gaza (except what is defined as 'humanitarian'). In the meantime, the imposed Fayyad Government in Ramallah became the darling of the US-Israel-Major Western transnational aid agencies-Palestinian and Zionist capitalists' configuration. Such a status allowed it (formally at least) to generate two neo-liberal plans: the PRDP (Palestinian Reform and Development Plan) in 2008 and "Ending the Occupation, Establishing the State" two-year Program in 2009.

This is the background against which the WA generated its "Strategic Plan 2008-2010".[93]

92 (http://www.ndc.ps; Kassabreh, 2010)

93 (WA, 2007)

Until the beginning of actual implementation of the new three-year Strategic Plan 2008 – 1010, WA committed in its 25 –year history a total of nearly $280 million in support of self-proclaimed goals of Palestinian "steadfastness [*sumoud*]", "self-reliance", "development", "reconstruction", and "humanitarian and emergency needs". Mostly, the aid was brokered from external sources. Except for a minimal response to "humanitarian and emergency needs", the remaining self-proclaimed goals rest in the realm of rhetoric. This is so, unless new definitions are invented for "sumoud", "self-reliance" and "development", which are underpinned on the occupation-sanctioned return of corrupt self-proclaimed leaders, propped up by their own capitalists and intellectuals; rapidly escalating and imperative dependence on the political aid from transnational agencies and on Zionist economy; rapidly increasing poverty and unemployment; and priding ourselves with generating a public and conspicuous culture of consumerism.

I maintain below that the new WA strategic plan reveals in a much clearer, yet convoluted, way WA's entrenchment as an 'extraterritorial' agency of the PA. Let us examine how this is being effected. [94]

The new three-year strategic plan 2008 – 2010 (SP) aimed at sharpening the focus of WA's work, "benefiting from the lessons learned from previous and cumulative experiences", particularly the experience gained from the implementation of the previous two strategic plans of 2002 – 2004, and 2005 – 2007. The new SP relies on "the Palestinian national goals as well as the UN millennium development goals and the needs of the partners, which imbue it with national and international dimension." The stated WA vision is "to see Arab Palestine independent, free and democratic where the Palestinian individual enjoys progress and good living ...". As for the mission statement, "WA aims to be the pioneering Palestinian non-governmental development organization by contributing to the development of the capaci-

94 All quotations below refer to the full text of the Plan and the Executive Summary submitted by the Research and Planning Department to WA BOT, September 2007; WA, 2007.

ties of the Palestinian individual, safeguarding his heritage and identity, supporting his living culture, and the building of civil society ...".

At another level, completely unrelated to the "vision" and "mission statement", the SP delineates WA "strategic objectives" and the subsequent "paths" for these objectives. The strategic objectives are limited to four that aim at consolidating and strengthening the organizational structure: (1) the cost- effectiveness and competence in programmatic work, (2) strengthening the organizational frameworks, (3) increase and diversification of financial resources, and (4) effective and strong cooperation and communication at the internal and external levels. Four "strategic paths" were identified: (1) preserving Palestinian culture and identity, (2) human resource development, (3) institutional empowerment, and (4) emergency support.

Despite the SWOT analysis exercise conducted as a basis for this SP, especially the analysis of the environment of continued and unending occupation, none of that was translated, or reflected in the "strategic objectives" defined in this plan. No eminence was given to the need to direct WA support towards enhancing Palestinian society's resilience in resisting occupation; in playing an active role in educating potentially responsive aid agencies to redirect aid to Gaza against the political positions of their governments; in achieving a viable and well fortified social fabric; and making substantial strides towards freedom, independence, self-reliance, and productivity.

The proposed budget for the 3-year plan is $73,350,000, about 76 percent of which is to be brokered from external resources. There is dissonance between the actual plan of action for the three years and the society under occupation. Is this an accidental omission? I don't believe so. It is a plan intended to be congruent with the PA government plan, i.e. talk about empowering institutions for an unclear and ambiguous goal, while by-passing the overall and pressing fact that the Palestinians—individuals, institutions and society—struggle to live day in and day out under an oppressive occupation. Their real development cannot be effected without ending the occupation.

In a self-assessment of the first 25 years of WA (in 2008), one of the key founding members and current honorary chairman of the BOT, summarized the achievements of the organization in the following words:

> *We had to confront questions about the political ambitions of WA ... but we kept away from being involved in Palestinian politics ... [??] We came not as an alternative [to the PLO] but to support the 'Palestinian national project' through supporting and strengthening the steadfastness of Palestinian society. ... WA was successful in making a smooth transition from the 'founding fathers' to the new generations [Basically sons, and in some cases daughters!].*[95]

With perhaps the possible exception of the last statement, the current situation does not hold the above self-assessment true!

INTERPLAY BETWEEN TRANSNATIONAL NGOs AND INDIGENOUS "DEVELOPMENTAL" NGOs: SUSTAINING MILITARY OCCUPATION AND THEIR WESTERN GOVERNMENTS' POLICIES BY OTHER MEANS?

The presence of Western transnational NGOs in the Occupied Palestinian Areas is correlated directly with the Western-Israeli political plans imposed on the Palestinians. Following the Camp David Accords between Egypt and Israel, brokered by the Americans in 1978, the American Department of State decided to allocate US funds to be spent in the Occupied Areas, under the guise of "improving the standard of living" of the Palestinians, but, indirectly, to entice the Palestinians to go along with the Camp David Accords. The mechanism to implement that decision was to channel USAID funds through five American Private Voluntary Organizations (PVOs). These American

95 (WA, 2008)

agencies established offices in the West Bank and Gaza, and started coordinating the allocation of this funding with the Israeli occupation authorities.[96]

Following the Israeli onslaught on the PLO in Lebanon in 1982, expressions of Western support to the Palestinians under occupation mounted. The agents to channel such support, of course, are agencies and associations from the West. Support from official European sources came through the European Commission, the Executive arm of the EU, and a number of European NGOs.

The third noticeable step in the visibility of Western aid and its ubiquitous agencies, in terms of volume and physical presence of Western transnational NGOs, coincided with the beginning of the popular uprising, the *intifada,* at the beginning of 1988.

The biggest leap, however, followed the establishment of the Oslo-invented PA in the West Bank and Gaza. Then, hundreds of international organizations and associations, governmental and non-governmental alike, non-profit and for-profit alike, etc., "invaded" the occupied, but the euphemistically-heralded as a "self-governing" Palestinian Areas. These organizations permeated the various sectors, ranging from health and education to the economy, financial institutions, the judiciary, the legislature, the security, and the executive offices of the President and the Cabinet. These organizations were deeply involved in training, strategic planning, organizational structuring and restructuring, setting up legal administration, setting up improvised institutions, etc. In this process, these organizations worked simultaneously with Palestinian governmental and non-governmental organizations. This influx of international organizations found welcoming and wide open doors, basically in relation to the volume of funds they brandished, the level and influence of the political and economic clout that their govern-

96 For further details, see (Nakhleh, 1989: 113-124), (Nakhleh, 1991:45-49), and Nakhleh, 2004).

ments manifested, and the degree of visible influence on decisions taken by the occupation structure.

In a recent study on "*International Charitable Associations and Non Governmental Organizations in Palestine*", the Palestinian Coalition for Integrity and Accountability AMAN sought "... to examine the work environment of these organizations and the level of transparency and accountability as decisive factors in determining the efficiency of their integrity systems".[97] The study showed a number of revealing aspects.

According to the data obtained from the Ministry of Interior, the competent agency for registering Palestinian and foreign associations and NGOs, there are 110 branches of foreign NGOs registered in the West Bank. Until 2007, additional 7 branches were registered in Gaza, but since then the Ministry cannot keep track of organizations in Gaza, and, consequently, they have no updated information to that effect. Of the branches of foreign NGOs in the West Bank, slightly over 85 percent are European and American. And nearly 89 percent of all the branches of the foreign organizations are concentrated in the central areas of Ramallah, Jerusalem and Bethlehem.[98] These organizations work "through partnerships with existing local institutions, or through opening and registering independent branches, or even through conducting direct operations without registration."[99]

SHIFTING TRENDS

Having been an active participant-observer in this scene, it is very evident that there is a clear shift in the pattern of Western funding, and the role of transnational NGOs (TNGOs), as the conduits for disbursing these funds. Prior to the beginning of the "Oslo Process", funds allocated from American and European official sources were channeled and supervised, by and large, by European and American transnational NGOs and

97 (AMAN, 2010:3)

98 (Ibid: 15)

99 (Ibid:14)

PVOs, on the ground, on behalf of their governments. These TNGOs were in effect the extended arm of their governments, their parties, their corporations, etc, in the field: in the occupied Palestinian areas, as in other parts of the Third World, regardless of whether those parts are directly occupied by foreign military power, or colonized subtly by remote control, or oppressed by the hegemony of their own economic and political elites and governments. These TNGOs reported directly to their governments—the source of their funds—in their home capitals. Just like their field military commanders in the past, and their diplomatic missions, in the past and the present, these TNGOs submitted to their capitals their reports, analyses and observations. They were, and continue to be, a valuable source of "intelligence-useful" information about what transpires on the ground.

The local people, on the other hand, regardless of how they are classified by these funding sources—poor, marginalized, disempowered, intellectuals, elites, etc, were always the object of this aid. They were part of the project being funded, nothing more nothing less. As part of the project, and beholden to the source of funds, they were controlled; and they were expected to be submissive recipients of aid, as submissive as the policy and strategy of the "mother" government stipulated.

The shift occurred on different levels, which, when combined, portrays, with clarity, the role of TNGOs and funding agencies as the real executive arm on the ground that enforces their governments' policies and strategies. I can summarize these levels in four, as follows:

LEVEL ONE

NGO funding shifted to funding administered directly by official agencies of their "mother" governments, who opened offices on the ground. These offices of international aid span almost all major Western countries committed to support the Oslo Process. They encompass the American USAID, the Swedish SIDA, the Swiss Agency for Development and Cooperation (SDC), The French Agence Francaise de Developpement (AFD), the Austrian Agency for International Development (AusAID), the Belgian Technical Cooperation (BTC), the Dutch Development Cooperation, a wide array of German organizations (including the German Technical Cooperation (GTZ) who works mainly with PA ministries, KfW who does financial cooperation, etc), the British Department for International Development (DFID), the European Commission for the EU, etc. The presence of these official aid agencies became indistinguishable from the official embassies, consulates or Representative offices. In some cases, the aid agencies are embedded in the same diplomatic representative office or consulate, e.g., Denmark's DANIDA, Sweden's SIDA, France's AFD, Belgium's BTC, etc.

What this did, in effect, it peeled off any illusion about the nature and process of funding. It placed the NGOs, as funding conduits, into a subservient role to the official aid agencies, and it redefined the external funding as "government to government", rather than the earlier and implicit claim of "people to people", notwithstanding, of course, USAID's false marketing slogan "from the American People to the Palestinian People", or the notion of an illusory government under the Oslo-invented PA.

As indicative for the above, it is worth noting what the AMAN study revealed about the special status the PA granted USAID institutions. Officially, USAID acknowledges publically that it disbursed to the West Bank and Gaza for the period 1993 – 2007, $1.7 billion. Framed in this context, "all USAID institutions, branches, bodies and companies operating in the PNA area received an exemption from registering at any PNA ministry", based on a decision taken by then president Arafat and his then Prime-Minister, Mahmoud Abbas (the current President) early in 2005 . "Decisions such as these gave USAID institutions immunity against any intervention that may obstruct its activities in the Palestinian Territory."[100]

100 (Ibid: 15)

Furthermore, "many USAID branches are granted registration permits from the Ministry of National Economy as non-profit companies without submitting any official documents. Their names are not even on the list of registered companies at the Companies' Controller at the Ministry. ... USAID non-profit companies do not report or submit budgets, and are not subject to the oversight of the Palestinian Companies Controller. ... Employment contracts of USAID with Palestinians stipulate that conflicts which may occur at work are subject to the United States judiciary system."[101] It must be clarified, however, that the sad irony is that many of those registered as "non-profit companies" with the Palestinian Ministry of National Economy are indeed for profit companies in the US, and the contracts they won from USAID for projects in the Palestinian areas (like everywhere else globally) are designed to increase their profits, and they do. Otherwise, they would not be here!

Furthermore, many of the founders and owners of these American for-profit companies who compete for official USAID funds, and who work here, either directly or through local affiliates, emerged from the official corporate, policy, or intelligence side. As an indicative example, see Chemonics (mentioned below).

> *Chemonics International is a private, for-profit company that focuses exclusively on international development. This Washington, D.C.-based firm provides economic, legal, trade and infrastructure assistance to developing and war-torn countries. Chemonics relies on the U.S. Agency for International Development for 90 percent of its business.*
>
> *Thurston F. Teele founded Chemonics as a small agricultural consulting firm in 1975. Today, the company employs nearly 1,000 people and has annual sales reaching $185 million. Since it was founded, Chemonics has completed at least 600 projects in 130 countries for USAID. The com-*

101 (Ibid: 16)

> *pany's first major contract was a USAID-funded livestock management project in Mali. From 1997 to 2002, Chemonics had 62 contracts (120 transactions) with USAID, the U.S. Trade & Development Agency and the U.S. Customs Service, worth more than $220 million. The company has worked in Albania, Armenia, Botswana, Bangladesh, Bolivia, Belarus, Colombia, Ecuador, Egypt, Guatemala, Guyana, Indonesia, Jordan, Madagascar, Macedonia, Mexico, Mozambique, Nigeria, Peru, Romania, Philippines, Russia, South Africa, Somalia, Uganda, Ukraine and the West Bank. Before founding Chemonics, Teele served as a Foreign Service Officer with the State Department. He then moved on to work as an international development consultant for Washington, D.C.-based international development firm Checchi and Company Consulting Inc. Teele served as Chemonics' president for 27 years.*
>
> *In December 2001, Chemonics reorganized its structure in order to 'renew' its 'focus' on its 'principal client'—USAID."*[102]

Palestinian Ministry of Interior claims that not more than 40 percent of INGOS actually operating in the PA areas are registered with it. Only 10 of the operating American organizations are actually registered.

LEVEL TWO

Since the beginning of the Oslo Process, Western aid has become "privatized". It relies for the implementation of its projects on a number of agents, including indigenous "developmental" NGOs, TNGOs, local consulting firms, Western consulting firms and other companies, individual consultants, etc. It's a mixed bag of agents running hard to qualify for bidding according to criteria posted on the Western funders' web sites. The net result is that TNGOs and transnational cor-

102 (http://www.publicintegrity.org/)

porations became competitive to indigenous NGOs and firms in the bidding process for implementation. This is lucrative business. To qualify for bidding, let alone winning, the bidder has to show a mastery of English, as well as a track record of experience in a similar business. By definition, of course, such a process excludes a priori indigenous, small, inexperienced, and not managerially-trained NGOs or grassroots organizations or community-based movements. It does not take much guessing in this case to know who will have the advantage in this "international" bidding game!

What the shift at this level did is to privatize and formalize the process of extending Western aid. It enticed the creation and proliferation of local managerially professional consulting and management firms, stocked with Anglophone-trained and formally-dressed technocrats, who are adept at mastering this game. The Ramallah based Massar International, who is the West Bank affiliate of Chemonics International, who was the consulting body for the USAID "tamkeen" project, and who markets itself under the slogan "We work locally and think globally", is a very good case in point for this process.[103]

LEVEL THREE

In this context, there is a noticeable trend of "indigenizing", albeit by name only, certain big new projects (referred to as 'programs'), especially in institutional development, health care and the judiciary, mainly funded by the USAID, the EU, and the World Bank. These projects were given indigenous vernacular names, such as, "*Tamkeen*" (empowerment), "*Hanan*" (compassion), "*Nidham*" (order), and "*Siyada*" (sovereignty), or the "Welfare Association Consortium" for the Palestinian NGO Project (PNGO), etc. This is basically to show, in my view, that these donors are really concerned about the indigenous cultural particularities, as expressed through language. And to show, further, how deeply engaged the Western donors are in the culture of the people. This is another approach of mythologiz-

103 (http://www.massar.com)

ing and reifying the entire matrix of control imposed by the provision of political aid.

LEVEL FOUR

The Oslo Accords formalized an elaborate structure for coordination of Western aid (e.g. LACCs). In reality, the formal aid coordination structure failed and did not evolve into much more than elaborate bureaucratic, time consuming meetings of donors with Palestinian counterpart ministries and local implementing agents. More specific attempts at "harmonizing" of aid sources were initiated by "like minded" groups of donors, as the case discussed earlier, and the "cluster approach to humanitarian assistance" initiative. These attempts were initiated to give a pseudo impression that donors were interested in cost-effectiveness of their funds, decentralization and transfer of decision-making functions to the field. This entailed a shift in surface terms and discourse only. For example, the observed linguistic communication shifted from "recipients" to "partners"; from "project" funding to "program" funding; from "short-term" funding to "longer term" funding; from "temporary" support to "sustained" support, etc. In reality, this shift in approach was based on deception and lies; it is intended to give a misleading impression that Western donors have serious, sincere, and solid commitment to the organizations they fund. Complicit in the maintenance of this process are their collaborators among the indigenous "developmental" NGOs, indigenous consultants, both individuals and firms, whose main interest is to secure lucrative jobs and contracts.

It is instructive to look, in this regard, at the so-called "cluster approach to humanitarian assistance", which was introduced in the occupied Palestinian areas in January 2009. Such a "cluster approach" was decided between Western international agencies working in the West Bank and Gaza and their headquarters, in an attempt "to reform humanitarian assistance".[104]

104 (Cluster Approach Evaluation, Phase 2, 2010:14)

The unpublished "zero draft" evaluation report of Phase 2 of this approach concluded:

> *The introduction of the cluster approach has intensified the humanitarian approach to the situation in oPt, which is neither in line with the Palestinian political agenda (f. e. building a state), nor does it empower relevant stakeholders in country. On the contrary, the definition of the situation as a humanitarian one undermines national ownership, disempowers and weakens national approaches and organizations, distracts attention away from many of the central political problems, creates dependency and may even help perpetuate the current crisis.*[105]

"Humanitarianism: A Non-Governmental Government" is the title of Fassin's chapter in the volume *NonGovernmental Politics.*[106] Indicative by this title is the analytical focus on the primacy of the role of governments in humanitarian interventions under the sheer cover of non-governmental organizations. And this is not unique to humanitarian interventions by Western governments in Third World countries, but it applies to such interventions in their own countries. (See, for example, the debacle of the Katrina disaster in the USA city of New Orleans). By and large, however, "... the wide usage of the term 'humanitarian' to describe the interventions of actors from Northern countries in Southern ones is not limited to nongovernmental organizations. States and supranational institutions have each in turn taken up the symbolic mantle of humanitarian reason **in order to justify and legitimate their actions, including military ones.**" [107]

In this regard, and keeping the above admonition that such intervention could be a justification for other actions, includ-

105 (Ibid: 39)

106 (Feher, 2007)

107 (Fassin, 2007:152); emphasis added

ing military-type intervention, some basic questions have to be raised, particularly in our Palestinian context. Notwithstanding situations of very clear natural disasters, there is a basic issue of who defines, and who has the right to define, when a situation is a "humanitarian disaster", thus warranting a special kind of intervention? Or, when such a definition is a justification for something else? The situation in Gaza, for example, following the election of Hamas in 2006, but, more specifically, in the aftermath of Hamas's control of Gaza in 2007, is a very clear case in point. After major Western powers, in conjunction with Israel and the Fateh-controlled PA, took a decision to besiege the entire population in Gaza, and then to destroy it in a ruthless military onslaught in 2008/2009, the situation was declared a "humanitarian disaster". This, consequently, was internalized by Western governments, which were responsible for creating this situation in the first place, who directed their major transnational aid agencies and all UN agencies to treat it as such. As a result, the volume, type and channels of "aid" were redefined and altered; an emergency humanitarian sub-culture was created and encouraged; the traditional notion of work, as a source of livelihood, was undermined; ordinary people were rendered completely dependent on emergency "aid coupons" handed out by Western donor agencies; total dependence on external aid was entrenched; and indigenous attempts and initiatives by the people to break away from the imposed "siege culture" were viewed by the same forces that are responsible for it, in the first place, as a threat to regional stability justifying additional military interventions. Thus, the cycle that was initiated and defined externally, is maintained externally!

NGOS, GOVERNMENTS, DONORS, AND PEOPLE: CHANGING RELATIONSHIPS AS A BASIS FOR TIGHTENED CONTROL AND DEPENDENCY

In 1997, David Hulme and Michael Edwards published an edited volume, titled *"NGOs, States and Donors: Too Close for Comfort?"* in which eighteen different papers were included on the trends of changing relationships between "NGOs, States and Donors".[108] The authors concluded that, at the bottom line, NGOs are "losing their roots". They are getting closer to donors and governments and more distant from the poor and the disempowered.

In a very challenging article on how "progressive" Canadian NGOs have become a "tool of the military" in the invasion and occupation of Afghanistan, Yves Engler[109] addresses the more generalized issue of the "overt ties between international development NGOS and Western military occupation", which he titled "the humanitarian invasion of Afghanistan: occupation by NGOs". The article raises questions about how the independence of NGOs is compromised when they rely on government funding. It states that "one important problem for … 'progressive' government-funded NGO community is that their benefactor's money is often tied to military intervention. A major principle of Canadian aid has been that where the USA wields its big stick, Canada carries its police baton and offers a carrot. To put it more clearly, where the U.S. kills Canada provides aid."

The supporting role of NGOs to the occupying armies, especially their own armies, became so flagrant with the Western invasion and occupation of Afghanistan and Iraq, and with the simultaneous privatization and outsourcing of those occupations, and the tremendous increasing availability in official funds to those privatized agents of maintaining the occupation, including NGOs. In her influential book, *The Shock Doctrine*, Naomi Klein [110] analyzes in great detail the function of NGOs as "the charity wing of the military, silently mopping up after wars". The Bush administration was not reticent about the value of NGOs for the wars in Afghanistan and Iraq. The NGOs were bluntly viewed by USAID officials as "an arm of the U.S. government".

108 (Hulme and Edwards, 1997)

109 (Engler, 2010)

110 (Klein, 2007, esp. chapters 19, 20, 21)

> *In the lead-up to the invasion of Afghanistan, U.S. Secretary of State Colin Powell explained: 'I am serious about making sure we have the best relationship with NGOs who are such a force multiplier for us and such an important part of our combat team.' ... In April 2009 U.S. Special Representative for Afghanistan and Pakistan, Richard Holbrooke, told the Associated Press that most of their information about Afghanistan and Pakistan comes from aid organizations. They are an important source of intelligence.*[111]

In light of the above discussion regarding the military destruction and control of certain Third World countries by Western imperial military machine; and in light of the use of "developmental" NGOs and funding agencies as the "soft" tool for maintaining that control and occupation; and in light of the ongoing gradual Zionist occupation and control over Palestine, as a part of this Western global onslaught on non-acquiescent peoples through the use of the "Oslo manufactured and imposed" political and economic agenda to maintain that occupation under a different guise; and in light of the flooding over the last seventeen years of nearly $ 18 billion, [112] in support of the imposition of this agenda; and in light of the proliferation of hundreds (if not thousands) of well financed Western and indigenous agents (NGOs, companies and individuals) for outsourcing this agenda, there is an urgent need to deconstruct certain critical sets of relationships. For the sake of this analysis, I focus on three sets of relationships, where "Developmental" NGOs stand at the center.

The first set is the relationship of NGOs with the PA (or central authority or government). The second set is the relationship of NGOs with their external (or international) funding sources, i.e. "donors. The third set is the relationship of NGOs with their traditional constituencies, or local and grassroots communities.

111 (Engler, 2010)

112 For an analysis of this "aid", see (Malhis, 2010)

I maintain from the onset that the more detached, distant, or removed "developmental" NGOs become from their traditional constituencies, the more coherent and consistent they become with their Western funding sources. Likewise, the closer the distance between "developmental" NGOs and the PA (or its agencies) becomes, the greater is the likelihood that they will become amenable agents or actors to impede the process of PCLD development.

Let us examine these relationships in view of the shifting trends discussed earlier. Indigenous "developmental" NGOs constitute one of the new elite classes generated by the "Oslo process", and funded from its dividends. They are becoming more entrenched in the officially prescribed "aid-development" paradigm as they become an integral part of the rising, Oslo created, privileged, political-economic elite. To succeed in this role, they seek and aspire openly to be endorsed by the PA as a legitimate target for international aid. To do that and to survive, they have to be part and parcel in the PA's acquiescence to the externally imposed political agenda. Furthermore, they gradually removed themselves from advocating for their traditional grassroots constituencies of the poor and the disempowered. The more they placed themselves in that category of being estranged from the ordinary people, the more they are inclined to coalesce their forces with the Oslo political, economic and intellectual elite in impeding PCLD development.

In this role, they become more of a substitute for progressive political parties and grassroots social movements. Otherwise, they cannot be an acceptable target for Western political aid, where they have become recipients of around 10% of all incoming international aid, over the last 10 year period? [113]

In the meantime, they are leading the "civil society" discourse. However, it is interesting to note that while the level of discourse about "civil society", or "civil society organizations" (CSOs) has notably increased; escalated and publicly surfaced, in practice, there is an emerging conscious behavior and push

113 (DeVoir and Tartir, 2009)

to extricate and distance "developmental" NGOs from the rest of civil society, and the gamut of other community-based CSOs (e.g., political parties, trade unions, social movements, active grassroots organizations, etc). Such a trend is being encouraged and rewarded ostensibly and simultaneously by major Western funding agencies and the Palestinian central authority (the PA). Insisting on a "civil society" discourse, in the self-definitions and auto-perceptions of "development" NGOs, is only a veneer for post-modernist discourse, which emits messages of "professionalism", "neo-liberalism", "openness", "democracy", "secularism", "pluralism", etc. These messages, while not posing any threat to the "liberal" Oslo-invented, political, intellectual, and economic elite, they are loved and cherished by Western transnational aid agencies and NGOs.

In this regard, I agree with Challand's generalization about Palestinian "developmental" NGOs:

> *In order to keep receiving funding from donors and to adapt to the new ways of working (professionalization, managerialization and increased institutionalization) some NGOs ... have experienced a gradual dislocation of their previous alignment with the local population from which they originally emanated through the many popular committees. Through this process of dislocation it resulted that certain sectors of civil society gradually became cut off from their popular bases, exacerbating heteronomy for the local population.* [114]

Also, it was observed in Latin America that

> *During the ascendency of the military dictatorships and continuing under the neoliberal regimes, while social movements and trade unions were suppressed, non-governmental organizations (NGOs) flourished. Billions of dollars flowed into*

114 (Challand, 2010:15)

> *the accounts of the NGOs from 'private' foundations. Later the World Bank and US and EU overseas agencies viewed the NGOs as integral to their counter-insurgency strategy.*[115]

In an earlier study on "Imperialism in the 21st Century", Petras and Veltmeyer concluded that

> *the real mushrooming of NGOs has occurred in times of rising mass movements that challenge imperial hegemony. The growth of radical socio-political movements and struggle has provided a lucrative commodity which ex-radical and pseudo-popular intellectuals have been able to sell to interested, concerned and well-financed private and public foundations closely tied with European and US TNCs and governments."*[116]

In both of their books, which appeared in the mid-nineties, "*Beyond the Magic Bullet*" and "*NGOs, States and Donors*", David Hulme and Michael Edwards grappled with the "relationships between NGOs and governments and official donor agencies," and their impact on poor people, especially in light of the fact that "NGOs that are not dependent on official aid for the majority of their budgets are now the exception rather than the rule". [117] "If NGOs are becoming more responsive to external concerns, what is happening to the links—to their values and mission, and to their supporters and others—through which they claim their right to intervene in development?"[118]

In the various analyses and discussions of these relationships, a central issue of "NGO accountability" looms large, and begs deeper analysis. As Edwards and Hulme maintain, "it is the *quality of the relationships* between GROs [grassroots Organiza-

115 (Petras, 2009:4)

116 (Petras and Veltmeyer, 2001:130-131)

117 (Edwards and Hulme , 1996:3)

118 (Ibid:14)

tions], NGOs, donors, and governments that determines whether patterns of funding and accountability promote or impede the wider goals of all these organizations in development."[119]

In his book "*The Role of NGOs Under Authoritarian Political Systems*" (1997) Cleary raises a number of very valid questions about NGOs' accountability. For example, "to what extent have NGO actors reflected the interests of the 'poorest of the poor' as opposed to some other group's interests, possibly including their own."[120]

CONCLUDING REMARKS

Like the previous chapter on the capitalist class, analysis in this chapter highlighted and assessed the emergent trends with the creation of "developmental" NGOs by transnational "aid" agencies, in terms of their destructive impact on the evolution of a PCLD environment. I maintained in the Introduction to this work that a PCLD environment strengthens and enhances the indigenous resources of the society; aims to create self-dependency, maximization the use of indigenous human resources; aims to liberate the people from external oppression, colonialism and hegemony, and from internal abuse, exploitation and social, political, economic apartheid; thus safeguarding a coherent and non-fragmented social fabric.

Through a detailed micro-analysis of five case studies, the cumulative evidence in this chapter points heavily to the direct role of international political "aid" in the establishment of "developmental" NGOs, as the new primary constituent of civil society, while fragmenting and dismantling the other necessary civil society components, namely political parties, active labor unions, grassroots social movements, and independent press and media. Being totally dependent on this external "aid", and insisting on being a beneficiary of it, these depoliticized, professional NGOs, some of whom act as "brokers" to this "aid" machinery, end up playing a pernicious role in impeding the realization of PCLD.

119 (Ibid:255)

120 (Cleary, 1997:227)

Chapter Four

THEORETICAL EXCURSIONS: A SORT OF ANNOTATED GLOSSARY

The analysis in this book is anchored in the body of critical social thought. It is not a Marxist treatise per se; nor is it a Gramscian treatise per se; it benefits from available literature inspired and enlightened by preceding critical thinkers. Thus, based on their analyses that deconstructed the bases of colonial structures in the non-Western world (so-called 'third world'), I was able to develop a clearer understanding of colonial processes of hegemonic control over peoples whose power was stripped from them through political and economic oppression. I am able to understand and analyze that colonization of other peoples was not a freak of history, which happened at one period in the nineteenth century, to expedite the robbery by Western powers of non-Western natural resources and wealth. But I can now see it as an ongoing and continuous process of decimation and social genocide, being effected successfully through military and non-military means alike, and targeting all kinds of disenfranchised, dis-empowered, poor people, regardless of whether they are beyond the physical national boundaries of the colonizing powers, or within their boundaries, e.g., native Americans (in North and South America), the Palestinians on their land. Relying on these critical analyses, I came to understand that "national" political boundaries are not only mutable, but, in the current wave of re-colonization, they have become immaterial and inconsequential.

The notion of "center" and "periphery", which was elaborated originally brilliantly by Samir Amin, Andre Frank, and others, and that had a perception of being separated by immutable boundaries of North and South, today, thanks to them, we look at it in fluidity. The perception of a rigidly polarized global structure is becoming blurred and intermingled. As Robert Cox and Timothy Sinclair claimed, "the North is generating its own internal South, and the South has formed a thin layer of society that is fully integrated into the economic North. The social core and the social periphery cut across national boundaries".[1] I find this notion very amenable to the current analysis in this book, especially as it pertains to the process of financial and cultural "re-colonization", with its well-funded localized agents and sub-agents for implementation. Furthermore, this notion pertains directly to the onslaught of the well-oiled and well- financed "re-engineering" process of our "national" consciousness that we, as a colonized people, as a people whose consciousness is predetermined by social, political and economic apartheid, are currently experiencing. The main agents of this process are our own South-North, North-South contingent of intellectuals and academics; our own self-proclaimed leadership of subservient political elites; as well as Western transnational funding agencies and states that encourage and fund activities whose aim is to normalize relations and contacts with the Israeli occupation structure, in order to humanize it and, consequently, to accept it as a benign "legitimate" partner.

I will focus in what follows on four thematic concerns to amplify the contexts and frameworks of some of the major concepts used in this work, to help annotate the glossary of ideas reiterated throughout, and to allude to the trends that we will be forced to adopt, currently and in the future, unless our people are empowered to reverse them.

---

1 (Cox and Sinclair, 1996:531).

LESSONS FROM FANON: POSSIBLE COMPARATIVE ADVANTAGE IN HINDSIGHT?

During the Algerian revolution against the French settler colonial rule, Frantz Fanon was assigned to a hospital in Algeria. Fanon, who died at the early age of twenty seven, was described by Noam Chomsky as a "tragic figure who struggled with some of the most critical problems of the present era ..."[2] Fanon's reflections on the Algerian revolution, and the conclusions he drew from his first hand engagement in that struggle and his astute observations of the colonized peoples in Africa, both during and post-colonization, require thorough contemplation. For example, his understanding of the meaning of the struggle for liberation was not limited to political independence. Liberation for him "was the regeneration of men and societies ... the process of self-liberation and rebirth ... the travail of people undoing the effects of colonization and restructuring their relations with one another and with the former colonizing power on the basis of their new situation."[3]

His Algerian experience, however, confronted him with a much harsher reality than his dream of liberation. On this bleak reality he observed:

> *During the struggle for liberation the leader awakened the people and promised them a forward march, heroic and unmitigated. Today, he uses every means to put them to sleep, and three or four times a year asks them to remember the colonial period and to look back on the long way they have come since then. Now it must be said that the masses show themselves totally incapable of appreciating the long way they have come. The peasant who goes on scratching out a living from the soil, and the unemployed man who never finds employment do not manage, in spite of public holi-*

2 In support of Gendzier's book, (Gendzier, 1973)

3 (Gendzier, 1973: xi)

days and flags, new and brightly-colored though they may be, to convince themselves that anything has really changed in their lives. ... During the period of the struggle for independence there was one right enough, a party led by the present leader. But since then this party has sadly disintegrated, nothing is left but the shell of a party, the name, the emblem, and the motto. The living party ... has been transformed into a trade union of individual interests. ... Today, the party's mission is to deliver to the people the instructions which issue from the summit. ... The party has made itself into a screen between the masses and the leaders. There is no longer any party life. ... The local party leaders are given administrative posts, the party becomes an administration. ...

The intellectuals, who on the eve of independence rallied to the party, now make it clear by their attitude that they gave their support with no other end in view than to secure their slices of the cake of independence. The party is becoming a means of private advancement.

There exists inside the new regime, however, an inequality in the acquisition of wealth and in monopolization. Some have a double source of income and demonstrate that they are specialized in opportunism. Privileges multiply and corruption triumphs, while morality declines. Today the vultures are too numerous and too voracious in proportion to the lean spoils of the national wealth. The party, a true instrument in the hands of the bourgeoisie, reinforces the machine, and ensures that the people are hemmed in and immobilized. The party helps the government to hold the people down. It becomes more and more clearly anti-democratic, an implement of coercion. The party is ... the accomplice of the merchant bourgeoisie. In the same way that the national bourgeoisie conjures away its phase of construction in order to throw

> *itself into the enjoyment of its wealth, in parallel fashion in the institutional sphere it jumps the parliamentary phase and chooses a dictatorship of the national-socialist type.*[4]

Irene Gendzier noted, in her "critical study" of Fanon that "while Fanon's political writing is indispensable to an understanding of the third world and specifically to the politics of decolonization ... [there is] universality" to the themes he addresses. The attraction to his ideas, she believes, derives from this universality[5]. Note, for example, his specific observations about third world colonized countries in Africa, and see how closely they reflect the current state of affairs in the occupied Palestinian areas that succumb to Israel's settler colonialism. Fanon describes, with caustic accuracy, in the following quotations about poverty, hording of wealth by the new elites, conspicuous consumption, corruption, and relations with the colonizers.

> *In these poor, underdeveloped countries, where the rule is that the greatest wealth is surrounded by the greatest poverty, the army and the police constitute the pillars of the regime; an army and a police force ... which are advised by foreign experts. The strength of the police force and the power of the army are proportionate to the stagnation in which the rest of the nation is sunk. By dent of yearly loans, concessions are snatched up by foreigners; scandals are numerous, ministers grow rich, their wives doll themselves up, the members of parliament feather their nests and there is not a soul down to the simple policeman or the customs officer who does not join in the great procession of corruption.*
>
> *The ranks of decked-out profiteers whose grasping hands scrape up the bank notes from a poverty-stricken country will sooner or later be men of*

4 (Fanon, 1963:169-172).

5 (Gendzier, 1973: xiii)

> *straw in the hands of the army, cleverly handled by foreign experts. In this way the former mother country practices indirect government, both by the bourgeoisie that it upholds and also by the national army led by its experts, an army that pins the people down, immobilizing and terrorizing them.*
>
> *In underdeveloped countries, we have seen that no true bourgeoisie exists; there is only a sort of little greedy cast, avid and voracious, with the mind of a huckster, only too glad to accept the dividends that the former colonial power hands out to it. This get-rich-quick middle class shows itself incapable of great ideas or of inventiveness. It remembers what it has read in European textbooks and imperceptibly it becomes not even the replica of Europe, but its caricature.*[6]

Fanon had no hope in the emerging national bourgeoisie in developing the country, as long as it continues to pursue its own profit. His views, as interpreted by Gendzier[7]:

Accustomed to playing an intermediary role during the colonial period, it had been active in trade and commerce within the system of production instituted by the colonizing country; it had never developed the instinct for productive initiative characteristic of the European bourgeoisie at a comparable stage in its national development. The colonial bourgeoisie did not invest in the nation. It was not inclined to take risks if it could profit more safely elsewhere. Hence, this role was also avoided and invariably left to foreign capital.

Being completely disenchanted and disappointed by the role of the political party after political independence, he arrived at the depressing conclusion that independence did not really change the lot of the masses. The new party and the government in an underdeveloped country act "as a barometer and as

6 (Fanon, 1963: 172-175)

7 (Gendzier,1973: 219-220)

an information service. The militant is turned into an informer. He is entrusted with punitive expeditions against the villages."

> *The party, instead of welcoming the expression of popular discontent, instead of taking for its fundamental purpose the free flow of ideas from the people up to the government, forms a screen, and forbids such ideas. The party leaders behave like common sergeant-majors, frequently reminding the people of the need for 'silence in the ranks'. ... It becomes, in fact, the tribe which makes itself into a party. This party which of its own will proclaims that it is a national party, and which claims to speak in the name of the totality of the people, secretly, sometimes even openly, organizes an authentic ethnic dictatorship. We ... see the rise of a ... tribal dictatorship.*
>
> *The ruling classes who have abdicated in favor of the leader, irresponsible, oblivious of everything and essentially preoccupied with the pleasures of their everyday life, their cocktail parties, their journeys paid for by government money, the profits they can make out of various schemes—from time to time these people discover the spiritual wasteland at the heart of the nation.*[8]

AS PERIPHERIES, WE ARE A PART OF A GLOBALIZED PROCESS OF "RE-COLONIZATION OF THE 'THIRD WORLD" BY HEGEMONIC WESTERN FINANCIAL SYSTEMS

Regardless of the blurry lines separating the North from the South in certain aspects, there is no doubt that, in totality, there is an eminent Center of capital and capitalism, from which imperial designs to control and re-colonize the weak and dependent Peripheries emerge and get implemented. These dependent peripheries, by and large, are what is classified as the third world, as well as the huge pockets of marginalized, disem-

8 (Fanon, 1963: 182-184)

powered and "irrelevant" populations dispersed throughout the capitalist Center. These pockets encompass remnants of native indigenous populations, the poor, the refugees, the migrant workers, the various ethnic, sectarian and racial human groupings that do not fit within the prevailing ideology and value system of the structure in which they exist. We are clearly and undoubtedly part of these peripheries.

Since the global debt crisis was set off in the 1980s, following the decision of Carter appointee Paul Volcker, as the Chairman of the Federal Reserve, to raise interest rates from 2 percent in the early seventies to 18 percent in the early eighties, many third world countries "across Latin America, Africa and parts of Asia" collapsed in debt[9]. This fabricated situation opened the door for the IMF and the World Bank to come "to the 'assistance' of the Third World with their 'structural adjustment programs'". In such a forceful intervention, Third World countries were forced

> *to privatize all state owned industries and resources, devalue their currencies, liberalize their economies, dismantle health, education and social services; ultimately resulting in the re-colonization of the 'Third World' as Western corporations and banks bought all their assets and resources, and ultimately created the conditions of social genocide, with the spread of mass poverty, and the emergence of corrupt national elites who were subservient to the interests of Western elites. The people in these nations would protest, riot and rebel, and the states would clamp down with the police and military* [10].

While Third World countries fell into the re-colonizing "debt trap", Western financial institutions and corporations were basking in "record-breaking profits". As people were pushed to consume, without any commensurate rise in wages, they fell

9 (Marshall, 2010)

10 (Ibid)

more and more in debt. The "middle class became a class based entirely on debt" [11].

In his recent article "From global depression to global governance", from which these quotes were extracted, Andrew Gavin Marshall presented a sober and awakening analysis of this potentially destructive process of "record-breaking" corporate profits, on the one hand, and what he referred to as "social genocide" of Third World peoples and all vulnerable populations, on the other. Yet, "there is a dim and growing beacon of hope."

> *At the recent G20 meeting in Toronto, the major nations of the world agreed to impose fiscal austerity – or in other words, commit social genocide – within their nations, in a veritable global structural adjustment program. So now we will see the beginnings of the Great Global Debt Depression, in which major western and global nations cut social spending, create mass unemployment by dismantling health, education, and social services. Further, state infrastructure – such as roads, bridges, airports, ports, railways, prisons, hospitals, electric transmission lines and water – will be privatized, so that global corporations and banks will own the entirely of national assets. Simultaneously, of course, taxes will be raised dramatically to levels never before seen. ... Simultaneously, of course, the middle class will in effect have its debts called in, and since the middle class exists only as an illusion, the illusion will vanish".*[12]

The hope he foresees in breaking this vicious cycle, however, lies in "what Zbigniew Brzezinski has termed ... the 'global political awakening'.

11 (Ibid)

12 (Ibid)

> *The global political awakening is representative of the fact that for the first time in all of human history, mankind is politically awakened and stirring, activated and aware, and that generally ... is aware of global inequalities, exploitation, and disrespect. ... As the middle classes realize their consumption was an illusion of wealth, they will seek answers and demand true change ... [change that is] inspired, and empowering.*[13]

Our ruling Palestinian economic and political elite are insisting on following this trend, with pride of accomplishment, and local and international claim that they are laying the institutional foundations for an independent state, albeit imaginary! However, since they insist on tying our future, with conscious and explicit determination, with the same imposed policies of the World Bank, the IMF and other Western aid agencies, aren't they insisting on mortgaging our society and our future generations to a permanent state of economic colonization and dependency?

BENEFITING FROM A CRITICAL ANALYSIS OF SOUTH AFRICA SINCE 1994, REGARDING THE NEO-LIBERALIZATION AND BUREAUCRATIZATION OF A LIBERATION MOVEMENT, THE FAILURE OF ITS "WAR ON POVERTY" PROGRAM, AND THE WESTERNIZATION OF ITS TOP RULING ELITES

Palestinians, like the rest of the oppressed world, have looked with admiration to Nelson Mandela for enduring 27 years in prison, and for waging a successful liberation struggle with the African National Council (ANC), culminating in the formal termination, after 46 years, of the apartheid system in South Africa. Much concern has been expressed in numerous different studies about the lessons Palestinians can learn from the methods used, and approaches followed, in the South

13 (Ibid)

African struggle for liberation and freedom. However, my concern in this analysis is to draw approximate comparisons between the evolving situation in South Africa since it was "liberated" in 1994, but more specifically since 1997 when Thabo Mbeke acceded to power as South Africa's new president, and our situation since 1994, when many of us were sold the idea that we were on the path towards a "free" and "independent" state of our own.

Reading and reflecting on two main critical works on South Africa post 1994, namely, a group of 18 studies published in an edited volume by Maharaj, Desai, and Bond [14]and the book by William Mervin Gumede on Mbeke "and the battle for the soul of the ANC"[15], forced me to draw alarming similarities that, in spite of the huge differences between the two cases, are revealing and very pertinent to the current analysis. The underpinning assumption, which evolved from these critical reflections, is that the path being charted by the current Palestinian ruling elites, as is the case in current South Africa, is being determined and shaped by Western global economic forces, in favor of the control of international capital, and disregarding the average citizen, particularly the poor. Similar, if not the same, forces contributed to the termination of the racially-defined apartheid, as well as the relocation of already defeated and demoralized PLO leadership to a portion of Palestinian land, in order to transform the historical Palestinian struggle for liberation to a "globalized economic-political enterprise". Hence, "the national sell-out" is the sub-title of this work.

In the absence of formal military occupation in current South Africa, and in the heavy presence of it in Palestine, the emerging political elites in both have succeeded, with the obvious and visible support of Western capitalist centers, directly or through local agents, in consolidating their hold on the population, and in emaciating and emasculating the liberation movements that buoyed them into their current leadership

14 (Maharaj, Desai, and Bond, 2010)

15 (Gumede, 2007)

positions, all under the guise of fulfilling "national" aspirations. In both situations, the guiding covenants of basic principles (the ANC's Freedom Charter, and the PLO's Covenant), on the basis of commitment to which many people lost their lives in the struggle to liberate their societies and their lands, basic principles were deleted or altered under pressure in order for the new entities to be accepted by the prevailing Western powers as a legitimate "globalized economic-political enterprise".

ON MBEKE AND THE FAYYAD-ABBAS DUO ...

Mbeke, who was rightly labeled "the joint CEO of SA, Inc, and ANC Ltd"[16], has aligned himself ideologically with Blair, Schroeder and the Swedish Social Democratic leader, who "embraced a common theme, known as the Third Way. It amounts to less government, using the market to deliver, distancing themselves from the unions and moving closer to business." [17] He "was seen initially, as the 'Mr Delivery' of transformatory goals, such as the creation of jobs and alleviation of poverty."[18]

In a three-part series in the *New York Review of Books* on our "Mr. Delivery", Nathan Thrall wrote:

> *Fayyad received a Ph.D. in economics from the University of Texas at Austin and held positions at the Federal Reserve Bank of St. Louis, the World Bank, and the IMF before becoming finance minister under President Yasser Arafat. His reputation as a fiscally responsible and trustworthy manager ensures the steady supply of international aid on which the Palestinian economy depends. Though he has neither a popular following nor backing from a large political party (his Third Way list received a mere 2.4 percent of the votes in the 2006 legis-*

16 (Gumede, 2007:163)

17 (Ibid:152)

18 (Maharaj, Desai, and Bond, 2010:14)

> *lative elections), today he is responsible for nearly every aspect of Palestinian governance. Yet he is not participating in the negotiations over a settlement with Israel, which are the province of the PLO (of whose leadership Fayyad is not a member) and are handled by its chairman, the seventy-five-year-old Abbas.*
>
> *Fayyad is criticized at home for many of the same reasons he is lauded abroad. He has condemned violence against Israel as antithetical to his people's national aspirations, stated that Palestinian refugees could be resettled not in Israel but in a future Palestinian state, and suggested that this state would offer citizenship to Jews. He is praised in the opinion pages of The Washington Post, The Wall Street Journal, and The New York Times, and has good relations with foreign leaders unpopular in Palestine.*[19]

Although technically Fayyad is appointed by the president (Abbas), informally, and in reality, he has been appointed by the World Bank, the IMF, the USA and the EU, through Abbas, as the West's "economic hit-man" in the Palestinian Authority, starting as a minister of Finance and ending as the prime minister. Fayyad and Abbas constitute an artificial duo with a manifest division of labor (economic and political); in effect, so far, they are a double-headed solo, one focusing on economic policies, and the other on political policies. Both coalesce in implementing the imposed Western-Israeli political and economic agenda in reversing and gutting Palestinian historical struggle for liberation.

Mbeke, who can be viewed as the equivalent of the joint Fayyad-Abbas combination, in our context, kept a tight rein on the party where "the state and party blurs into one, and the president becomes the 'keeper of the chalice cup of wisdom'. Those who challenge the wisdom of the president, challenge

19 (Thrall, 2010, pt.1)

the people"[20]. Mbeke's presidency "resembles a royal court with minions jockeying for position and jostling one another to gain access to the king."[21] As is the case with Abbas's president's office, which is stacked with "yes men", the Mbeke's presidency was characterized as "...once an individual is appointed to high political office [Read 'mustashar" = 'advisor'], it appears that they cannot be sacked for poor performance. Differing with the president is a more sackable offence." [22]

In both situations, the visible approach, over the last five to ten years at least, is to concentrate all effective power in the office of the president, to destroy the political party as a legitimate forum for people's participation, and to kill any dissenting voice, through a heavy use of security. "The ANC as a party has itself been 'presidentialised', with the office of the presidency being given new and stronger authority, without any countervailing checks and balances".[23]

Describing the ANC 2002 conference, Gumede[24] commented:

> *The gathering has become nothing more than a jamboree where the delegates network and leaders show off their newfound wealth. Those who attend are carefully screened at branch level in advance to weed out potential rebels and dissenters, draft policies are prepared beforehand, candidates for office are presented to delegates by the leadership, and all that remains is for decisions to be rubber-stamped.*

Note the obvious similarity with the sixth Fateh conference held in August 2009 in Bethlehem:

20 (Maharaj, Desai, and Bond, 2010:15)

21 (Gumede, 2007:150)

22 (Ibid: 157)

23 (Ibid:165)

24 (Ibid)

> *The conference was a spectacle on many levels: 2300 delegates with their accompanying entourages crammed Bethlehem, many in a fleet of fancy cars with flashing lights and hidden sirens. Virtually all the city's water was directed to various hotels where delegates stayed, resulting in massive water shortages throughout the rest of the city. There was an intriguing gradation between Fateh delegates who got to stay in the five-star suites, versus those for whom the two-star rooms sufficed. 2500 Palestinian Authority robocops were bussed in, quite literally stationed at every 50 meters of Bethlehem's streets.*
>
> *In fact Abu Mazen [Abbas] appears to have strengthened his position by taking a page from the ruling style of his predecessor, Yasser Arafat. That meaning, though the new 21-person Central Committee indeed features 14 fresh faces (and potentially 17, when three more political appointments to the Committee are finally handpicked by Abu Mazen), it nonetheless craftily balances the competing interests, personalities and powers that compose Fateh. Thus, relics of the 'old guard' ... are balanced by a nationalist current ... a diplomatic current ... a collaborationist/ security current ... and a financial current.*
>
> *This is quintessential Arafatism: forcing political rivals to compete amongst themselves horizontally for influence and power in order to access Abu Mazen vertically. In the end, Abu Mazen holds all the strings – particularly the purse strings, through his Prime Minister designate Salam Fayyad ... . Abu Mazen sits atop them all, tightening or loosening each string pending the needs of the political circumstance.*[25]

A comparable reflection to what happened to the PLO since 1974 through 1988, and more openly and visibly since 1994,

25 (Haddad, 2009)

where its liberation raison d'etre was extracted and transformed, under the guise of 'modernizing' it, is evident in the Mbeke ANC. Mbeke's "strategists called it 'modernizing' the ANC from a broad-based liberation movement to a governing political party, with centrist political, social and economic policies firmly orientated towards the market."[26] This led to a situation of 'double-speak' of talking "left" and "right" simultaneously, which, under the most charitable evaluation, I call hypocrisy, deception and lies. A South African sociologist depicted this state as follows: "Today the rhetoric about the 'national democratic revolution' and 'delivery' often creates the impression that what we are witnessing are unprecedented revolutionary changes".[27] Doesn't this explain the dissonance we are experiencing in Palestine between official speech and action?

ON POLICY APPROACH, CONCERNS FOR CAPITAL AND LACK OF CONCERN FOR THE POOR...

In a situation of "presidential" tight reins on free ideas and subservience to externally imposed political and economic agendas, creative policy options are determined by the allowable margin for political and economic action. The excessive centralization of authority in the office of the president and the prime minister is an effective means of control and weeding out critical and dissenting ideas. Under Mbeke's rule, "increasingly, policy is formed by directors general of government departments and their senior management, or even worse still, by external and very often private sector consultants from the EU or North America or whatever." [28]

Examining the available literature, big similarities surface between the economic approach of the neoliberal economist Mbeke in responding to the challenges confronting current South Africa, and that of the neoliberal economist Fayyad. It would be instructive to draw the comparison between the

26 (Gumede 2007: 149-50)

27 (Ibid: 152-53)

28 (Ibid:168)

"reform" plans that were marketed to external funding agencies and governments, by Mbeke for South Africa and Fayyad for occupied Palestinian areas: Mbeke's government plan, titled "Growth, Employment and Redistribution" (GEAR) , and Fayyad's government latest plan, titled "Ending Occupation, Establishing the State", which replaced, in effect, the Palestinian Reform and Development Plan (PRDP) of 2008[29].

Just as GEAR "was presented to parliament as non-negotiable, and even the National Economic Development and Labour Council (NEDLAC), established in 1995 to build consensus between government, labour, business and civil society on social and economic issues, was bypassed"[30] Fayyad's plan of "Ending Occupation, Establishing the State" somehow surfaced to the fore from behind closed doors. It was not deliberated by the elected Palestinian Legislative Council. It is not clear whose initiative it was. But what is clear is that Fayyad was its address and implementing tool to divert people's attention from struggle against the occupation, through a public show of hyped up foreign interest in investing in institution building, regardless of the presence of occupation.

The crux of the GEAR plan was this:

> *The higher growth path depends in part on attracting foreign direct investment, but also require a higher domestic saving effort. Greater industrial effectiveness, a tighter fiscal stance, moderation of wage increases, accelerated public investment, efficient service delivery and major expansion of private investment are integral aspects of the strategy. An exchange rate policy consistent with improved international competitiveness, responsible monetary policies and targeted industrial incentives characterises the new policy environ-*

29 (PNA, 2009)

30 (Gumede, 2007:167)

> *ment. A strong export performance underpins the macroeconomic sustainability of the growth path.* [31]

As Gumede concluded, "the entire strategy depended heavily on new investment, particularly from foreign sources, pouring into South Africa." [32] Further elaboration of this plan was presented by Hart[33]. He maintained that "elements of this project include the consolidation of conservative forces working in alliance with white corporate capital to create a black bourgeoisie nominally more responsive to 'development'". For contextualization, we should read this in the context of the active and ongoing collaboration between Jewish Israeli and Palestinian capitalists.

In their article on "debating the first and second economy", in the same volume focusing on "Losing South Africa's 'War on Poverty', Desai and Maharaj [34] maintained that "the essence of Mbekism is to depoliticise the social order, to transmute the class character of the state and to spread the market into the very life of the poor through the commodification of basic services, and the turning of the poor into micro-entrepreneurs relying on micro-credit."

The renewed interest in South Africa and here in the ideas of micro-financier Muhammad Yunus have become popular since winning the Nobel Peace Prize in 2006. His ideas were well received in South Africa in the prevailing approach of depoliticizing poverty which, instead of focusing on the causes of poverty, lumped them all in one category, namely the poor's inaccessibility to credit, and re-focused the attention on the shortage of credit. However, as Ferguson[35] maintains, "we need to be skeptical about the facile idea that problems of poor people can be solved simply by inviting them to participate

31 Quoted in (Ibid:107)

32 (Ibid: 109)

33 (Hart, 2010:83)

34 (Desai and Maharaj, 2010:56)

35 (Ferguson, 2010:415)

in markets and enterprise. Such claims (which often ascribe almost magical transformative powers to such unlikely vehicles as 'social entrepreneurship' or 'microcredit') are almost always misleading, and often fraudulent." Discussion of the entire issue of power in relation to poverty is absent. The problem is not ideological. But in situations, like in current South Africa and Palestine, where there is a huge gap between the poor and the rich, the poor cannot afford to repay the credit made accessible to them. Thus, they become mired deeper in debt, and, consequently, availability of microcredit does not help them alleviate their poverty. Gumede is correct in stating that "poor people understand their needs better than anyone, and government must take its lead from them, not the other way round"[36].

Notwithstanding the huge differences in the two situations of South Africa and the occupied Palestinian areas, there are major similarities, as discussed earlier. Yet in spite of failures and warnings advanced by various studies, we, in the Palestinian situation, keep insisting on not learning from them. "South Africa's wholehearted embrace of neoliberalism left its economic growth path especially fragile, relying on asset bubbles and subject to capital flight at the first sign of trouble."[37]

The number of studies I reviewed for this analysis proposed possibilities of responding to some of the vexing issues confronting current South Africa. For example, "regarding the relationships between NGOs and grassroots social movements", a major issue is "how to build an autonomous people-centred organization that can context powerful forces which support global capital; who should build this organization; what is the relationship of the poor to those who support them ... ." [38]. To broaden this thought, Patrick Bond challenged us to think of alternatives globally. He questioned: "are we ready for social movements that fight not 'from below' but 'across', using their 'foreign policy' to fight struggles not against 'the state' but

36 (Gumede, 2007: 146)

37 (Bond, 2010:65)

38 (Hendricks and Ntsebeza, 2010:234)

against that hydra-headed transnational apparatus of banks, international agencies, and market institutions through which contemporary capitalist domination functions?"[39]

Whether our focus is on South Africa or Palestine, we cannot today analyze poverty by limiting ourselves to the national political boundaries. Poverty has to be analyzed globally, otherwise we cannot address correctly power relations, global control of resources, and how vulnerable and colonized people in the world are being impoverished. Our analysis has to rely on, and benefit from, critical analyses such as Chossudovsky's "*The Globalization of Poverty and the New World Order*", and Samir Amin's discussion of "The gap between the poor and the rich". To bridge this gap, regionally and globally, Amin concludes, "requires a process of double liberation, from liberal globalization and American hegemony. These are two sides of the same coin and it is impossible to separate them". [40] In this regard, it is most useful to study Patrick Bond's most recent article on the failing path of "development" in South Africa since the liberation from apartheid, 16 years ago, and particularly over the last two years, since Zuma acceded to power.[41]

TRANSNATIONAL FUNDING AGENCIES, NGOS, AND CORPORATE FINANCIAL AGENCIES: THE MILITARIZATION OF HUMANITARIAN DISASTERS

In this section, I shall explore certain aspects of transnational funding agencies and their interaction with NGOs around the funding axis. I shall explore, further, how the provision of foreign aid, through this interaction, shapes and determines the conflict between "professionalized" NGOs and mass-based social movements, and skews it in favor of the former. And why it is important analytically to situate this discussion in the globalization context. I will contextualize this analysis in what has been termed "philanthropic imperialism", by focusing on

39 (Bond, 2007:83)

40 (Amin, 2008)

41 See (Bond, 2010)

the re-invention and militarization of humanitarian disasters. All this is put in the context of increasing levels of funding, the mushrooming of Western NGOs, and their rapid expansion and active "invasion" of 3rd world countries, as well as the ensuing increasing control of these transnational funding agencies in those countries.

I depended in this analysis on a number of studies and reports, but, primarily, I benefited from the critical analyses of James Petras, Michel Chossudovsky, Firoze Manji, and Didier Fassin, to name but a few.

ON TRANSNATIONAL FUNDING AGENCIES, NGOS, SOCIAL MOVEMENTS, AND CORPORATE FINANCIAL AGENCIES...

I use the term "transnational" funding agencies advisedly, because I want to distinguish it from the benign message conveyed by the use of the term "international". My concern here is to show the uneven power relations in this process of "transnationalism", where these agencies overstep national boundaries with unmitigated determination and total disregard for the national entities, merely because they are cloaked with the political and financial power of their Western mother countries. I use the term "transnational funding agencies" throughout this analysis to refer to a big basket of organizations, encompassing official governmental agencies, tax-exempt foundations and charities, and major intermediary funding NGOs. The official governmental agencies are by definition the extended arms of their governments in the 3rd world, in which they enforce their official foreign policy through the offering of financial "aid", be it "developmental" or "humanitarian". In our case, these include, *inter alia,* the American USAID, the European Union's EC, the Japanese JICA, the British DFID, the Norwegian NORAD, the Swedish SIDA, the Danish DANIDA, the German GTZ, the Canadian CIDA, the Swiss SDC, the French AFD, etc.

The World Bank and its Bretton Woods sister organization, the IMF, should be viewed as a class by themselves. They interfere in the 3rd world with unchallenged global authority and impunity, in the name of powerful countries, but primarily enforcing the approach of their creators—the major Western capitalist centers. The IMF sits inside the Palestinian Ministry of Finance, while the World Bank roams freely intervening in what it assumes the country needs. Since 1993, the World Bank set the tone for transnational and UN funding agencies for which areas to intervene, and how, etc.[42]

Since 1994, and particularly over the last ten years or so, we have been invaded by some of the major US tax-exempt foundations and charities which, in their connection with Western corporate capital, are rendering this part of the world (and us included), "safe for capitalism", as McGeorge Bundy, the former president of the Ford Foundation, claimed early on. Some of the best known American tax-exempt foundations, which were created by corporate capital, and which operate in Palestine, are Ford Foundation, the Rockefeller Foundation and Soros Open Society Institute. We are "benefitting" from the global trend starting in the 1990s, as Chossudovsky analyzed in his excellent article on "manufacturing dissent" [43]. He stated:

> *Following the deregulation of the global financial system in the 1990s and the rapid enrichment of the financial establishment, funding through foundations and charities has skyrocketed. In a bitter irony, part of the fraudulent financial gains on Wall Street in recent years have been recycled to the elites' tax exempt foundations and charities. These windfall financial gains ... have ... been channeled to NGOs, research institutes, community centres, church groups, environmentalists, alternative media, human rights groups, etc.*[44]

In the meantime, to put these funds to their desired use, as originally foreseen, two things were happening simultaneously: using

42 Refer to the 6-volume work, Developing the Occupied Territories, An Investment in Peace (WB, 1993), and other subsequent reports.

43 (Chossudovsky, 2010)

44 (Ibid:3-4)

American and European non-profit organizations as funding agencies, thus creating a buffer between the real source of funds (government or corporate) and the intermediary; and utilizing these same funds to entice the creation of "professional" NGOs on the ground, as the receptacles of these funds, while destroying existing grassroots social movements, and not facilitating the rise of others. To do this effectively, however, many foreign NGOs had to be physically present and "open shop" in the field of operations. With the increased levels of funding, "about 40 percent of the development NGOs working in Kenya today are foreign organizations". Consequently, "African countries found that their social and economic policies were being controlled no longer by the citizen, but rather by the international finance institutions in the interest of enabling the transnational corporations to increase their rate of profit." [45]. Furthermore, "many NGOs", as Chossudovsky maintains, "are infiltrated by informants often acting on behalf of western intelligence agencies".[46]

It must be kept in mind that, with very few exceptions, all American and European NGOs working in the Palestinian areas are secondary or tertiary funding sources, acting as intermediaries on behalf of their political parties, their governments or corporate capital in their mother countries, vis-a-vis Palestinian NGOs. The Canadian International Development Research Center (IDRC), or the Norwegian Chris Michelsen Institute (CMI), for example, fund research institutes and publications, inside and outside Palestinian universities, as independent, not for profit, research institutes committed to the generation of new ideas, etc. They present themselves as Non-Governmental Organizations independent of their governments. The real fact is that they, like most others, exist thanks to governmental funding from CIDA and NORAD, respectively, and the research programs they fund here would cease to exist, if perceived to deviate from the official position of either government.[47]

45 (Manji, 2010:4)

46 (Chossudovsky, 2010: 4)

47 For example, in 2010, about two years after it had approved funding for MADA, the Arab Center for Applied Social Research in Israel, IDRC

The basic question this discussion raises is this: why is there a need for funding intermediary? Is it for a more efficient use of funds? For more effective monitoring and evaluation? For less chances of misuse of funds and corruption? Etc. None of these possible answers seems to be the case. But there seems to be a need to erect insulation layers in order to deflect the true political, or partisan, or security, or corporate nature of the funds that get disbursed on the ground for "developmental" or " humanitarian" concerns. The NGOs are an effective tool for this purpose. Through them, "filthy" aid funds get laundered, so to speak.

So far, and by and large, the NGOs have performed this prescribed function successfully.

> *The recipient grassroots organizations are invariably unaware that their partner NGOs in the United States or the European Union, which are providing them with financial support, are themselves funded by major foundations. The money trickles down, setting constraints on grassroots actions. Many of these NGO leaders are committed and well meaning individuals acting within a framework which sets the boundaries of dissent. The leaders of these movements [however] are often co-opted, without even realizing that as a result of corporate funding their hands are tied"*[48]

On the question of broad-based mass movements and NGOs, there is no inherent contradiction or opposition between the two organizational categories: mass movements and NGOs. Their evolution shows that both were voluntary configurations of people who coalesced under certain conditions to respond to certain needs, or to defend certain important issues that affect

---

decided abruptly to freeze its financial commitment for this project under the guise of fabricated excuses. It was proven later on that IDRC's decision was taken as a result of pressure from the Israeli consulate in Canada, and the Zionist organization, NGO Monitor in Tel Aviv.

48 (Chossudovsky, 2010:17)

people's lives. Both are components of the arc constituting civil society organizations. The oppositional stance and the antithesis between the two types of social organizations is directly connected to the rapid dumping of the so-called "developmental aid" from Western centers of corporate capital into the third world, and using it to establish "developmental" NGOs, while assisting in choking off the politicized broad-based mass movements.

Broad-based mass movements are basically advocacy organizations, seeking to alter the prevalent oppressive and colonial status quo, and to liberate themselves from that oppression. There would be no contradiction if social movements get coopted by external "aid", and get transformed into "developmental" NGOs. Generally, genuine broad-based mass movements are antithetical to corporate capital and imperial designs. What we are observing in the 3rd world is that with the increase in availability of foreign aid, these mass movements are being choked off, and "developmental" NGOs are funded to replace them. As it was discussed earlier, this is clearly in line with increasing the receptivity of the people to normalize their situation with foreign capital, and get distracted from purposeful political struggle against their oppression towards forming managerial organizations of "aid".

See for comparison what is happening in Latin America, as an example:

> *During the ascendency of the military dictatorships and continuing under the neoliberal regimes, while social movements and trade unions were suppressed, non-governmental organizations (NGOs) flourished. Billions of dollars flowed into the accounts of the NGOs from 'private' foundations. Later the World Bank and US and EU overseas agencies viewed the NGOs as integral to their counter –insurgency strategy."* [49]

49 (Petras, 2009:17)

Furthermore, "the real mushrooming of NGOs has occurred in times of rising mass movements that challenge imperial hegemony."[50]

Our situation in Palestine is following that same direction. In that case, the fundamental question becomes how to mobilize a new generation of engaged and radical intellectuals and activists to re-engineer and re-configure new radical social movements and "avoid the NGO temptation"? [51]

ON THE INVENTION OF HUMANITARIAN CRISES, THEIR MILITARIZATION AND POLITICIZATION AS CHANNELS OF CONTROL AND HEGEMONY OVER VULNERABLE 3RD WORLD PEOPLES

Didier Fassin suggested that 'humanitarian' interventions open the door for military interventions:

> *The wide usage of the term 'humanitarian' to describe the interventions of actors from Northern countries in Southern ones is not limited to non-governmental organizations. States and supranational institutions have each in turn taken up the symbolic mantle of humanitarian reason in order to justify and legitimate their actions, including military ones."*[52]

"Technologies of disaster", to use Adi Ophir's term, "became political technologies, and their control and operation were at stake in political struggles." [53] If so, this generates a number of critical questions about Western interventions in non-Western countries under the guise of "humanitarian" intervention. For example, one can ask has the situation in Palestine been perceived all along by Western powers as a politico-humanitarian

50 (Petras and Veltmeyer, 2001:130-131)

51 (Ibid: 138)

52 (Fassin, 2007:152)

53 (Ophir, 2007:162)

situation, to provide a pretext for intervention and ultimate control? Similarly, Alex de Waal raised the question about US intervention in Somalia: "Did the US Marines who stormed up a Mogadishu beach in December 1992 represent the vanguard of the 'humanitarian international' or the shock troops of **philanthropic imperialism? ...** Free of their straitjacket, humanitarian agencies ... could set a real political agenda. 'Humanitarian intervention' was emblematic of that ambition: using the hardware of the world most powerful states to pursue philanthropic goals." [54] Doesn't this blur the distinction between 'political' and 'humanitarian'? And, if so, it legitimizes the use of all traditional and non-traditional tools to achieve specific and latent political goals, disguised as a response to 'humanitarian crises". Further, it sets the scene to justify transforming the role of humanitarian actors (individuals and agencies, for example, UNOCHA), concomitantly with the hundreds of millions of humanitarian aid, into virtual agents of hegemonic control.

The most recent disastrous earthquake that hit Haiti is a clear case in point. Many legitimate questions were being asked whether the US's response was a "humanitarian operation or an invasion"? It is legitimate to raise this question if one considers that, from day one, the overall humanitarian operation was being led by the Pentagon, and the entire mission was placed under the US Southern Command (USSOUTHCOM), headquartered in Miami.

> *Prior to the earthquake, there were, according to US military sources, some 60 US military personnel in Haiti. From one day to the next, an outright military surge has occurred: 10,000 troops, marines, special forces, intelligence operatives, etc., not to mention private mercenary forces on contract to the Pentagon. In all likelihood the humanitarian operation will be used as a pretext and justification*

54 (de Waal, 2007:184; emphasis added)

> *to establish a more permanent US military presence in Haiti.*[55]

Reports indicate that this was done without consultation with the Haitian government. With the destruction of the institutions of civilian government, local people's initiatives for rescue and support sprung into action. It is feared that "the militarization of relief operations will break the organizational capabilities of Haitians to rebuild and reinstate the institutions of civilian government ... [and] will also encroach upon the efforts of the international medical teams and civilian relief organisations."[56]

55 (Chossudovsky, 2010, 15 Jan)

56 (Ibid)

Bibliography

(2010, April 19). *CNN* .

Abdalla, S. (2010, September 23). Director General of MAS. (K. Nakhleh, Interviewer)

Abdul Karim, N., Tamari, S., & Farraj, K. (2010). The Palestinian Economy and Future Prospects:Interview with Mohammad Mustafa, Head of the Palestine Investment Fund. *Journal of Palestine Studies, Vol XXXIX, No.3* , 40-51.

Abunimah, A. (2010, May 6). *Electronic Intifada* .

Al-Aref, R. N. (2010, April 5). Sharekat Al-Shamal. (B. Center, Interviewer)

Al-Dabbagh, M. M. (1970). *Biladuna Filastin (Our Country Palestine), Part II, section two.* Beirut: Dar al-Tali'ah.

Al-Wazir, J. (2010, November 26). Governor of Palestinian Monetary Authority (PMA). (Shalabi, Interviewer)

AMAN. (2010 (February)). *International Charitable Associations and Non Governmental Organizations in Palestine.* Ramallah: AMAN.

Amin, S. (2008, December 3). Retrieved March 12, 2009, from Center for Marxist Studies and Research Web site: http://www.ahewar.org

Asmus, R. D., Diamond, L., Leonard, M., & McFaul, M. (2005). A Transatlantic Strategy to Promote Democratic Development in the Broader Middle East. *Washington Quarterly 28:2* , 7-21.

Bahour, S. (1998, January 2000). Telecommunications in Palestine: Growing Pains. *Al-Quds Newspaper* .

Bahour, S. (2000, November). *Telecommunications in Palestine: Self Inflicted Paralysis.* Ramallah: Unpublished.

Bergsten, F. (2009, Jan -Feb). Think Tank Second Thoughts. *Foreign Policy* .

Bond, P. (2007). "Two Economies", Microcredit and the Accelerated and Shared Growth Initiative for South Africa. *Africanus, 37 (2)* , 216-230.

Bond, P. (2010). Limits to class apartheid. In B. Maharaj, A. Desai, & P. Bond, *Zuma's Own Goal: Losing South Africa's 'War on Poverty'* (pp. 59-69). Trenton, NJ: Africa World Press and The Red Sea Press.

Bond, P. (2007, November, No.49). Linking below, across and against: World Social Forum weaknesses, global governance gaps and the global justice movements' strategic dilemmas. *Development Dialogue* , 81-95.

Bond, P. (2010, October 6). *Neoliberalism in South Africa: Dead in the Water*. Retrieved October 29, 2010, from Global Research Center Web site: http://www.globalresearch.ca

Byrne, A. (2011, January 18). Building a police state in Palestine. *http://www.conflictsforum.com* .

Chesters, G., & Welsh, I. (2006). *Complexity and Social Movements.* London: Routledge.

Cleary, S. (1997). *The Role of NGOs Under Authoritarian Political Systems.* London: MacMillan Press.

Cox, R. W., & Sinclair, T. J. (1996). *Approaches to World Order.* New York: Cambridge University Press.

de Waal, A. (2007). Humanitarianism Reconfigured: Philanthropic Globalization and the New Solidarity. In M. Feher, *Nongovernmental Politics* (pp. 183-195). New York: Zone Books.

Declaration. (2005). *Paris Declaration on Aid Effectiveness.* Paris.

Desai, A., & Maharaj, B. (2010). Debating the first and second economy. In B. Maharaj, A. Desai, & P. Bond, *Zuma's Own Goal: Losing South Africa's 'War on Poverty'* (pp. 37-57). Trenton, NJ: Africa World Press and the Red Sea Press.

DeVoir, J., & Tartir, A. (2009). *Bridging the Gap between Research and Policy Making in the Palestinian Territories: A Stakeholders' Analysis.* Ramallah: Palestine Economic Policy Research Institute (MAS).

Engler, Y. (2010, September 5). The Humanitarian Invasion of Afghanistan: Occupation by NGO. *http://www.globalresearch.ca* .

Fanon, F. (1963). *The Wretched of the Earth.* New York: Grove Press, Inc.

Faten, T. P. (2009). *Annual Report 2008.* Ramallah: Faten.

Faten, T. P. (2010). *Annual Report 2009.* Ramallah: Faten.

Ferguson, J. (2010). Rethinking poverty and assistance in Southern Africa. In B. Maharaj, A. Desai, & P. Bond, *Zuma's Own Goal: Losing*

South Africa's 'War on Poverty' (pp. 399-416). Trenton, NJ: Africa World Press and The Red Sea Press.

Freire, P. (1971). *Pedagogy of the Oppressed.* New York: Herder and Herder.

Gendzier, I. L. (1974). *Frantz Fanon: A Critical Study.* New York: Vintage Books.

Giacaman, G., Bishara, A., Ghalioun, B., & Zeidani, S. (1993). *On the Decmocratic Option: Critical Studies.* Ramallah: MUWATIN the Palestinian Institute for the Study of Democracy.

Gumede, W. M. (2007). *Thabo MBEKI and the Battle for the Soul of the ANC.* London and New York: Zed Books.

Haddad, T. (2009, August 29). *Fateh's Sixth Conference: The Wrap Up.* Retrieved September 5, 2009, from http://the fastertimes.com/palestine

Hart, G. (2010). Provocations of neoliberalism: Contesting the nation and liberation after apartheid. In B. Maharaj, A. Desai, & P. Bond, *Zuma's Own Goal: Losing South Africa's 'War on Poverty'* (pp. 71-99). Trenton, NJ: Africa World Press and The Red Sea Press.

Hedges, C. (2010, November 9). *A Recipe for Fascism.* Retrieved November 12, 2010, from Truthdig: http://www.truthdig.com

Hendricks, F., & Ntsebeza, L. (2010). Black poverty and white property in rural SA. In B. Maharaj, A. Desai, & P. Bond, *Zuma's Own Goal: Losing South Africa's 'War on Poverty'* (pp. 213-239). Trenton, NJ: Africa World Press and The Red Sea Press.

Hudson, M. (2010, October 8). *Boiler rooms, foreclosure mills:The story of America's mortgage industry.* Retrieved October 10, 2010, from Center for Public Integrity: http://www.publicintegrity.org

Hudson, M. (2010, November 15). *The coming sell-out to the super rich and what it means for us.* Retrieved November 17, 2010, from Information Clearing House: www.informationclearinghouse.info/article 26827.htm

Hulme, D. (1997). *NGOs, States and Donors: Too Close for Comfort?* New York: St. Martin's Press in association with Save the Children.

Jayyousi, A. (2010, September 8). General Manager of FATEN. (K. Nakhleh, Interviewer)

Jayyousi, M. (2010, September 20). Executive Director of Muwatin. (K. Nakhleh, Interviewer)

Kassabreh, G. (2010, March 27). Director General of NDC. (K. Nakhleh, Interviewer)

Khalidi, W. (2010). Remembering Hasib Sabbagh:1920-2010. *Journal of Palestine Studies, Vol. XXXIX, No.3* , 52-65.

Khouri, Z. (2006, November 10). A simple road to Middle East peace. *San Diego Union-Tribune* .

Khouri, Z. (2006, September 30). Things go better with rights. *Wall Street Journal* .

Khoury, B. (2010, July 1). Putting the Palestinian carriage behind the horse. *http://mideast.foreignpolicy.com* .

Maan Developmental Center. (2010, May). *Environment and Development Horizons" magazine, No. 25* .

Maan. (2010, August 31). *Mazen Sinoqrot announces Al-Quds Share Holding Company*. Retrieved September 4, 2010, from Maan News: http://www.maannews.net

Maan. (2010, May 18). *Yedioth Aharonoth report on al-Rawabi town.* Retrieved May 15, 2010, from Maan News: http://maannews.net

Macintyre, D. (2008, June 26). King of the West Bank. *The Independent* .

Maharaj, B., Desai, A., & Bond, P. (2010). *Zuma's Own Goal: Losing South Africa's 'War on Poverty'.* Trenton, NJ: Africa World Press/Red Sea Press.

Malhis, G. (2010, 25 March). International Assistance in Support of the Palestinain Economy: The Role of Regional Partners. *UN Seminar on Assistance to the Palestinian People.* Vienna: UN.

MAS. (2010). *Annual Report 2009.* Ramallah: MAS.

MAS. (2004). *Assessment of the Institute's Performance for the period 1994-2004.* Ramallah: MAS.

MAS. (2007). *Mapping Palestinian Non-Governmental Organizations in the West Bank and the Gaza Strip.* Ramallah: MAS.

MAS. (2007, issue 10). *Palestinian Economic Bulletin.* Ramallah: Portland Trust.

MAS. (2007, Issue 4). *Palestinian Economic Bulletin.* Ramallah: Portland Trust.

MAS. (2007, Issue 7). *Palestinian Economic Bulletin.* Ramallah: Portland Trust.

MAS. (2007, Issue 8). *Palestinian Economic Bulletin.* Ramallah: Portland Trust.

MAS. (2007, Issue 9). *Palestinian Economic Bulletin.* Ramallah: Portland Trust.

MAS. (2008, Issue 17). *Palestinian Economic Bulletin.* Ramallah: Portland Trust.

MAS. (2008, Issue 19). *Palestinian Economic Bulletin.* Ramallah: Portland Trust.

MAS. (2008, Issue 20). *Palestinian Economic Bulletin.* Ramallah: Portland Trust.

MAS. (2008, Issue 22). *Palestinian Economic Bulletin.* Ramallah: Portland Trust.

MAS. (2008, Issue 23). *Palestinian Economic Bulletin.* Ramallah: Portland Trust.

MAS. (2008, Issue 27). *Palestinian Economic Bulletin.* Ramallah: Portland Trust.

MAS. (2009, Issue 29). *Palestinian Economic Bulletin.* Ramallah: Portland Trust.

MAS. (2009, Issue 31). *Palestinian Economic Bulletin.* Ramallah: Portland Trust.

MAS. (2009, Issue 33). *Palestinian Economic Bulletin.* Ramallah: Portland Trust.

MAS. (2009, Issue 35). *Palestinian Economic Bulletin.* Ramallah: Portland Trust.

MAS. (2009, Issue 36). *Palestinian Economic Bulletin.* Ramallah: Portland Trust.

MAS. (2009, Issue 38). *Palestinian Economic Bulletin.* Ramallah: Portland Trust.

MAS. (2010, Issue 43). *Palestinian Economic Bulletin.* Ramallah: Portland Trust.

MAS. (2010, Issue 44). *Palestinian Economic Bulletin.* Ramallah: Portland Trust.

MAS. (2010, Issue 46). *Palestinian Economic Bulletin.* Ramallah: Portland Trust.

Munib al-Masri. (2007, May 14) BBC, Interviewer.

Murad, N. L. (2010). Indigenous resource mobilization for Palestinian-led social change and development. *Geographies of Aid Intervention.* Birzeit University: Unpublished.

Nakhleh, K. (1989). Non-Governmental Organizations and Palestine: The Politics of Money. *Journal of Refugee Studies, vol.2, no.1* , 113-124.

Nakhleh, K. (2009). *Occupation and Development: A Conflict-related Development Analysis in the WBG. Draft unpublished report submitted to Center for Development Studies, Birzeit University.* Ramallah: Unpublished.

Nakhleh, K. (2004). *The Myth of Palestinian Development: Political Aid and Sustainable Deceit.* Jerusalem, Ramallah: PASSIA, Palestinian Academic Society for the Study of International Affairs (English edition), and MUWATIN, the Palestinian Institute for the Study of Democracy (Arabic edition).

NDC. (2010). *Strategic Plan 2010 - 2014.* Al-Ram/Ramallah: NGO Development Center.

Ophir, A. (2007). The Sovereign, the Humanitarian and the Terrorist. In M. Feher, *Nongovernmental Politics* (pp. 161-181). New York: Zone Books.

PCBS. (1998). *The Establishments Report 1997- Final Results.* Ramallah: PCBS.

Peraino, K. (2007, December 3). Messiah on a Hill. *Newsweek* .

PIPA. (2010, May). *Palestine Investment Conference: Inspiring Business.* Ramallah: PIPA.

PNA. (2008, May). *International Assitance to the Palestinian People 2005-2007.* Ramallah: Palestinian Authority, Ministry of Planning.

PNA. (2008). *Palestine Investment Conference: Project and Concept Profiles.* Ramallah: PA.

PNA. (2007). *Palestinian Reform and Development Plan (PRDP).* Ramallah: Palestinian Authority.

PNA. (1996). *Palestinian Development Strategy.* Ramallah: Palestinian Authority.

PNGO. (2008). *ENP Workshop Executive Summary.* Ramallah: PNGO.

Reuters. (2010, August 18). *PADICO cautious amid rising profits.* Retrieved August 25, 2010, from Sahem Investment: http://www.sahem-inv.com/news.php?archive=1

Riyahi, I. (2011). *Two years after Palestinian Reform and Development Plan.* Ramallah: Bisan Center.

Samara, A. (1993). *"Capital" Class Re-Ordering.* Jerusalem: Al-Mashriq for Economic and Development Studies.

Sayigh, Y. (2007). Inducing a Failed State in Palestine. *Survival, 49:3* , 7-39.

Shoman, A.-H. (1982). *Al-Isami: The Biography of Abdul- Hameed Shoman.* Beirut: Arab Society for Studies and Publications.

Sidoti, C. L. (2007, 7 July). *External Review Report of Mu'assasat.* Ramallah.

Thrall, N. (2010, October 14). Our Man in Palestine. *The New York Review of Books* .

WB. (2010). *Evaluation of the World Bank Group Program: The World Bank Group in the West Bank and Gaza, 2001-2009.* Washington, DC: The World Bank.

WA. (2009). *Minutes of Programs and Projects Committee Meeting, Amman, 6-7 March.* Ramallah: WA.

WA. (2008). *25th Year Anniversary Document.* Amman: Welfare Association.

WA. (2007, September). *Strategic Plan 2008-2010.* Ramallah: Welfare Association.

WB. (2007, 3 April). *Completion Report, PNGO II.* Jerusalem: The World Bank.

WB. (1993). *Developing the Occupied Territories, An Investment in Peace.* Washington, DC: The World Bank.

Zanotti, J. (2010). *U.S. Foreign Aid to the Palestinians.* Washington, D.C.: Congressional Research Service (www.crs.gov).

Index

171111-200-1-60W